W9-BSJ-648

Expert Advice from Start to Finish

PAINTING *and* FINISHING

MICHAEL DRESDNER

DISCARD

DISCARD

The Taunton Press

Text © 2002 by Michael Dresdner
Photographs © 2002 by Sandor Nagyszalanczy, except where noted
Illustrations © by The Taunton Press, Inc.

All rights reserved.

The Taunton Press
Inspiration for hands-on living™

The Taunton Press, Inc., 63 South Main Street, PO Box 5506, Newtown, CT 06470-5506

e-mail: tp@taunton.com

Distributed by Publishers Group West

Taunton's Build Like a Pro™ is a trademark of The Taunton Press, Inc.,
registered in the U.S. Patent and Trademark Office.

DESIGNER: Lori Wendin

LAYOUT ARTIST: Potter Publishing Studio

ILLUSTRATOR: Mario Ferro

INTERIOR PHOTOGRAPHER: Sandor Nagyszalanczy, except where noted

COVER PHOTOGRAPHERS: Alec Waters ©The Taunton Press, Inc. (front cover top left); Roe Osborn ©The Taunton Press, Inc. (front cover right and bottom left and back cover bottom); Sandor Nagyszalanczy (back cover top and center)

Library of Congress Cataloging-in-Publication Data
Dresdner, Michael M.
    Taunton's Build like a pro : painting and finishing : expert advice from start to finish / Michael Dresdner
        p. cm.
    Includes index.
    ISBN 1-56158-480-0
    1. House painting. 2. Finishes and finishing. I. Title.
TT320.D697 2002
684.1'043—dc21   2001046469

Printed in the United States of America
10 9 8 7 6 5 4 3 2

To my father, William Dresdner, who proved that you don't have to be a professional to do exemplary work, and also to my readers, the legions of dedicated amateurs like him.

Acknowledgments

AS USUAL, A HOST OF wonderful friends stepped forward to help me out at every turn, offering information, advice, tools, materials, and, most of all, their own time and efforts whenever I needed them. Below, in alphabetical order, are the people, groups, and companies that went so far out of their way for me. Every one of you has my heartfelt thanks.

Don Bollinger, Gillian Brook, Andy Casillas, Del Cover, Drew Dresdner, Kaitlin Dresdner, Ken Gilitzer, Roger Goad, Gene Hoyas, Jim Kucharzak, Berj Martin, Jane McKittrick, Chris Minick, Bob Mitchell, Sandor Nagyszalanczy, Terry Nelson, Tim Neville, JR Reding, Bob Senior, John Swanson, George Woodruff, 3M Corp., Evergreen Woodworkers' Guild, McLendon Hardware, Purdy Brush Co. The Woodworking School, Wolman, WoodFloor Pro, and Zinsser.

Contact Information

You can reach me on the web at: www.michaeldresdner.com

Contents

Introduction

AS I WAS GROWING UP, I watched my dad fix and finish most everything around our house. We weren't well off, so what he did was a necessity, not a hobby. But his workmanship was so exemplary that to me, "do-it-yourself" came to mean "do it right." I also discovered that even though finishing or painting seems confusing when you first approach it, with some clear instructions about what to buy and how to apply it, it's just not that hard. Now, after thirty years as a professional in this field, it is time for me to share what I've learned.

This book is for you, the homeowner who wants to tackle the painting and finishing projects around your house. It's for people of all abilities, and for those with no prior experience. I've set down clear, easy-to-follow instructions on how to paint and finish everything inside and outside your home, from the deck, fences, walls, and patio furniture outside, to the floors, wainscoting, cabinets, and furniture inside. If it is made of wood, this book will show you how to coat it so that it looks great and lasts a long time.

While we're at it, I'll help you cut through the confusing terminology on finish and paint can labels. Instead of being misled by conflicting claims, I'll make sure you know what is on the shelf, what it is used for, and how to apply it. In short, I'll be your guide through this jungle of finishing options.

So take the plunge and tackle that project. I know it seems a bit daunting, but I'll be beside you, in spirit at least, with lots of helpful tips to get you through the sticky parts. In the end, you'll find that the fear of getting started is nothing compared to the ultimate satisfaction of having done it yourself. Give it a try. You'll be amazed at how well you do.

Start to Finish: The

CHAPTER ONE
First Steps

"How do you swallow an elephant? One bite at a time." That is a good adage to remember when you are faced with household finishing tasks. Take any finishing job one step at a time and you'll find it's not so intimidating. Whether you're painting a house, refinishing a kitchen, or coating a recently made shop project, start each job by getting a handle on what it will entail. Next, decide whether or not you even want to do it. After all, some jobs really are better left to the pros. If it is something you feel comfortable tackling, you'll want to know in advance how much money and time you should allocate. After that, it is down to the nitty-gritty of choosing the right finish, gathering the gear you'll need, and preparing the surface.

TOOLS AND MATERIALS

**Don't Buy
Too Much Paint**

Disposing of leftover coating materials is difficult these days, so buy just what you need, with no more than 10% extra for wiggle room. You can always go back and buy a bit more if you run short, and even custom colors can be remixed accurately with today's color matching equipment.

IN DETAIL

**Should You
Remove Old Finish?**

Removing old finish is a messy, labor-intensive job. Before you launch into a major stripping project, first make sure that it's necessary. Many defects and damages can be repaired and surfaces brightened and re-newed without stripping. Even in cases where you want to change to a darker color, you can often finish over an old coating if it is in good condition and there is no flaking or peeling.

Assessing the Job

Before starting any kind of painting or finishing job, it makes sense to understand what is involved before jumping in. In some cases, this will affect your decision whether or not to do the job yourself. At other times, it will affect when you start the work. Stripping, painting with solvents, and other smelly jobs are best left to seasons when the house can be adequately ventilated. Weather also affects outside jobs. For example, you can't paint or finish outdoors when it is too cold for the coating to cure.

Estimating the cost

The simple truth is that some jobs are better left to professionals. You may encounter a job that requires specialized equipment that is expensive to buy, impossible to rent, or dangerous to an inexperienced operator. You may also have a particularly bad reaction to certain solvents or chemicals that the task requires. And finally, it may simply be cheaper to have a pro do it. An honest estimation of the costs and time involved, factored in with what you feel your time is worth, will let you compare your cost to the estimate of a professional.

It's fairly easy to estimate the monetary costs involved in a project. First, start with a list of all the equipment you will need for the job. This may include putty and knives, caulking and caulking guns, sandpaper, masking tape and plastic, drop cloths, brushes, rollers, spray equipment, ladders and scaffolding, scrapers and wire brushes, respirators, and gloves and goggles in addition to paint,

varnish, stripper, and cleaning solvent. At the beginning of each chapter, there is a list of things you'll need for each type of job. Once you have your list, check off the items you already own.

A trip to a local paint or home store will help you fill in prices for the materials you need to buy. Coatings typically list coverage rates on the label. To figure out how much finish to buy, measure the surface area you need to coat and multiply it by the number of coats you need. Bear in mind that spraying is a lot less efficient than brushing or rolling, so you may need as much as 50% more finish if you go that route.

Painting in a stairwell—safely—may require a complex scaffolding arrangement and may be a job better left to a professional contractor.

"An honest estimation of the costs and time involved, factored in with what you feel your time is worth, will let you compare your cost to the estimate of a professional."

TRADE SECRET

A paint pro confided that when he estimates a paint job for a house exterior, he first counts the windows. "What with caulking, cutting in, masking, painting a contrasting color, and then cleaning the glass, the windows are by far the most time-consuming. I figure one hour per win-

dow on top of what I estimate for the house's surface footage." And unless you plan to spray, figure in more time for lapped siding than for flat surfaces, due to the fact that you have to paint the underside of each board before moving on to the flat side of the next board.

GOOD APPLICATION PRACTICE
• Protect everything you do not wish to coat, including plants and shrubs.
• Transfer leftover CWF-UV to smaller, sealed containers to prevent gelling.
• Apply between 50°F and 90°F.
• Do not apply if cold, wet weather is expected within 48 hours.
CUSTOM TINTING
• Do not add more than one ounce of all-purpose tinting color per gallon.
• Test your color on a small section of wood before coating the entire surface.
COVERAGE
• Each gallon will cover from 150 square feet (for rough sawn or very porous wood) to 250 square feet (for smooth wood).
DRY TIME
From 24 to 48 hours, depending on temperature and humidity.
CLEANUP
• Clean up with soap and water. If CWF-UV is allowed to dry, it can be removed with paint remover.
• Danger – Rags, steel wool or waste soaked with this product may spontaneously ca fire if improperly discarded. Immediately after each use, place rags, steel wool or was in a sealed water-filled metal container.

LIMITED WARRANTY

A paint can's label tells you how many square feet a gallon of paint covers.

Estimating your time

While estimating the monetary cost for a project is pretty easy, estimating the time it will take is not. For a professional, the most important factor in accurate time estimation is experience, and that is the one thing you are not likely to have.

One strategy is to break the job down into separate components, such as stripping the finish, sanding, disassembling, masking, staining, and so on. Picture yourself doing each task and guess how long it will take you. Consider whether the parts are simple, flat areas that are easy to sand and coat, or more time-consuming carved, turned, or fluted surfaces. Given the same surface, a clear, one-coat wipe-on finish will take much less time than a thick, filled-pore, high-gloss, polished finish. Don't forget to add time for trips to the store to buy materials. When you have estimated all of the component hours, add them up and multiply the final number by three.

Another strategy that may be worthwhile for especially complex or large jobs is to pay a professional for a time estimate. Have a pro estimate the job in hours by writing a task-by-task job description coupled with how long it will take him or her to do it. Multiply the pro's estimated hours by five to get an approximation of how long it will take you to do it. Be fair, though, and pay for this service. Everyone's time is valuable, and asking someone for a free quote just to help you do the job is unethical at best. To get you started, I'll provide some typical professional job time estimates at the beginning of various chapter segments. But remember: Each job is different, so these are only jumping-off points.

A complex chair with turned spindles and stretchers takes more time to finish than one with a flat, simple surface.

Painting the underside of lapped-board siding can be tedious and adds time to the job. Plan for it.

SAFETY FIRST

Don't forget to figure in the cost of good ladders, sturdy scaffolding, and other equipment that make the job safe. No matter how much you save by doing it yourself, one trip to the hospital can change everything. If you are not certain whether you can do a job without putting yourself in danger, call in a pro.

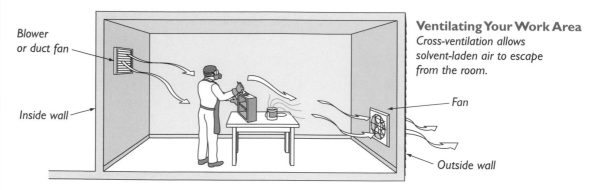

Blower or duct fan

Inside wall

Ventilating Your Work Area
Cross-ventilation allows solvent-laden air to escape from the room.

Fan

Outside wall

TRADE SECRET

Oil-based polyurethanes form a skin when exposed to oxygen, which is how they coat wood. It doesn't matter whether you leave a can open or reseal it with some space left inside. Either way, there is enough oxygen to turn at least some of the liquid into a solid poly-urethane film. One way to avoid this dilemma is to lay a sheet of plastic wrap directly on top of the finish before you close the lid. Press the film onto the surface of the polyurethane, making sure the entire area is covered. When it is time to use the finish again, take off the lid and discard the plastic wrap.

TRADE SECRET

Most oil-based poly-urethanes and varnishes are sold as ready to brush, but I find that they handle a whole lot better if you thin them out just a bit. Add 10% to 15% mineral spirits and stir it thoroughly. Try it both ways on scrap wood, but I bet you'll prefer the thinned-out version.

> *"The important variable is what the finish will have to endure."*

Environmental challenges

Virtually all finishing materials contain solvents, and therefore require ventilation if you're working indoors. Latex paints and other water-based coatings contain lower amounts of less dangerous solvents and require less aggressive ventilation. A couple of open windows and a gentle breeze may be enough. However, solvent-based coatings or strippers require good ventilation. That term means that you, the operator, should always be standing in a strong flow of forced fresh air produced by an ample fan moving clean air in from one window or doorway and pushing solvent-laden air outside through another.

Many paint strippers and solvents, such as alcohol, lacquer thinner, acetone, toluene, and naphtha, are flammable. Working with these products always requires strong ventilation, and they should be used in an area where there are no open flames or sources of sparks. Self-cycling motors, stove and hot water heater pilot lights, and furnaces are sparking sources that are easy to overlook. You should also wear an appropriate respirator. However, a respirator is not a substitute for good ventilation, only an added measure of safety.

Ventilation is not a problem when you work outdoors, but weather is. Finishes will not cure if it is too cold, and most coatings will blister if they are applied in strong, direct sunlight. Apply oil-based coatings above 50°F and water-based finishes above 60°F. In addition, paint the west side of the house in the morning and the east side in the afternoon.

Choosing a Finish

The sensible way to choose a finish is the same way you would choose a car: Decide what you expect in the way of performance coupled with how you want it to look. The important variable is what the finish will have to endure. The finish for a heavily trafficked floor has different needs than the "for looks only" coating on a prized jewelry box, and both will differ from the paints and deck coatings that are expected to weather the effects of sun, wind, and water.

Exterior walls

Outdoor wood exists in an environment with wide variations in humidity and, as a result, it expands and contracts through the seasons. Therefore, it needs a finish that is flexible enough

WHAT CAN GO WRONG

Working Outside

Both heat and humidity affect drying time. Heat speeds it up; high humidity slows it down. Brisk winds drive dirt and dust into a wet finish, and a sudden rainstorm can destroy a still-wet paint job or newly coated deck. When working outside, a reliable weather report is a must-have tool.

TRADE SECRET

For the most part, sanding wood to 180 grit is about as fine as you need to go before applying the first coat of paint or clear finish. However, an oil finish is the exception. Since it is applied so thin, it tends to show scratches more. Under an oil or Danish oil finish, sand the wood to at least 220 grit and up to 320 or finer if it is a very hard wood, such as rock maple.

to adjust without cracking. The wood is also subject to mold and mildew, strong sunlight, rain, snow, and worse. Indoor coatings are simply not designed to be both tough and flexible enough to hold up under such conditions. A good quality exterior paint is able to resist fading and deterioration in direct sunlight, contains mildewcide and fungicide to prevent growth on the surface, and can withstand the abrasion of rain, snow, and wind. These days, water-based latex paints are formulated to be as durable as oils, easier to apply, and faster drying, so they have become the first choice in almost all paint jobs.

If you want to maintain the natural look of the wood, you have several other choices. Clear coatings slow the erosion and graying of wood siding and shingles while retaining the wood's natural appearance. However, they don't hold up as long as paint does and, depending on your area, have to be renewed every few years. Semitransparent stains offer the same basic protection with some color added, and usually last a bit longer than clear finishes. They are typically offered in wood-tone colors, such as redwood, cedar, and even driftwood. Opaque or fully pigmented stains retain the texture of wood but look like paint. They tend to be more durable than clear finishes but less resilient than paint. All of these finishes are available in both oil- and water-based formats.

Decks and fences

Decks suffer the same assaults as walls with one extra challenge—people walk on the surface. As a result, the film-type finishes that work so well on

Mildew on this second story deck starts just past the drip line of the roof overhang.

walls would be rubbed off in no time if used on a deck. The best strategy is to use a thin, clear, penetrating finish that will not rub off, and recoat the deck every year or so.

There are two major categories of deck finishers. Rain blockers primarily shed rain and make water bead up. They are cheap, go on fast, soak in completely, and last a year or less. Deck sealers are more expensive, but they block dirt better and last longer. They come in semitransparent wood-tone color stains and clear coatings in both oil- and water-based formats. You can use the same treatments for patio and deck furniture, but for especially nice pieces, I prefer to use old-fashioned spar varnish.

WHAT CAN GO WRONG

Oil Bleed

Woods with large pores, such as oak, ash, mahogany, and walnut, present a particular problem for Danish oil finishes. The finish soaks into the pores; several hours after you have wiped off the excess, it starts to bleed back out. It collects at the mouth of the pores in tiny wet spots that harden overnight to small, rough nibs. There are two ways to avoid this, the second of which is practical. The first (unpractical) way is to continue to rewipe the surface every hour or so until the finish is dry or until it stops bleeding out of the pores. The practical way is to instead use boiled linseed oil, tung oil, or a liquid or gel wipe-on varnish on large-pore woods.

For outdoor exposure, use only stains with "exterior" printed on the label.

Semitransparent stain in a driftwood color gives this suburban home a seaside feel.

Doors, windows, and trim molding

Trim paint is not the same as wall paint. It is designed to be more durable for surfaces that get regular wear. A window sash that is raised and lowered would quickly wear out normal interior or exterior paint, but trim paint will take the abuse. Use it both indoors and out for frames, doors, windows and sashes, railings, and trim molding. It comes in both oil- and water-based versions. Water-based trim paint dries faster and smells less, and is the more common first choice.

For natural wood, use an exterior oil- or water-based polyurethane. It will hold up to the abrasion and sunlight erosion that plague windows and doors. If you want to stain the wood first, use only exterior or 100% pigmented stains. Indoor stains often contain dyes, which may fade in sunlight.

Floors

We ask a lot of floor finishes. We want them to be fine enough to show off the beauty of our wood floors yet strong enough to let us walk on them. That demands a coating that is both very tough and very flexible. It should come as no surprise, then, that some furniture-grade varnish is not appropriate for floors. Sure, you can get away with putting garden-variety polyurethane on the floor, but it simply won't hold up as well as a specially formulated floor finish.

Polyurethanes, both oil- and water-based, are the most common types of floor finishes on the market today and are adequate for most situations.

These garage doors are a natural choice for clear exterior coatings.

"Polyurethanes, both oil- and water-based, are the most common types of floor finishes on the market today."

IN DETAIL
UV Absorber/Inhibitor

UV absorbers/inhibitors are chemicals that are added to clear finishes to absorb the UV energy from sunlight and render it harmless. Sunlight is the bane of clear finishes, because it breaks them down prematurely, fades stains, and alters the color of the wood below. Exterior finishes are formulated so that UV light does not affect them very much. However, while a finish may be immune to UV light, that does not mean that it protects the wood beneath it. That is where UV absorbers come in. They offer some degree of protection both to the finish and to the wood. However, UV absorbers don't last forever and are not foolproof. Given enough time and exposure, the sun always wins.

Among professionals, so-called "Swedish" finishes are favored because they are the most durable, but they are also more difficult to apply. A new alternative, called Danish Finish, combines outstanding endurance with the ease of application typical of other water-based finishes. Chemically reacting shellac is also sold as a floor coating, and many people feel it is the most beautiful finish of all. Finally, you may opt for the traditional pure oil or wax-over-shellac finishes. They are easy to apply and look thin and woody, but they don't hold up well and require much more maintenance.

Furniture and cabinets

Furniture and cabinet finishes offer the most choice, from simple paint to a wide range of clear finishes. In descending order from most to least durable, you can choose from oil-based or water-based polyurethane, lacquer, traditional varnish, paint, shellac, oil and Danish oil, or wax. Each of the clear finishes has a slightly different appearance, so looking at or making samples is well worth the time.

For areas that are subjected to heat, chemicals, or serious abrasion, such as kitchen cabinets, bar tops, bathroom vanities, and kitchen tables, stick with one of the polyurethanes. Living room and bedroom furniture will do fine with shellac, lacquer, or varnish, as well as the more durable options. Pieces that receive little or no wear, such as mirrors, picture frames, small boxes, and ornamental turnings, can get away nicely with just a coat or two of oil or wax, though there is no reason you can't opt for something tougher.

Gathering the Gear

There are few things more annoying than having to stop in the middle of a job to go fetch some piece of equipment that really should be close at hand. Once you get varnish or paint on a brush, the last thing you want to do is watch it dry and harden while you run out to the store for masking tape, a respirator, or a ladder. So be prepared, and gather the drop cloths, masking tape, and other preparation tools along with your brushes, rollers, and pads. Don't forget goggles, gloves, ladders, and anything else that you'll need to make the job safe and efficient. This section will help you make a checklist of all the right stuff.

Masking and cleaning tools

If you're working on anything attached to the inside or outside of the house, chances are you will have to protect some adjacent areas from dust, spray, splatters, or solvents. For most vertical sheeting, I like to use thin, one- or two-mil plastic. Sold as folded drop cloths or rolls, this sheeting is convenient to have around. Rubberized canvas works well for protecting carpets and is not as slippery as plastic sheeting. For hardwood floors, a roll of heavy pink rosin paper is ideal.

Before you repaint finished wood—especially kitchen cabinets—scrub them first with trisodium phosphate (TSP) or some other grease-removing soap. A nylon abrasive pad, scrub brushes, several rolls of thick paper shop towels, and clean buckets are sure to come in handy. For outdoor scrubbing, you may want to rent or buy a pressure washer to clean large surfaces quickly. If you use a pressure

Trim paint is formulated to last longer on exterior doors and molding.

| TAKE YOUR PICK |
Oil or Water?
Polyurethane comes in oil-based and water-based versions. Both are equally durable but look quite different. Oil adds an amber tone and brings out the depth in most woods. It looks especially good on darker woods, such as walnut. Water-based finishes dry almost completely clear and don't alter the color of white woods, such as maple.

TRADE SECRET

I know what it says on the can. It tells you to brush on two or more coats of varnish or polyurethane. But if you want a thin, natural-looking finish, you can wipe polyurethane onto wood instead. Treat it like a Danish oil mixture, using a nylon abrasive pad and then wiping off the excess immediately. It's not a highly durable finish, but it looks great and is easy to do. Besides, you can just as easily add another coat the next day or renew it a year later.

WHAT CAN GO WRONG

Oil and Water Don't Mix!

You can apply an oil-based finish over a water-based one, but doing the reverse may not work as well. Water-based finishes don't always stick well to the slippery surface of old oil paints and varnishes. Sanding the old surface helps, but it is best to rely on a "tie coat," a special coating that helps tie the two finishes together. For clear finishes, the best tie coat is wax-free shellac. For painted finishes, water-, oil-, and shellac-based primers in white and other colors will do the job.

Rosin paper is a great non-slip masking material for hardwood floors.

washer, set it on low and use a wide fan spray. A narrow stream of high-pressure water can strip off paint and drill holes into softwoods.

Once you start painting, you'll need an assortment of drop cloths and masking tapes to protect nearby areas. You can use those cheap blue plastic tarps, but if you want to go first class, opt for good canvas ones. They are great for protecting plants and sidewalks outdoors and are easier to handle and less slippery to walk on. Indoors, cover furniture and drapes with plastic sheeting, and use thin plastic film to mask walls and areas that may get splattered. Hang the film with low-tack masking tape if you are working near wallpaper or old finishes. It is designed to come off easily without pulling wallpaper or finish with it. Otherwise, blue painter's masking tape is your best ally for most masking jobs. It leaves a clean line and comes off easily, even after several days.

Sanding tools

There are a number of sandpapers on the market, and for good reason. Each one is best at some particular task. To choose the right sandpaper, you'll need to know some of the terminology used with abrasives.

Closed coat/open coat. Closed-coat sandpaper has grit covering the entire surface. Open-coat sandpaper has grit covering only 40% to 70% of the surface. The spaces between the grit act like the gullets between saw teeth, clearing out sanding dust (called swarf) as it cuts. For woodworking and finishing, use only open-coat sandpaper.

Grit types. Aluminum oxide and garnet are the most common grits used for sanding raw wood. Silicone carbide and aluminum oxide are frequently used on sandpapers designed to sand between coats of finish. Aluminum oxide is sometimes called production paper.

Number of grits. Printed on the back of sandpaper is a number that tells you how coarse or fine the abrasive is (this number may or may not be preceded by the letter P; e.g., 120 or P120). The larger the number, the finer the grit. 50 grit is coarse, 80 is medium, 120 is fine, 240 is very fine, and 320 is super fine. In most cases, start with 80 on raw wood and use 220 or finer when sanding between coats of finish.

Paper grade. A letter grade, usually A, C, or D, indicates how thick the paper backing is. A-grade, the thinnest and most flexible type, is handy for sanding curved surfaces. I use it almost exclusively. Sanding media also come in cloth-back belts (for belt sanders) and in 5-in.- and 6-in.-diameter

"The right application tool is as important as the right finish or paint."

IN DETAIL

All Masking Tapes Are Not Created Equal

Have you ever noticed that if you leave regular tan masking tape on something too long, it is almost impossible to remove, tearing and leaving adhesive residue behind? And besides, it often makes a ragged line with some stains and coatings instead of a crisp, clean one. That's not your fault. You are simply choosing the wrong tape. There are several specialty tapes that work better.

One company, 3M, color-codes their specialty tapes, making the differences easier to see. Their blue Long Mask tape is designed to remain on for a week and still come off clean, with no residue. For a clean, masked line when staining or painting, use 3M's bright green Lacquer Tape. If you need to mask a curved line, you'll find that their pale green Fineline tape, a flexible film tape, is just the ticket.

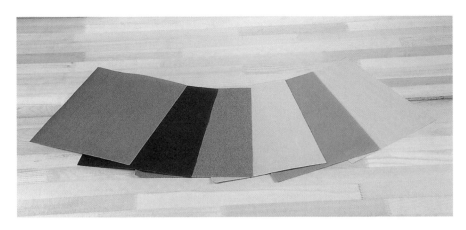

A variety of sandpapers: Shown from left to right are garnet paper, latex paint paper, wet-and-dry paper, two types of self-lubricated paper, and aluminum oxide production paper. The first and last examples are for sanding raw wood; the rest are for sanding finish.

disks for electric random orbit sanders. The backings for the disks are either peel-and-stick pressure-sensitive adhesive (PSA) or reusable hook-and-loop material. The latter can be removed and replaced more easily, but it is more expensive. Most power sanders come with a pad that takes PSA paper as well as replacement pads if you want to switch to hook-and-loop disks.

Fairly new on the market are an assortment of sanding sponges. These flexible sponges are covered with sanding grit and can be used wet or dry. They are very comfortable to use, especially on curved or convoluted surfaces, and generally outlast sandpaper many times over.

Application tools

The right application tool is as important as the right finish or paint, and you have quite a few choices. Spraying is the fastest method, especially if you need to cover convoluted surfaces, but it is also the most expensive and least efficient in terms of material usage. Rollers are cheap, fast, and efficient, provided you are covering more or

less flat surfaces and the finish you are using works well with a roller (most paints do, but most clear finishes don't). Rollers certainly shine when it comes to applying latex paint to large flat areas, such as walls. Paint pads are also efficient but not quite as fast; however, they are more versatile in terms of the shapes they can cover. I also find that paint pads are ideal for clear waterborne coatings. And last but certainly not least are brushes, the venerable standby of the finishing world. They are incredibly versatile, efficient, and a joy to use and own.

Spray guns. Spraying is the fastest way to coat wood. However, the equipment is costly and it wastes finish in the form of overspray—the finish that misses the wood or bounces off it as airborne mist. For large surface areas, like the outside of a clapboard house, the fastest tool is a high-pressure airless spray rig. This sprayer uses a high-pressure fluid pump to force a fan of paint out of the spray gun tip and onto the wood. A rig like this is quite expensive, but you can rent one if you need to spray a building. You'll also find small, rea-

Printed on the back of sandpaper is the type and size of grit, the thickness of the paper, and whether it is an open or a closed coat.

The right tape for the job: Shown from left to right are Lacquer Tape (green), masking tape (tan), Long Mask tape (blue), and low-tack tape (white).

TRADE SECRET

If I'm using oil-based paint or if I am just not up to a big cleanup job, I'll buy a paint tray, several cheap plastic tray liners, and throwaway roller covers. At the end of the job, I let the paint dry and then toss out the tray liners and roller covers. Both liners and roller covers are cheap enough to justify the quick cleanup they afford.

TOOLS AND MATERIALS
HVLP Conversion Guns

If you own an air compressor, you may want to consider buying an HVLP conversion gun. If so, first check the amount of air the new gun will require and make sure your compressor can produce it. Air volume is measured in cubic feet per minute (cfm) at a particular pressure rated in pounds per square inch (psi). A typical HVLP conversion gun might require 7 cfm at 60 psi, which is more than many of the smaller portable compressors can produce.

Flexible sanding sponges, which eliminate the need for sanding blocks on both flat and curved surfaces, can be washed out and reused.

sonably priced, hand-held airless sprayers at the store, but these are low-volume applicators and really not much faster than using a brush. They are certainly handy for small painting jobs, though.

Airless spray systems are good for paint, but for finer indoor work, such as spraying lacquer or varnish, look into air-supported guns. There are three types and they all work by mixing pressurized air with the finish to form a fine, atomized mist of coating. A conventional spray gun can handle any type of finish and operates from a standard air compressor. A high-volume, low-pressure (HVLP)

conversion gun also sprays any type of finish and creates much less overspray, hence wasting less material. These guns use far more compressed air, so you need a large compressor (typically 3 hp or bigger) to operate them. The third type of gun is an HVLP turbine gun. This portable, self-contained rig comes with a gun, an air hose, and a turbine to produce large volumes of low-pressure air. It is handy, efficient, and portable, but often has trouble spraying thick coatings.

Rollers. Nothing beats a roller for quickly covering large, flat areas with paint, especially latex. Roller covers are cheap and come in several lengths and nap thicknesses. Typically, short-nap (bristle height) covers are used for smooth surfaces, while high-nap covers work better on rough substrates. You can even get specialty roller covers that leave a textured surface. High quality roller covers and frames cost more, but they also hold up longer and apply paint more smoothly with less reloading and fewer problems. All good roller frames accept extension handles that let you reach a lot higher and make rolling ceilings and even standard-height walls much easier.

Paint pads. A paint pad is like a roller spread out into a flat square instead of cylinder. It has a short nap that works great with paints (for which it was designed) and clear, water-based furniture finishes. It gets into smaller spaces and tighter corners than rollers do. I use a paint pad to get the corners and edges that rollers won't reach, then follow up with a roller for the large areas. Like rollers, paint pads come in a variety of sizes and shapes; some even come with flexible foam back-

" A brush is the most versatile applicator ever invented. It can coat any shape, gets into tight corners without going 'outside the lines,' and comes in a wealth of sizes and shapes."

A good brush (left) forms an even line at the end of the bristles when they are deflected.

TAKE YOUR PICK

Good Brushes vs. Cheap Varieties

There is no reason why you can't use cheap throwaway or foam brushes for jobs where the quality of the surface does not matter. Putting on stain that will then be wiped off is a good example. And some folks really like those gray foam-on-a-stick brushes for putting down the first coat of primer or oil varnish. For anything that requires a smooth layout with no brush marks and no hairs in the finish, good brushes are an important investment. You'll appreciate the difference.

ers that you can bend to accommodate almost any surface. Better paint pads have replaceable pad covers on a plastic handle that accepts an extension pole for hitting the high spots. You can load a paint pad from any paint tray, but the ones specially designed for pads contain a roller that loads them more evenly.

Brushes. A brush is the most versatile applicator ever invented. It can coat any shape, gets into tight corners without going "outside the lines," and comes in a wealth of sizes and shapes. Choose the style and format based on what you need to do and what is comfortable in your hand. A 3-in. or 4-in. brush covers a wider swath, but I personally find a 2-in. brush more comfortable to hold. I use an angled sash brush for painting trim and windows, plus several sizes of small artist brushes for touchup work.

A good brush has even ends, plenty of long bristles, and a supple, springy feel when you deflect it. When you tug lightly on the bristles, no hairs come out. Use only synthetic nylon or polyester brushes for water-based paints and finishes, because natural hair tends to splay in water. For oil- and solvent-based finishes, I always use natural bristle brushes. They are more expensive, but if you care for them properly they'll last for years. My favorite all-around brush is a 2-in. black

China (hog) bristle brush with a chisel-shaped end, but some finishers prefer softer, ox-hair blends or badger for thin finishes.

Safety gear

You'll get a lot more pleasure out of a job if it is done safely. When you need to reach high areas, set up scaffolds and ladders on sturdy, level ground. If the ground is uneven, use a leveling foot on the ladder and make sure it is secure before you climb up on it.

When you sand either finished or raw wood, wear a dust mask. When you work with materials that are high in solvents, such as lacquer and paint remover, or any time you spray finish, wear a respirator. Most respirators come with a variety of replaceable cartridges that list which solvents they protect against. If any finish is likely to splash into your eyes, such as when pouring or stripping, wear goggles. I usually wear cheap, vinyl or latex throwaway gloves for any operation that requires my hands to come into contact with finish. Gloves keep my hands clean and prevent my skin from drying out. When you use strong paint stripper, upgrade to neoprene gloves for added protection. They are thicker and somewhat clumsier, but the protection is worth the trouble.

A leveling foot lets you use a ladder on uneven ground.

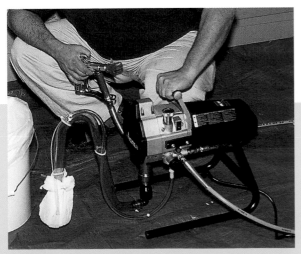

A high-pressure pump spray rig can make short work of house painting.

Inexpensive, self-contained pump sprayers are great for small jobs, such as painting fences and garage doors.

TRADE SECRET

When it comes time to remove masking tape, don't just tug it straight off. That could tear the tape or, even worse, pull up the paint or finish you just applied. To get a clean edge and easy removal, pull the tape back over itself and at a 30-degree angle away from the painted or stained edge.

Unlike synthetic bristles, natural bristles (left) splay when soaked in water.

Disposal and clean up

Once the job is done, you'll need to throw away the masking and drop cloths and clean up the tools. Paper, plastic, and masking can go right into the trash, provided the paint on it is dry. The same is true for the sludge left after stripping off old finish. Once the sludge is dry, it is landfill safe, but before that it is not. Spread it outdoors on newspaper or cardboard and let it dry completely before you add it to the trash can.

Any remaining paint or varnish that you don't want is considered a hazardous material in its wet form and is not safe for landfills. Most cities have paint recycling centers that take excess materials. Call your city or county trash disposal center and find out where and how to get rid of it. Otherwise, you can paint the remainder on paper or cardboard and let it dry. Leave the lid off the

Throwaway gloves are great for most work, but tougher neoprene gloves (shown in black) are best when handling strong solvents, such as paint remover.

empty paint can and let the residue sticking to the sides and bottom dry. Then the can is safe to deposit in the trash or a steel recycling bin.

Paint pads and rollers can be cleaned in the sink if you used them for water-based coatings or latex paint. Wash them with lots of warm, soapy water, rinse them well, and hang them up to dry. If you used oil-based paint or enamel, it is probably cheaper and easier to let the pads dry and then toss them. Brushes are a different story; unless you used disposable foam brushes, they should be properly cleaned after each use.

"If it comes apart, take it apart. But as you do, label each piece so that you'll be able to put it back together again later."

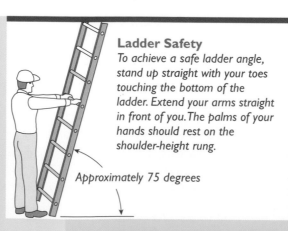

Ladder Safety
To achieve a safe ladder angle, stand up straight with your toes touching the bottom of the ladder. Extend your arms straight in front of you. The palms of your hands should rest on the shoulder-height rung.

Approximately 75 degrees

SAFETY FIRST

A ladder set at too steep or too shallow an angle is dangerous. Here's a quick, no-measure way to place a ladder at the right angle. Stand with your back straight, your toes touching the foot of the ladder, and one arm straight out at shoulder height. The ladder will be at the correct angle when both your toes and your palms are touching it.

Preparing the Surface

You're almost ready to start. You've looked the job over, chosen the finish, and collected all the tools you'll need. Now it's time to get the wood ready to accept the finish. That means taking off the hardware and loose parts, cleaning the surface, stripping off the old finish, patching up any defects, and sanding the wood.

Disassembly and marking

It is much easier to finish small, simple pieces than large, complex ones. Whenever possible, take your project apart as much as you can. If you're redoing kitchen or bathroom cabinets, desks, bookshelves, or chests, remove all the doors, drawers, and shelves, and pull off the hinges and handles. If it comes apart, take it apart. But as you do, label each piece so that you'll be able to put it back together again.

For doors, pencil a number or letter under the spot where the hinge was and cover it with a piece of masking tape so the finish solvent won't erase it. Eventually, the hinge will hide the mark. If there is no hardware to hide it, make a mark where it won't show—the top or bottom of a door, for example, or the end or back of an inside shelf.

Make a drawing of the room or piece of furniture with the corresponding marks on the sketch. This will come in handy later if you need to match colors on a series of doors or drawers. I even mark the parts of a chair on the glue joint area when I take it apart for regluing prior to finishing. That way I can get all the spindles and stretchers back where they belong.

If hardware comes apart, remove it when you refinish the woodwork. Most hinges, knobs, and pulls are easily disassembled.

Powerwash or simple scrub

Before you recoat your house or deck, wash off any dirt or grime. Here's where a powerwasher comes in handy. Set it on low, open the nozzle to a fan pattern, and work from the top down. If you have lapped siding, be careful to aim the water spray downward, not upward, or the water will get between the boards and soak the sheathing and insulation. You can also wash the house or deck with a pressure nozzle on your garden hose.

If there is any mildew, take it off with a mixture of one part bleach to three parts water, then rinse well. Go after stubborn areas of dirt with a scrub brush, then rinse it again with the hose. Of course, let everything dry thoroughly before you move onto painting.

Hold your brush by the ferrule for more comfort and control.

IN DETAIL

How to Hold a Paintbrush

Choosing the right brush is important; so is how you hold it. Rather than grabbing the handle, wrap your hand around the ferrule with the base of the handle in the notch between your thumb and first finger. With your thumb on one side and your fingers on the other, your hand will be in line with the direction of the bristles. That way, the bristles will feel like an extension of your fingers, making the movement of the brush feel very natural. You'll find you can use a brush all day like this without getting a cramped hand or having your wrist twisted in odd configurations. Try it!

TRADE SECRET

Do you have a paint-brush that is too good to throw away but has a line of crusty, dried paint about an inch down from the ferrule? You can return it to almost new condition. Drill a hole in the handle, thread a thin dowel or rod through the hole, and hang the brush over a can of good paint remover. Make sure that the bristles soak all the way up to the ferrule. Make a cardboard lid with a cutout for the brush, cover the can, and let the brush soak for an hour or two. When all of the crusty paint has softened, rinse the brush in lacquer thinner until the bristles look completely clean. Now take it to the sink for the soapy wash sequence.

When using a pressure washer on lapped siding, aim down, not up.

Cleaning is also necessary if you plan to recoat your kitchen or indoor furniture. Kitchen cabinets may have grime, grease, or cooking oils on them, and indoor furniture may have wax or polish on the surfaces. To clean finished surfaces indoors, scrub them with TSP diluted in water or with naphtha and steel wool. If you use TSP, rinse off any soapy residue with clear water. For naphtha, simply wipe off the surface with a damp cloth, and then dry it with paper towels.

Off with the old

There are times when you can simply apply a new finish over an old one, provided the surface has been properly prepped. But whenever possible, it is always better to get down to raw wood. In a nutshell, if the finish is peeling or cracking, it will have to come off. If it is in good shape and sticking solidly to the wood, you can coat over it. There are many mechanical and chemical methods for stripping finish. The best one depends on the surface and what you prefer using.

Scrapers. Metal scrapers are quick and easy if you are working on flat surfaces. Some have shaped heads to get into curves and grooves. However, it is easy to gouge or damage wood—especially softwood—with a sharp metal scraper. It is also difficult to get into every little groove and corner with scrapers. At times, I'll scrape off the bulk of a finish, then switch to chemicals to get that last bit clean.

Heat guns. If you have a heat gun, you can use it to strip paint. Heat a section of the surface, then shovel off the softened finish with a paint scraper. Heat guns are particularly handy for multiple layers of paint. Just be careful of where you aim the gun. You can melt plastic sheeting or set paper masking on fire as quick as a wink. When I work with a heat gun, I always keep my kitchen fire extinguisher within arm's reach. I haven't had to use it yet, but you never know.

Heat guns make short work of multiple coats of paint.

> "In a nutshell, if the finish is peeling or cracking, it will have to come off. If it is in good shape and sticking solidly to the wood, you can coat over it."

IN DETAIL

Soap, Water, and Pressure

Virtually all pressure washers accommodate detergent and mix it with the water stream. Small pressure washers have a soap reservoir while larger ones have a plastic tube (see photo, right) designed to siphon cleansers directly out of their containers. There are several brands of specialty house cleaning detergents that remove grime without harming shrubbery or leaving residue behind.

Scrapers quickly remove paint from flat surfaces.

Chemical strippers. For smaller pieces, or for wood that has too many grooves and curves to scrape, there is an assortment of chemical strippers you can use. The strongest and fastest contain methylene chloride, which will go through several layers of paint or varnish in as little as 10 minutes. Next in line are the slower but less odorous strippers, which are often advertised as safer (though that claim is arguable). These take substantially longer to soften finishes, especially when there are many layers. They are typically based on n-methyl-2-pyrrolidone (NMP) and may declare on the label "Contains no methylene chloride." Figure on two hours or more for them to work. You'll also find an even slower, safer stripper based on dibasic esters (DBE). This is a water-based stripper and may take up to 24 hours to do the job.

Next in line are the so-called "refinishers," which are fast-acting mixtures of common solvents, such as methanol, acetone, and toluene.

Marking Parts

Create a marking system to help you identify the location of parts after you've disassembled an item. For example, I use a code to identify four similar stretchers on a chair. This code tells me which side faces up, which end goes forward, and whether the stretcher is on the left, right, front, or back. I place the marking on the tenon, which will be hidden once the chair is reassembled. LF, for left front, means the tenon is to the left (when facing the chair), and that the tenon goes toward the front. The first letter signifies the position; the second letter distinguishes the orientation. The left side of the adjacent stretcher, which goes across the front, is marked FL. The side facing up is always opposite the marking. If there are two stretchers per side, they have an extra letter, T for top or B for bottom, at the end of the string of letters.

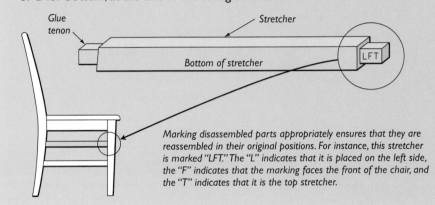

Marking disassembled parts appropriately ensures that they are reassembled in their original positions. For instance, this stretcher is marked "LFT." The "L" indicates that it is placed on the left side, the "F" indicates that the marking faces the front of the chair, and the "T" indicates that it is the top stretcher.

Refinishers are highly flammable and say so on the can. In addition, they usually work on just shellac, lacquer, and some spirit varnishes. There are a few other types, such as caustic mixtures, that are designed for special uses. Lye-based stripper, for example, is dangerous to use and can actually erode wood, but it is about the only thing that will take off milk paint. By reading the warnings and ingredients, you can figure out which is best for your project.

SAFETY FIRST

Despite paint remover's notorious reputation, you can use it safely with some sensible precautions. Wear goggles to protect your eyes from splashes, use a respirator to protect your lungs, wear an apron and neoprene gloves, and most important, make sure the room is well ventilated. If you can, put an exhaust fan at floor level, perhaps with the garage door open just enough to clear it. Most stripper solvents are heavier than air, and thus collect near the floor.

SAFETY FIRST

When you strip paint that was put on prior to 1970, you may be dealing with lead-based paint. In that case, stick to chemical strippers. Sanding and scraping can put lead dust in the air and heat guns will vaporize the lead, creating very dangerous fumes.

TRADE SECRET

If you're rolling on multiple coats of paint or have to leave a paint job for a few hours, you don't need to clean up your roller. Just put it in a plastic bag and twist the bag tightly shut to keep any air out. Don't try to reuse the bag, though, the next time you want to store your roller; bits of dried paint will peel off the old bag and embed in your roller, ruining your paint job.

IN DETAIL
Tent It

Drape polyethylene or polypropylene plastic sheeting like a tent over pieces that are too large to enclose in a bag. Line the floor with newspaper to catch the drips, and weight the edges with 2x4s to keep the solvent in place. The stripper won't melt the plastic, so the sheeting can be placed directly on the wet surfaces.

> "Be patient and let the stripper do the work."

How to use stripper

Strippers work only while they are wet, so the key to using them is to keep the wood wet until ALL the finish has softened or lifted. Some furniture may be small enough to strip in a metal tray, and for those pieces you may opt for a liquid stripper. Wash the stripper over the piece again and again, keeping it wet until the finish is all off.

For larger pieces or built-ins, buy a thicker paste or semipaste stripper. It is more likely to stay where you put it. Apply the stripper liberally, daubing it on with an old paint brush or a nylon abrasive pad, then cover the piece with plastic to prevent the stripper from drying out. For small objects, like a chair, simply make a tent with a large plastic garbage bag.

In other cases, you can press plastic polyethylene sheeting directly onto the stripper-laden surface. The stripper will not melt polyethylene sheeting or garbage bags, but it will dissolve a vinyl tablecloth, so choose your plastic wisely. Pull up a corner and test the finish now and then, but don't take off the plastic until you get all the way down to the wood with a gentle push of a putty knife. If you try to scrape it before the finish has completely softened, you will have a mess on your hands. Be patient and let the stripper do the work.

When the finish has softened, scrape off the bulk of it with a putty knife. Get the gunk off of grooves and spindles with a scrub brush, nylon

You can "tent" small projects by sealing them in a plastic garbage bag.

abrasive pad, or handful of coarse wood shavings. To clean out the grooves in turned spindles, I use a piece of coarse twine. For reveals, tight corners, and grooves in flat sections, nothing beats a wooden dowel honed to a point in a pencil sharpener. Get off the bulk of the old finish and, if there are some stubborn areas that won't budge, rewet the piece with stripper and do it again.

Five categories of stripper: Shown from left to right are safe DBE stripper, refinisher, two types of NMP strippers, three types of methylene chloride strippers, and caustic stripper.

Once you are down to bare wood, scrub the surface with a nylon abrasive pad soaked in mineral spirits and wipe it dry with paper towels. Then scrub it with a solution made from one ounce of household ammonia to one pint of warm water. Once again, wipe it off and let the wood dry overnight. When you strip off an old finish, you end up with raw wood. However, it will most likely be smooth, since it was probably sanded before it was finished the first time.

Putty and patching

Rare is the job that makes it through with no dings, dents, or gouges. When you find them (hopefully before you put on the finish), fill them and sand them level. There are a variety of different putties on the market, both ready to use and ready to mix, in a range of colors. If you can't find the color you need, buy a neutral or natural putty and turn it into a custom shade by stirring in a drop or two of universal tinting color. Mix a small amount at a time to meet just your immediate needs.

Press the putty into the gouge and smooth it so that it is just slightly proud of the surrounding surface (most putties shrink as they dry). When the spot is dry, sand it flush to the surface. You can test to see if the putty is ready to sand by pressing your thumbnail gently into the deepest part of the patch. If it moves or leaves a groove, let it dry longer.

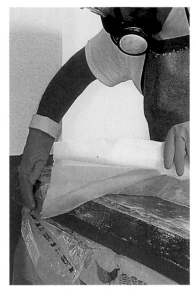

Press plastic sheeting directly onto the wet stripper to prevent it from drying prematurely.

A handful of wood shavings scrubs stripper gunk out of hard-to-reach areas.

Coarse twine acts like dental floss to remove gunk from spindle grooves.

TRADE SECRET

If a piece of wood is dented but the wood fibers aren't broken or torn, you can usually steam the dent out. This works only on raw wood, so don't even try it over a finish. Put a drop or two of water into the dent and let it soak in for a few seconds. Cover the area with a damp cloth and press a hot iron over the spot.

The iron will turn the water in the dent into steam, which will swell the crushed wood fibers back to their original shape. Not sure if the dent will steam out or not? Try it. If it doesn't work, you can always go back and putty it afterward.

TOOLS AND MATERIALS
Finish Compatibility and Wood Putty

Most people wonder if they should select wood putty to match the finish. The answer is no. There are a number of wood putties available, including fast-dry, slow-dry, oil-based, water-based, and UV-cured putties, and as long as they dry, they will work under any finish. But be aware that there is also a type of putty that is designed to stay flexible indefinitely. It is meant to be used under flexible exterior paint or on top of a painted surface to hide finish nail holes. It is usually called oil putty and sometimes painter's putty. If you are not sure which type you have, take out a small dab, spread it on some scrap wood, and wait a bit. If it dries in less than two hours, you can use it under any finish.

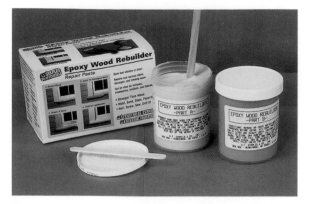

Two-part epoxy repair putty is great for rebuilding rotted wood.

For large areas of missing or rotted wood, especially on outdoor work, either replace the section with new wood or use an epoxy-based repair putty. It does not shrink, but it usually needs to be left overnight to cure completely. I have also used auto body filler to rebuild sections of missing wood that I planned to paint a solid color, and it works like a charm.

Sanding

Once the surface has been scrubbed clean, stripped if necessary, and repaired as needed, it's time to sand it. Of course, this isn't practical if you are repainting a house exterior or recoating a deck, but it is definitely in order for furniture and built-in indoor pieces. Prefinished surfaces that are in good shape can be lightly scuff-sanded with 220- or 320-grit self-lubricating sandpaper or with nylon abrasive pads. Scuff-sanding—lightly and quickly roughing up the smooth surface of the existing paint or varnish—helps the new coating stick better to the original finish.

But try not to get too aggressive. If you sand through to raw wood, you will have to seal or prime those spots or they will have a duller sheen after the next coat of finish.

When you are finishing new wood, start with 80- or 100-grit aluminum oxide sandpaper to remove power tool or chisel marks, then move up through the grits. The first sanding is to remove tool marks and flatten the surface, but each subsequent sanding has only one objective—to remove the scratches from the last sanding. A typical sequence of sandpaper is 80, 120, 180 or, alternatively, 100, 150, 180.

Scuff sanding is quick and easy to do if you use self-lubricating paper.

> **"When I sand flat surfaces with a hand-held block, I like to sand diagonally to the grain. This technique makes the grit cut faster and keeps the surface flat."**

IN DETAIL
Brush Cleanup

A good brush should last for many years if it is properly cleaned and cared for. Before you use it, soak it for a minute in the solvent appropriate for the coating (mineral spirits for oil-based finishes, alcohol for shellac, lacquer thinner for lacquer, and water for water-based or latex finishes), then squeeze out the excess. As you work, keep it from forming a dried crust of paint

Wash brushes as you do your hair—lather, rinse, and repeat.

Use a power sander if you have it, or sand by hand with a block. When I sand flat surfaces with a handheld block, I like to sand diagonally to the grain. This technique makes the grit cut faster and keeps the surface flat. Each time I change grits, I change direction 90 degrees. This makes it easy to see when I have removed all the previous scratches. The last grit I use is usually 180. After that, I follow with one more hand-sanding operation, and I do this one even if the other three were done with a power sander. The last sanding is done with 180-grit garnet paper and this time I sand with the grain. The garnet paper leaves a softer scratch pattern in the wood and helps burnish the end grain so it takes stain more evenly. Sanding with the grain also leaves the wood

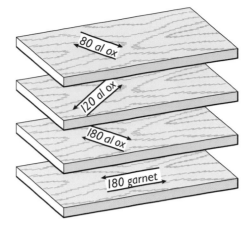

Sanding Sequence

- *Sand diagonal to the wood grain with 80-grit aluminum oxide sandpaper.*
- *Sand opposite to the diagonal with 120-grit aluminum oxide sandpaper.*
- *Sand opposite to the diagonal with 180-grit aluminum oxide sandpaper.*
- *Sand along the wood grain with 180-grit garnet sandpaper.*

smooth and free of visible scratches. For most woods, 180-grit is fine enough for the last sanding. For very hard woods, such as ebony and rock maple, you may want to sand to 220 or even to 320 grit.

Use universal tinting colors to make custom-colored putty.

along the bristles by periodically rewetting it in the solvent and squeezing it out. When you finish, wash it well in the solvent, shake it out, and take it right to the sink. It should still be wet with solvent but look clean. Wash it in copious amounts of warm water and plenty of soap or shampoo, rinsing it and repeating the process until the soap foams up nicely. Then rinse out all the soap and roll the brush up in a brown bag paper. Feel for the end of the bristles, and fold the paper over 1 in. past the ends. Let it dry, and it will be supple and reshaped by morning.

CHAPTER TWO

rooms

Kitchens and bathrooms are two of the most heavily used rooms in the house. Heat, water, steam, stains, abrasion, and chemicals abound, yet wood is still the material of choice for cabinets and tables. Countertops, too, are often made of wood, not only for its beauty and warmth, but also for its utility. And let's not forget the variety of wooden utensils and cutting boards that are found in most kitchens. Because they get so much daily use, these rooms—and the items in them—are frequently at the top of a homeowner's project list and are often the most challenging to finish. Appropriate finishes for kitchens and bathrooms can run the gamut from nothing (leaving the wood raw) to the most durable of coatings available. The key is choosing the right finish for the right project.

1 Cabinets and Shelves
page 24

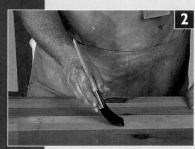

2 Countertops and Work Surfaces
page 30

3 Food Contact Surfaces
page 36

TOOLS AND MATERIALS
What You'll Need: Finishing

Best finish choices:
- Polyurethane (oil- or water-based)

Gear:
- Masking tape and plastic
- Paint remover (if stripping)
- Small stepladder
- Paint, glaze, or stain, and clear top coat
- Dropcloths or floor masking
- Putty and putty knife
- TSP and warm water
- Applicators (brushes, pads, spray guns)

Cabinets and Shelves

Heat, steam, water, grease, and constant handling define the world of kitchen and bathroom cabinets. And let's not forget the variety of chemicals and cleansers that are used in the kitchen and bath, all of which can potentially stain and attack finishes. Here's where we need a finish that is tough enough to scrub yet highly resistant to heat, stains, water, and contaminants on people's hands.

Whether you are installing new cabinets or, more commonly, changing the look of the ones you already have, there are lots of options. You can simply paint over whatever is there, alter the color of the finish without removing it, strip off the old finish and refinish it, or replace some or all of the cabinets with newly finished wood.

Painting over old finish

The simplest way to change the look of your cabinets is to paint over the existing finish.

Avoid painting over finishes that are peeling, cracked, or alligatored, like the one shown here. Strip them first, then paint.

Scrub the surface with TSP in water to remove dirt, grease, and oils.

Whether your cabinets are painted, stained, or finished with a clear coat, paint hides it all. But before you start, make sure that the paint will stick to the old finish and that the existing finish is still secure to the wood. If you manage to get a new coat of paint to stick to the old one but the old one is flaking off, both coats will soon lift away from the wood.

Check the existing finish to make sure it is not flaking, peeling, or alligatored. If so, it is probably not a good candidate for repainting without stripping. While it seems as if you could simply sand the loose areas, chances are that if one area is peeling, others are about to. If you are not sure whether the finish is secure enough to repaint, do an adhe-

"Here's where we need a finish that is tough enough to scrub yet highly resistant to heat, stains, water, and contaminants on people's hands."

TRADE SECRET

Water-based coatings require synthetic brushes, because water splays natural bristles. However, in some cases I find that paint pads work even better than brushes. Flat, low-nap paint pads seem to do a better job of smoothing on water-based coatings, especially on large, flat surfaces, such as cabinets and doors. Paint pads are inexpensive and easy to use and clean. For intricate recesses, corners, or flutes, I still keep a good nylon bristle brush at the ready, but nothing beats a paint pad for large surfaces.

Lightly sanding the old finish will help the new one stick better.

sion test on an area (see sidebar, below right). If it passes the test with 90% or better, go for it. Once you are sure the finish is secure, the next step is to prepare it for painting.

Prepare the old surface. Paint won't stick to grease, dirt, or wax, so you need to get the surface clean. Scrub down all the surfaces, inside and out, with a solution of trisodium phosphate (TSP) in warm water. Use a fine nylon abrasive pad or a scrub brush to help dislodge stubborn dirt. As you go, wipe off the surface with paper towels until it is obvious that no more dirt will come off. Then wipe down the surface with a damp cloth or a soft paper towel to make sure the wood is completely clean.

When the wood is dry, lightly sand the old finish with 320- or 400-grit sandpaper to rough up the surface. Don't go through the old finish—just score it so that the new finish will stick better. While you are at it, sand over any sharp edges as well.

SAFETY FIRST

When you set up a fan for ventilation, make sure that the airflow travels away from you after picking up fumes. That way you are always standing in the flow of clean air while the solvent-laden air is pushed outside.

Now is the time to putty any areas that are dinged. Use quick-drying putty and sand the area again after the putty is dry. Sections that are worn through can be spot-primed to feather in the edge of the existing finish so the transition is smooth. If you are changing hardware, this is a good time to fill screw holes, too. Once the surface is smooth, it is ready for primer.

Choosing the right primer and finish. Primer acts as a tie coat, helping the new finish tie into the old one, and as a barrier coat, blocking anything that is likely to bleed into or contaminate the new finish. Primers come in oil-based, water-based, and shellac-based versions. Oil-based primers are the only ones that lock in nicotine stains, but they dry more slowly and tend to smell. Water-based primers smell a bit better but allow some water-soluble stains to bleed through. My favorite primer for all indoor work is BIN, a

Simple Adhesion Test

Manufacturers use a cross-hatch adhesion test to determine whether coatings will stay on their substrates. You can approximate this test with a single-edge razor blade and a piece of duct tape. Using a new, sharp razor blade, cut six score marks into a 1-in. section of the old finish. Then cut six score marks in the

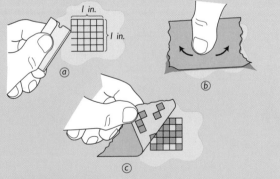

Cross-Hatch Test
a. Scratch a 1 in. × 1 in. cross-hatch pattern into the finish with a straight razor blade.
b. Cover the cross-hatch pattern with duct tape and burnish it well.
c. Lift the tape.

opposite direction to make a grid with 25 boxes in it. Press the duct tape onto the grid and burnish it with your thumb. Pull off the duct tape sharply and see how many of the squares of finish remain on the wood. If more than two of them are on the tape instead of on the wood, plan on stripping the old finish instead of going over it.

TOOLS AND MATERIALS
One-Step Finishes

Several companies offer one-step stain-and-finish poly-urethanes. Like glaze, you can wipe or brush a thin coat of these colored polyurethanes over an old finish. However, these products are less user-friendly and are almost impossible to remove or manipulate once they are on. If you feel you can add color in one shot with no mistakes, these poly-urethanes offer a glaze-and-seal operation in one coat. They dry pretty quickly, though, and there is no turning back. Don't say I didn't warn you.

Specialty primers and undercoats are offered in both water- and solvent-based mixtures.

white shellac-based primer that prevents stains from bleeding through new paint, hides the finish underneath, sticks extraordinarily well to almost any surface, and dries very quickly. Best of all, it leaves a surface that is perfect for oil-, solvent-, or water-based finishes. The bottom line is that

whichever product you choose, don't bypass the primer coat. It makes a big difference in how the job turns out.

Let the primer dry thoroughly, usually over-night, and then apply a good gloss or semi-gloss color coat. Your best bet is a scrubbable water-based paint specifically formulated for kitchen and bathroom cabinets. It resists stains and abrasions far better than standard wall paint. Don't be sur-prised to find that this type of paint costs quite a bit more than wall paint—sometimes twice as much—but it is definitely worth it.

Recoloring old finish

Next to painting, the easiest way to change the look of kitchen cabinets is to recolor them. If the existing finish is in good shape, you can recolor

BIN is my favorite primer for indoor projects, such as this kitchen cabinet.

Specially formulated kitchen and bathroom paints may cost more, but they are more durable and easier to clean.

> "The bottom line is that whichever product you choose, don't bypass the primer coat. It makes a big difference in how the job turns out."

TAKE YOUR PICK

Brushes vs. Pads

Water-based coatings require synthetic brushes, because water splays natural bristles. However, in some cases I find that paint pads work even better than brushes. Flat, low-nap paint pads seem to do a better job of smoothing on water-based coatings, especially on large, flat surfaces, such as cabinets and doors. Paint pads are inexpensive, easy to use, and quick to clean. For intricate recesses, corners, or flutes, I still keep a good nylon bristle brush at the ready, but nothing beats a paint pad for large surfaces.

A seal coat of wax-free shellac helps a water-based glaze adhere better to this old oil-based finish.

the cabinets without stripping off the old coating. Clean and scuff the surface, as you would to prepare it for painting, but this time use clear, wax-free shellac as the primer coat. If you can't find wax-free shellac, you can omit this step, but it does offer an extra degree of protection from chipping and delamination.

Any pigmented wood stain, as well as thinned paint, can be used as a glaze to recolor a cabinet. Use a dark glaze over light colors or a light glaze to brighten up dark cabinets. These days, most paint and home stores carry a line of specialty glazes that can be custom-colored to any hue. Water-based versions usually dry faster, while oil-based colors give you a bit more working time. Brush, roll, or wipe the stain onto the surface, blend it out, and then even up the color with a dry brush. You'll need to manipulate the color while it is still wet, so work on one section at a time, such as a door or a section of the case. Apply an even glaze for a uniform color or leave extra

color in the recesses to give the wood an antiqued look. When you like its appearance, let the glaze dry completely, then go over it with two thin coats of clear polyurethane for protection and durability. Use oil-based polyurethane over oil-based glaze and oil- or water-based polyurethane over water-based glaze. Water-based polyurethane is clear and doesn't change the color beneath it, but oil-based polyurethane adds an amber tone. Test the products on scrap wood first to make sure you'll get the look you want.

Complete refinishing

Not all finishes are in good enough shape to glaze or paint over. If the finish is badly worn, is peeling and chipping, or fails the adhesion test, your best bet is to strip off the old finish completely. Once you are down to raw wood you can stain your cabinets whichever color you like, then add a clear protective finish on top. If you prefer, you can paint them by following the primer and painting guidelines above.

Apply glaze with a roller, rag, or brush—whatever is fast and convenient.

IN DETAIL
Mixing Glazes

In a pinch, you can use thinned paint as a glaze. It works, but it tends to be a bit hard to handle. However, many stores now offer a clear, water-based glaze base that is specifically designed to add to latex paint. To get the color you want, choose a paint chip from the display and have the store make up a quart of it. When mixed with enough glaze base, one quart of paint makes three to four quarts of glaze.

IN DETAIL
What Is Glaze?

Staining is the process of putting color on raw wood. The color may be oil-based, water-based, dye-based, or pigmented, but if it goes onto raw wood, it's a stain. If you paint that same color on top of finish or in between layers of finish, it's a glaze. Same stuff, different locale. In a pinch, most any stain, and even thinned paint, can be used as a glaze.

WHAT CAN GO WRONG

Test the Stain Color

Stain combines its color with the wood beneath it, so the final color you get may be different from the sample in the store. Therefore, it's best to test the stain before you commit to the whole job, since this is one area where surprises are not so welcome. Buy a small container of the stain you plan to use and try it out on a hidden area, such as an inconspicuous spot on a cabinet, the back of a door, or the edge of a drawer. If you are doing a new set of cabinets, take some scrap wood from the case and doors, sand them the same as the real thing, and stain them to check the color.

TRADE SECRET

There is an easy way to get just the color stain you want without taking a course in color mixing. Have the paint store make up a quart of oil- or water-based custom-color paint. You can choose the color from the paint chips on display. Take the paint home and thin it about 50/50 with solvent (mineral spirits for oil-based paint, water for latex) and you'll have an ideal stain.

"If the finish is badly worn, is peeling and chipping, or fails the adhesion test, your best bet is to strip off the old finish completely."

Disassembly and stripping. Start by taking the drawers out and the doors off, then remove all the hardware. Mark the parts on a master chart so you can put them back together later. If you plan on changing the hardware, now is the time to plug the holes from the old handles and screws. Strip the doors and drawers as separate pieces. Cases usually don't come off the wall easily. If they do, you can strip them separately, too. If they don't come off, mask the adjacent walls, counters, and floors before you start, and use a thick, nondrip paste stripper on the vertical surfaces. Don't forget to provide plenty of ventilation and use gloves, goggles, an apron, and a respirator. (See Chapter 1, page 18, for guidelines on stripping old finish.)

Once the wood is clean and the old finish is off, you can either stain the wood or hide it completely with paint. Staining is a good option if the wood itself is attractive and in good condition, but if it is mismatched, loaded with patched holes and defects, or just plain ugly, consider painting the cabinets. All the steps from here on are the same whether you are finishing new wood cabinets or refinishing old ones.

Staining. Before you stain, sand the raw wood with fine 220-grit sandpaper so that the surface is uniform. This helps the stain cover more evenly. Liquid and gel-type stains are available in both oil-based and water-based formats. All of the products are fine for this project, but the gel-type ones are less drippy and make the job a bit less messy. For even coloration, brush or wipe on the stain liberally, then wipe off the excess while it is still wet. I always like to seal stripped wood by applying a thin coat of wax-free shellac over the stain. This prevents any future problems when it is time to add clear top coats. Think of wax-free shellac as clear primer. It is not absolutely necessary, but it helps.

Pickling. A pickled finish is a way to make wood lighter without painting it. Pickling is really nothing more than staining wood with white or pastel-colored stain. Most stain companies sell

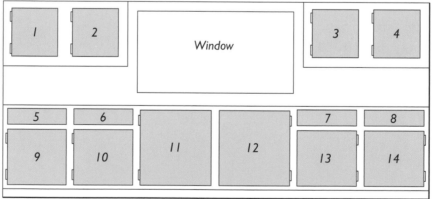

Map Your Kitchen before Removing Drawers and Doors
Before you disassemble your kitchen, draw a simple master chart and number (label) all the doors and drawers so that you can return them to their original positions.

IN DETAIL

Changing Hardware

If you are changing hardware on cabinetry or doors, plug the screw and handle holes before you strip off the old finish. Then, when you are down to raw wood, level the holes with putty when you fill other nicks and dings. For doors that will get a coat of paint, use a dowel dipped in glue to plug the holes. Cut off the excess flush (photo left), and putty the spot if you

Sand the wood before you stain it.

and are available only at commercial outlets—and polyurethanes. So, that leaves us with polyurethane as the prime candidate. Both oil- and water-based polyurethanes are durable enough, though oil-based polyurethane takes longer to dry, smells more, and adds a warm amber color to the wood.

Oil-based polyurethane is a perfect candidate for a natural China bristle or a blended China bristle/ox-hair brush. For water-based finishes, use a synthetic nylon bristle brush or a paint pad. Don't forget to stir the finish first, then pour some out into a tray or container. That way you won't contaminate the entire can by dipping the brush back into it. Reseal the can once you pour out what you need to keep the finish from getting thick or forming a skin. Apply at least two coats of polyurethane with plenty of drying time in between. Don't apply more than one coat of oil-based polyurethane per day or two coats of the faster drying water-based polyurethane per day.

white pickling stain and some also carry several pastel shades.

Brush or wipe the pickling stain onto the raw wood, then wipe off as much as you want while it is still wet. Typically, people leave extra white in the recesses to add character, but the stain also collects in the large pores of oak and ash and gives the appearance of highlights. Although you can pickle most any wood, the process is usually done on light-colored woods, such as oak, ash, maple, birch, and pine, to provide subtle contrast and a pale look. Let the stain dry overnight, then cover it with two coats of water-based polyurethane. You can use oil-based polyurethane, but its amber color tints the pickling to off-white.

Applying a top coat. Whether you stained, pickled, or glazed your cabinets, you must finish them with a clear, durable top coat. The only clear finishes tough enough for kitchens are conversion varnishes—which must be applied by spray gun

Pickling is easily achieved by applying a white or pastel-colored stain.

need to. Under clear finishes, you should use a plug cutter to make plugs that match the wood grain (see photo, right). You can drill new holes for the replacement handles and hinge screws either before or after you apply finish, depending on how secure you are with your drilling prowess. If you think you may tear out wood while drilling, do it before you apply finish, when it's easier to repair slipups.

Use a natural bristle brush for oil-based polyurethane and a synthetic bristle brush or a paint pad for water-based polyurethane.

TAKE YOUR PICK

Polyurethane vs. Conversion Varnish

Most professional shops apply conversion varnish (sometimes called catalyzed lacquer) to kitchen cabinets. This is a crosslinking two-part finish that is sold primarily at commercial supply outlets. You need to mix it first, then apply it with a spray gun. If you have any experience with spraying lacquer and can find a safe, explosion-proof booth to work in, it is indeed the most durable choice for kitchen and bathroom cabinetry. However, the low-tech alternatives of oil- and water-based polyurethanes are easy to find, require no mixing, and can be applied with brushes and paint pads. They dry overnight but take about a month to completely cure.

"Like a chain, a finish is only as good as its weakest link."

If you wait more than a week before recoating, you'll get better adhesion if you lightly sand between coats with fine 400-grit sandpaper or a very fine nylon abrasive pad.

Rubbing out

No matter how smoothly you apply the finish, it seems that there are always a few dust nibs that settle in, making the dried surface a bit rough. This is more common with clear finishes than with paint. Rubbing out the finish smoothes it. This technique is only for semigloss and satin finishes, not for gloss and matte finishes, because it alters the sheen.

Give the finish at least a week to cure. Scuff the surface very lightly with fine 500- or 600-grit paper—just enough to remove the nibs. Dip a 0000 steel wool pad or a very fine nylon abrasive pad into paste wax and rub it into the wood

with the grain (see top photo, p. 31). The pad leaves a uniform scratch pattern, like brushed brass, and the wax helps lubricate the surface. Go back and forth several times, and then immediately wipe off the wax with paper towels or a cloth. Work on one door or drawer at a time so the wax does not harden before you are able to wipe it off. The result is a satin finish that feels as smooth as it looks.

Countertops and Work Surfaces

Whether located in a kitchen, bar, or bathroom, countertops and work surfaces receive lots of wear. They're scrubbed with cleansers and water, and splashed with everything from acids (like vinegar and lemon juice) to bases (like baking soda and drain opener). Kitchen countertops also have to deal with grease and mustard and wine stains, while bathroom counters and vanities must endure acetone (nail polish remover) and alcohol (in perfume and mouthwash). On top of that, there is the wear and tear of daily use. If there was ever a place that demands a tough finish, a countertop is it.

As with the rest of the kitchen, the professional's choice for wood countertops, bars, and work surfaces is almost always conversion varnish. However, several coats of polyurethane will do the job quite nicely. In this case, though, I would not use a water-based one, nor would I go over an old finish. In short, strip it down to the bare wood and coat it with oil-based polyurethane.

TRADE SECRET

If you have experience spraying lacquer or varnish but not waterborne coatings, be prepared for some changes. Waterborne finishes often lay out better on vertical surfaces than on horizontal ones. It's also important to spray waterborne finishes in a lighter coat than you think you should. If you put on a thoroughly wet coat, the way you do with solvent-based coatings, the finish will not lay out smoothly and will probably drip and run. A coating of the proper density looks like the texture of an orange peel. As the finish cures, it will become smoother. Wait overnight to judge your work. As always, if this is your first time, practice on scrap wood before you do the real thing.

Using wax as a lubricant, rub with 0000 steel wool in the direction of the grain.

Use Old Brushes for Stripping

Stripping is a great opportunity to use a brush that you forgot to clean thoroughly and which now sports a crust of old paint. Not only will you be employing something that is otherwise useless, but you'll also get the chance to clean a brush that was probably destined for the trash. Once you've applied the remover and the stripper has softened the old gunk, rinse the brush well in mineral spirits. When it is clean, take it to the sink, wash it in warm soapy water, rinse it, and wrap it in a brown paper bag. Stripper will not harm either synthetic or natural bristle brushes.

Stripping

The first step in creating a durable countertop, bar top, or heavy-use kitchen table is to strip off the old finish. Like a chain, a finish is only as good as its weakest link, and in this case we want to make sure all the links are up to snuff. That means starting from raw wood and building a finish with only high-wear materials.

Stripping can be a messy process, so if you can remove the countertop and take it to a shop or garage, I recommend doing so. Prop it on sawhorses with plastic sheeting and newspaper below to catch any drips. If you can't remove it, take out the sink, range top, or anything else built in. Mask the walls, floors, adjacent cabinets, appliances, and the area underneath the sink cutout.

Take tables apart whenever possible. Remove the base and leaves, then strip each part separately. Treat the main tabletop as though it were a counter and prop it on sawhorses or a worktable.

Start with a strong paint and varnish remover, shaking it first to mix the ingredients. I prefer

using strippers with a high methylene chloride content. Removers without methylene chloride work, but they take a lot longer to do the job. Gather tools for stripping, plenty of newspaper on which to spread the stripped gunk, some plastic sheeting, and safety gear. Suit up with neoprene gloves, a respirator, an apron, and goggles. Most important, open some doors or windows and turn on a fan to get a healthy flow of air going.

Hot coffee pots, cleansers, acids, bases, alcohol, and stains from wine and mustard are just a few of the assaults waiting for the finish on this kitchen table.

WHAT CAN GO WRONG

Dealing with Drips

No matter how careful you are, it's inevitable that you'll get one or two drips in the course of your work. If you see them as they happen, pick them up immediately with the brush. First unload the brush by scraping it across the edge of the finish tray. Then go over the dripped area quickly and lightly to smooth it out. If you don't see the drip until it has started to dry, leave it alone. When it is fully hard (this may take several days), cut off the drip with a single-edge razor blade held at a low angle. Sand the area lightly, and follow up with another thin coat of finish to smooth it out.

TOOLS AND MATERIALS

What You'll Need: Stripping Tools

- Stripper
- Plastic sheeting
- Pan
- Brush
- Scrapers
- Newspaper
- Goggles, neoprene gloves, apron, respirator
- Ventilation fan
- Nylon abrasive pads
- Mineral spirits
- Water and ammonia
- Paper towels

Gather gloves, scrapers, goggles, pans, brushes, paper, an apron, a respirator, and stripper before you start a project.

Once the wood is clean but before it dries, remove the loose residue by scrubbing the surface with a nylon abrasive pad soaked in mineral spirits. Wipe the surface clean with a cloth or paper towels, then scrub it again with a solution made from one ounce of ammonia to one pint of warm water. This helps remove any silicone or nondrying oils in the wood. Wipe off the wood with towels and let it dry overnight.

Sealing the sink hole

The cutout for the sink is at least 50% end grain, so it is a prime place for water to seep into the wood and lift the finish. To prevent that, seal the edge with epoxy. Mask the top surface, mix some two-part epoxy according to the label's directions, and spread it onto the edge with a wooden Popsicle stick, taking care to force it into the end grain (see photo, right). Remove the masking tape when you are done spreading the epoxy but before it has completely set. Let it cure overnight and sand any overage flush with the countertop

so the sink seats properly. After you've finished the countertop and it is time to reinstall the sink, seat it with a bead of silicone caulk just inside the outer edge. This prevents water from seeping underneath it.

Sanding

As a general rule, you don't need to sand items that have been stripped clean but, with counters and tables, I find it is a good idea to do it anyway. Sanding helps eliminate irregularities in color and flatness. If the table or counter is new wood, sand through the grits, from 80 to 120 to 180 or 220.

Stripped pieces and veneered counters need only be sanded with 180- or 220-grit paper. Use a random orbit or vibrating sander, or sand by hand with a sanding block. In either case, the final sanding step should be by hand, with 180- or 220-grit garnet paper in the direction of the grain. Wipe off the sanding dust with a lightly dampened cloth.

Before setting a sink, spread epoxy on the edge of the sink cutout to stop water from migrating into the end grain.

"The cutout for the sink is a prime place for water to seep into the wood and lift the finish."

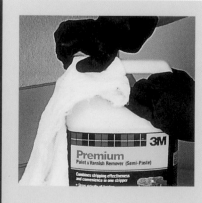

TRADE SECRET

Before opening a can of stripper, place a rag over the top and twist it off with the rag in place. This way, if a bit of stripper spurts out when you open it (which often happens), the rag will catch it.

Applying polyurethane

Buy a good, oil-based polyurethane, open the can, and stir it well. If it is a matte or satin finish, make sure all the flattening agent is stirred in (while the can sits, it settles to the bottom and looks like a hazy mass). Pour some out into a tray and close the can. I find that most polyurethanes brush out better when they are thinned about 10% to 15% with mineral spirits or naphtha. Thin only the finish in the tray, not the whole can. That way you can readjust the mixture if you need to by adding extra uncut material.

Prepare a good quality ox-hair blend or China bristle brush by soaking it up to the ferrule in a can of mineral spirits for about a minute. Squeeze out the excess and dip only the bottom third of the bristles into the varnish. Touch the bristle tips to the side of the tray to prevent drips, then place the brush at a 45-degree angle to the surface and deflect it just enough to bring wet finish to the top of the bristles. Starting just inside the edge, move smoothly and slowly in the direction of the grain. Continue to depress the bristles to feed finish evenly onto the wood until you run out of material. Lift off gently, redip the brush, and continue. After one pass, go back and blend the starting point out to the edge by brushing in the other direction. When the surface is coated, tip it off immediately (see p. 35).

Resist the temptation to lay a thick coat of finish; apply only a thin coat each time. Let each coat dry overnight before adding the next one. For counters and tabletops, apply at least three coats—four or five if you have the patience. Before the last

Make a Stripping Scraper

Here's how to make a handy scraper for taking off stripper. Cut a 45-degree angle at one end of a small section of a 2×4 stud. At the other end, attach a ¾-in. dowel with epoxy to make a handle. This scraper won't mar the surface the way a metal spackle knife can. (If you do use a metal scraper, be sure to round off the corners.)

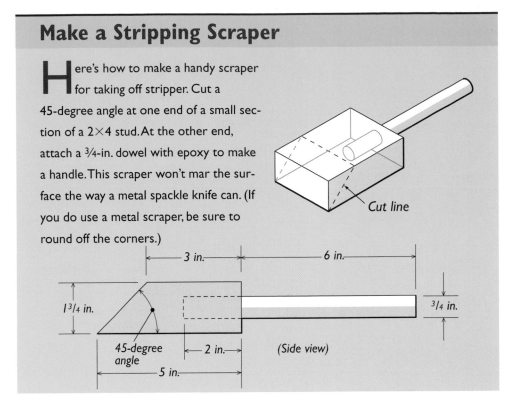

Cut line

3 in. — 6 in.

1³/4 in.

45-degree angle

2 in.

(Side view)

5 in.

³/4 in.

coat, sand the surface lightly with 320- or 400-grit lubricated sandpaper to make sure it is completely smooth and free of dust nibs, then tack it off with a rag lightly dampened with water.

Rubbing out

Rubbing out the top coat makes it feel silky smooth and looks great to boot. It may seem like a lot of work, but it's worth it. First, though, give the last top coat at least a week to cure for a satin rub, three weeks or more for a glossy one. The longer you let the finish cure, the easier it will be to rub it out. Rubbing to satin is fairly easy, but rubbing to gloss is a real chore. If you have a choice, pick satin.

SAFETY FIRST

Methylene chloride (DCM) is certainly the most effective stripper out there, but anything aggressive enough to go through paint that fast is bound to be dangerous. On the positive side, it is biodegradable and so nonflammable that when it is added to other flammable liquids, it renders them nonflammable, too. However, the fumes are dangerous if allowed to build up, especially to someone with heart disease. Make sure you work in a well-ventilated room. That means either outdoors in a breeze or inside with the windows open and a fan blowing. Keep the fan on exhaust so the fumes blow away from you, not toward you. A respirator is also a good idea, but it is not a replacement for adequate ventilation, only an added precaution. DCM can also enter your body through your skin, so wear good neoprene gloves and protect your eyes from splashes with goggles.

TOOLS AND MATERIALS

What You'll Need: Rubbing Compounds and Wax

- Buffing head (optional)
- Rubbing compound
- Polishing compound
- Glaze
- 0000 steel wool pad
- Paste wax
- Soft cotton rags
- Cold water

TAKE YOUR PICK

Tack Cloth vs. Damp Cloth

Tack cloths work well for solvent-based finishes, but they tend to leave a residue that adversely affects water-based coatings. Cheaper, and always effective, is a simple damp cloth. Not wet, mind you, but damp. What is damp? About as moist as a healthy dog's nose.

> *"Resist the temptation to lay a thick coat of finish; apply only a thin coat each time."*

Dip the bottom third of a brush's bristles into polyurethane, then gently touch the tips to the side of the container.

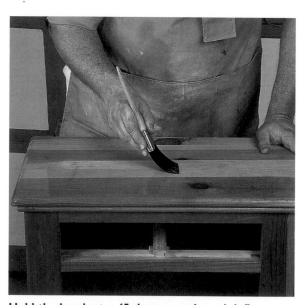

Hold the brush at a 45-degree angle and deflect the bristles just enough to bring the finish to the surface.

IN DETAIL

Avoiding Pigtails

First, understand that I am talking about a random orbit sander, not a belt sander. Leave the belt sander on the shelf. Random orbit sanders are designed to work under their own weight and to be moved slowly. If you press down on it or move it too fast, it creates coiled scratches in the wood that are called *pigtails*. Use only the weight of the sander itself and move it

about 1 in. per second. Try it. This page is about 8 in. wide. Move your hand so that it takes 8 seconds to get across the page. Slow, isn't it? Ironically, this will get the sanding done just as quickly, since you won't have to go back over spots again. Best of all, you won't have any annoying pigtails showing up under the finish.

Satin rub. First, sand very lightly with 400- or 500-grit sandpaper—just enough to remove any dust nibs. Then dip a piece of 0000 steel wool in paste wax and rub just the ends of the top in the direction of the grain (see drawing, facing page). If the top has a sharp edge, keep your hand flat so you don't rub through the corner. Redip the steel wool in the wax and rub the length of the counter or tabletop with the grain, going back and forth and keeping the strokes as straight as possible. Rub back and forth from the front edge to the back and from side to side to the ends, then back toward the front. That is one pass. Do that six times, pressing down with moderate pressure and adding wax as needed to get a smooth, even scratch pattern over the entire top. Wipe off excess wax with a clean cloth or a paper towel.

If you squeegee the top with your thumb, you'll notice that there is still too much wax on the surface. Sprinkle the top with cold water (it will bead up), then take a clean 0000 steel wool pad and repeat the rubbing action once more, but this time don't press down. Use only the weight of your hand, moving from side to side and from front to back, then flip the pad over and reverse the process. You'll notice that the pad fills with coagulated wax. The cold water helps the steel wool lift off the wax instead of smearing it around. When you're done, wipe the water off the surface of the wood.

Gloss rub. For a gloss rub, sand the surface with 600-, 800-, 1,000-, and 1200-grit sandpaper, using slightly soapy water as a lubricant. Wipe off the slurry in between the grit changes.

Rubbing Out a Satin Finish

1. Dip the steel wool in paste wax and rub just the ends in the direction of the grain.

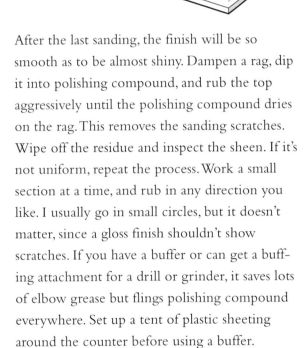

2. Dip the steel wool in paste wax and rub the surface end to end following the grain.

3. Overlap the passes on long strokes and repeat the process six times.

After the last sanding, the finish will be so smooth as to be almost shiny. Dampen a rag, dip it into polishing compound, and rub the top aggressively until the polishing compound dries on the rag. This removes the sanding scratches. Wipe off the residue and inspect the sheen. If it's not uniform, repeat the process. Work a small section at a time, and rub in any direction you like. I usually go in small circles, but it doesn't matter, since a gloss finish shouldn't show scratches. If you have a buffer or can get a buffing attachment for a drill or grinder, it saves lots of elbow grease but flings polishing compound everywhere. Set up a tent of plastic sheeting around the counter before using a buffer.

When the entire top is glossy and free of scratches, give it a coat of swirl mark remover. I like Meguiar's Number 7 Mirror Glaze (you can find it in the auto department of a home store or in an auto parts store). Shake it up, squeeze some

Tipping Off

After completely coating a surface with oil-based polyurethane, unload the brush by scraping the bristles over the edge of the tray. Then hold the brush at a 90-degree angle to the surface and, with only the tips of the bristles touching the still-wet polyurethane, gently drag the brush through the finish in the same direction in which it was applied. This operation, known as tipping off, pulls out dust and smoothes air bubbles.

Cold water congeals excess wax so a pad can remove it.

IN DETAIL
Aging with Oak

Ever wonder why wine is aged in oak casks? The tannins in the oak impart a flavor to the wine that, in the opinion of the experts, improves it. Two hundred years ago, virtually all foods—liquid and solid, wet and dry—were stored in oak casks that occupied much of the floor space of town stores. They gave us expressions such as "cracker barrel" and "cash on the barrelhead," and led Edgar Allan Poe to write about a "cask of Amontillado."

TRADE SECRET

The first time you open a can of finish, take a sharpened slot head screwdriver and punch a few holes in the recess of the rim. This lets the finish that collects there drip back into the can. A clean rim means that the lid fits snugly. It also saves you a fortune in finish that dries out because the lid doesn't fit right anymore.

IN DETAIL
Polishing to Gloss

There are any number of good polishing and rubbing compounds out there, and they all work pretty well. Try polishing compound first, as rubbing compound is coarser. It may do the trick by itself. If it doesn't get the sanding scratches out, try rubbing compound, then follow up with polishing compound again. Finish off with a coat of swirl mark remover.

TRADE SECRET

When the finish starts to thicken on your brush, especially up by the ferrule, stop and rinse it in mineral spirits. After you squeeze out the excess liquid, you'll have a brush as clean and supple as when you started. It takes only a minute to rinse it and the brush will be a breeze to clean at the end of the job.

> *"My kitchen boasts its share of wooden cutting boards, mixing spoons, and spatulas, and all of them have the same finish—nothing."*

Set up a plastic tent before buffing or you'll fling compound everywhere.

A coat of swirl mark remover adds just a bit more shine to an already polished top.

TRADE SECRET

If you put at least three to five coats of polyurethane on a countertop, you'll be able to rub out minor scratches the same way you originally rubbed them in. Sand lightly with 600-grit or finer sandpaper and follow up with steel wool and wax (for a satin finish) or with buffing compound (for a gloss finish). Now and again you can recoat the countertop as the finish wears thin. To do so, first remove the wax with a nylon abrasive pad soaked in mineral spirits, sand the surface well with 320-grit lubricated sandpaper, and then add a fresh coat of polyurethane.

out onto a soft cloth, and spread it liberally on the top. Wipe it off immediately with a clean cloth. This adds that extra fillip of shine to an already beautiful job.

Food Contact Surfaces

A hearty eater is sometimes called a trencherman, a term derived from the word *trencher,* which was a wooden platter used for serving food in days of yore. We haven't strayed so far from our roots it seems, because wooden objects still abound in most kitchens. These days they are most likely to be in the forms of cutting boards, salad bowls, spoons, and spatulas, but they still pose the question of how best to finish them. As it turns out, the easiest answer (and arguably the best) is to use nothing at all. Food contact items do not require a finish, but if you don't like the look of natural, raw wood, there are several alternatives.

Cutting boards, mixing spoons and spatulas

My kitchen boasts its share of wooden cutting boards, mixing spoons, and spatulas, and all of them have the same finish—nothing. They get used every day, several times a day. After each use, I scrub them with soap and hot water and stand them up to dry. Two of my cutting boards, one oak and one maple, have been in constant use for the past 25 years and are in better shape than I am. No finish will stand up to being cut with a knife and subjected to high heat, constant scrubbing, and strong acids and bases without losing the battle relatively quickly.

Now and again, though, you'll have a cutting board that you want to present in its best light, like those fancy striped ones made from different types of hardwoods. Wipe those down with mineral oil, which you can find at your local drugstore. Just flood it on and wipe it off. It won't turn rancid like vegetable oils, nor will it dry like nut oils. Mineral oil stays wet indefinitely and does not impart any flavor to food. Of course, after one or two scrubbings with soap and water, most of it will have been washed off, but you can reapply it as often as you like.

Chopping blocks

Unlike regular cutting boards, which display the flat side of the wood, chopping blocks are made with blocks of wood glued together so that the end grain provides the working surface. The one standard finish for them is paraffin, which you can find in the canning section of a grocery store or the candlemaking section of a craft store. Melt the paraffin in a double boiler and while it is still hot spread it thickly onto the end grain of the butcher block. The end grain soaks up the hot wax. Leave plenty of extra wax on the top. When the wax cools back to a solid, scrape off the excess with a flat scraper or the edge of a credit card to leave a smooth, wax-filled surface.

Bowls, serving platters, and sushi trays

These, too, can be left in the raw or treated with mineral oil, but since they aren't subjected to the abuse of cutting boards, you have a few more

options. Quite a few, in fact. The finish you apply depends on how the item will be used and what you want it to look like. Bear in mind that these finishes are for items that will be gently washed by hand and not subjected to strong alkaline cleansers, such as ammonia. Here are a few of the choices, going from the thinnest, most woody looking, to the thickest and glossiest.

Drying oil or Danish oil. Many turners who make bowls treat them with tung oil, boiled linseed oil, or Danish oil while they are still on the lathe. Flood the oil on, let it soak in for about 10 or 15 minutes, then wipe it off. It takes a day or so to dry, and you can add more coats if you like. Since the oil soaks in, it keeps the wood looking rich and there is no surface coating to chip or wear off. Oils look best on wood that has been finely sanded to at least 500 or 600 grit.

Wax. Paste wax, which you can find in the finish department of a hardware or home store, makes a simple finish all by itself. Apply it with a

Some well-worn wooden utensils rest on the author's 25-year-old cutting board.

IN DETAIL

Unfinished Wooden Bowls and Splinters

How come unfinished wooden plates, bowls, and utensils don't put splinters in the food—or do they? They could, and that would be no real hardship, since gnawing on most woods won't hurt you. I've been known to wander the house chewing on a stick of licorice root. But there are two good reasons why we usually

don't get splinters from unfinished wooden utensils. First, we get splinters from wood that is rough, not from smoothly sanded wood. Second, certain woods are less splintery than others are. We generally make our food-service items from well-sanded, non-splintery woods, such as maple, beech, and cherry.

TOOLS AND MATERIALS

Drying Oils vs. Nondrying Oils

Some oils, such as those used in your car's crankcase, are meant to stay liquid indefinitely. But in finishing, we coat wood with oils that dry to a solid film when they come in contact with air. As a rule, nut oils, including linseed (also called flaxseed) oil, tung oil, and walnut oil, are drying oils. Mineral oils and vegetable oils, such as olive oil, corn oil, and lemon oil, are nondrying oils and do not form a film. They are absorbed into wood but stay wet indefinitely. Incidentally, peanut oil, in spite of its name, is not a drying oil. Peanuts are legumes, not nuts, and are thus members of the vegetable group.

Even in a double boiler, hot wax can easily catch fire, so filling the end grain of a chopping block is a process best done outdoors.

0000 steel wool or a very fine nylon abrasive pad. Dip the pad into the wax and scrub it onto the wood. Wipe off as much as you can immediately. The result is a soft finish that does not darken the wood the way most oils do.

Wipe-on polyurethane. Another thin but easy-to-apply finish is oil-based polyurethane that is wiped on instead of brushed. Open the can, stir it well, and dip a nylon abrasive pad into the polyurethane. Wear thin, throwaway gloves for this. The finish won't harm you, but it sure makes your hands sticky. Scrub the polyurethane into the wood, then immediately wipe off the excess with a cloth or paper towels. Let it dry overnight and if it still looks "hungry," add another coat.

Shellac. Shellac gives you the choice of a thin, low-luster finish or a thicker, glossier one

that looks elegant on fancy sushi trays. For a thin version, reduce the shellac with denatured alcohol until it is the consistency of skim milk. Put on a pair of disposable vinyl or latex gloves and dip a rag into the thinned finish. Flood it onto the wood, and then immediately wipe off whatever does not soak in. Let it dry for about three hours, then very lightly sand it with 320- or 400-grit sandpaper—just enough to eliminate fuzziness. Then rub on a coat of paste wax and wipe it off immediately with a cloth or paper towels.

For a high sheen, omit the wax. After the fine sanding, add more coats of shellac with a brush or spray gun. You can buy shellac in an aerosol can if you don't own a spray gun. You'll need to apply at least two or three coats, but there is no need to sand between coats. Apply no more than two coats per day, and keep building the finish until you get the look you want. Let it dry for several days after the last coat, and then apply a coat of

It's easy enough to scrub some polyurethane onto this bowl, then wipe off whatever is not absorbed.

"Paste wax, which you can find in the finish department of a hardware or home store, makes a simple finish all by itself."

SAFETY FIRST

Rags soaked with drying oils, such as linseed oil, can spontaneously combust if they are left in a pile for even a couple of hours. Put oil-soaked rags one layer thick out to dry on a workbench, a clothesline, or the edge of a trash can. By the next day the rags will be hard, crusty, and dry—and safe for the household trash.

TRADE SECRET

Did you know that you've probably eaten shellac? Like honey, another product that comes from insects, shellac is completely edible, though nowhere near as tasty. It is used to coat pills to make them easier to swallow and to coat chocolate candy to make it shiny. It is listed on the label as confectioner's glaze or confectioner's resin.

paste wax with a rag. Let it dry for about 15 minutes, and then buff it to a shine with a soft cloth.

Lacquer. Clear lacquer also comes in spray cans and is an easy way to build a finish. After the wood has been sanded well, spray on several coats of lacquer. Stick to two coats a day, adding as many as you like until you get the depth you prefer. Once again, there is no need to sand between coats.

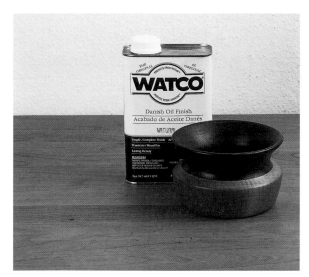

Danish oil is the perfect finish for this fancy nut bowl.

This ornamental walnut bowl sports nothing more than a thin coat of paste wax.

Shellac adds a glossy sheen to this ornate lidded bowl.

This delicate but elegant miniature goblet is protected with several coats of spray lacquer.

IN DETAIL

Definition of a White Cooper

A *cooper* is someone who makes barrels and buckets out of staved oak. A *white cooper* is someone who makes barrels and buckets to hold water as well as dry goods. The term comes from the fact that if you fashion a barrel out of red oak, no matter how well it is made, water can seep through the grain and "weep" onto the outside of the barrel. Not so with white oak. But those who used white oak to make water vessels had to be talented enough to make barrels that could hold water. As a result, the white cooper was regarded as more skilled than the run-of-the-mill cooper was. In the 17th century, ships carrying colonizing groups always hired for the voyage a white cooper, whose job was to make barrels for storing food and drink. Probably the most famous of these was John Alden, who came over on the Mayflower and fell for the lovely Priscilla.

White oak.

Built-Ins and Panel

CHAPTER THREE

ing

1 Prefinishes
page 42

2 Stains and Color
page 44

3 Top Coats
page 47

Say the word "den" and it conjures up a warm, inviting hideaway whose walls are lined with rich wood wainscoting and matching bookshelves flanking a carved fireplace. Yours may not be quite so quaint, but wood certainly lends a calm dignity to any room, even if it is nothing more than exposed beams or waist-high chair rails. Opt for the right finish and you can add a deep glow to the wood as well as make it more practical to use and clean. Most any finish is durable enough for paneling, wainscoting, and built-ins, which leaves plenty of options. You can go for a woody-looking oiled finish, the old-world shine of shellac and varnish, or a highly durable modern polyurethane.

TOOLS AND MATERIALS

What You'll Need: Finishing Built-Ins

- Brushes, paint pads, spray gun
- Masking materials
- Drop cloths, resin paper
- Polyurethane, shellac, lacquer, oil, varnish
- Paste wax
- Nylon abrasive pads
- Sandpaper
- Rags or shop towels
- Ladders
- Sawhorses or worktable
- Mineral spirits

Professional estimate
- Fireplace: 18 hours
- 6-ft. bookcase: 13 hours

IN DETAIL

Fluorescent Lights and Fading

While it is true that fluorescent lights emit some UV-range light, it is nowhere near enough to cause fading in wood or paint. A far more significant source of UV light is that which comes in your windows.

Setting a built-in on sawhorses for horizontal finishing means fewer runs and sags.

Prefinishes

Whenever you have the option, finish built-in woodwork before it goes in place. It is far easier and more convenient to treat it as separate furniture and finish it in your shop or outdoors. Trying to work without damaging carpet or pristine hardwood flooring adds one more potential problem and another level of stress. Besides, if you finish items separately, you'll be able to turn a large bookcase or a section of wall paneling on its side. When you have gravity working with you instead of against you, the fin-

ish flows out better and you are far less likely to end up with runs and sags (see photo, left).

Bookcases and built-ins

If you are building the piece yourself, you can take prefinishing to another level. In most cases, you can finish the parts of a cabinet or bookcase before the piece is glued up and assembled. When you finish the parts as flat objects, you can conveniently apply the entire coat and eliminate dreaded glue spots underneath the finish (see photo, below). Such spots occur because excess glue on the surface of the wood, which is invisible, blocks stain from penetrating the wood. The result is unstained spots that surprise you during staining or that show up after the finish is applied. Prefinishing lets you stain before glue up, thus eliminating glue spots entirely.

Start by cutting and sanding all the parts, then dry-fit them for accuracy. Take the pieces apart and mask off the glue joints carefully with blue

Glue spots are the bane of woodworkers because they show up only after the stain or finish is applied.

"Prefinishing lets you stain before glue up, thus eliminating glue spots entirely."

WHAT CAN GO WRONG

Right Tape, Wrong Tape

When you mask a glue joint for prefinishing, the tape has to stay put for a long time—through application, drying time, and maybe even rub out. Regular tan masking tape deteriorates after several days. It tears and leaves adhesive on the wood when you try to remove it. I've found that 3M's blue Long Mask Tape does a far better job. It is designed to stay on for many days and still come off clean with no tearing or adhesive residue.

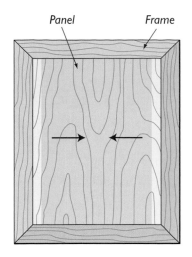

Panel   Frame

**Prefinish
Panels
if Possible**
*Wood shrinks
across the grain.
Panels that are
finished after they
are in the frame
often shrink
enough to show a
line of unfinished
wood at the edges.*

frame are set in the opposite direction, with
plenty of room for movement (see drawing,
left). Panels that are finished after they have been
set in their frames often shrink during the dry
heating season and show a white line of unfinished wood along the edge of the panel (see
photo, p. 44).

To accommodate expansion and contraction
of the wood, panels are often left to float in their

painter's tape. Glue does not stick to finish, which
will prove to be a big advantage later. Apply the
stain (if you are using any), then brush, wipe, or
spray on the various coats of finish. If you plan to
rub out the piece, do that too. Make sure you
finish both sides (see sidebar, right).

Once all the finishing is done, remove the
masking tape to reveal the raw wood where the
glue is applied. Then glue up the piece as you
normally would. You'll find that the glue
squeeze-out of most woodworking adhesives
does not stick to finish. You can easily wipe it off
with a damp cloth while it is wet or pop it off
with a sharpened dowel after it is dry. You could
use a chisel, too, but a dowel is less likely to slip
and mar the new finish.

Raised panel wainscoting

Solid wood wainscoting is made by setting large
panels of wood in frames. The rails of the frames
are made from the long grain, so there is no
shrinkage along them. However, the panels they

Prefinish Masking

Before you prefinish,
mask the glue
joints. This keeps the
joints free of finish so the
glue can adhere, but pre-
vents white unfinished
lines from peeking out of
the joints later on. Lay
out the joints during the
dry-fitting stage and
make a light pencil mark
at the ends of the joints.
Mask 1/16 in. inside the
line. Remove the pencil
lines with a quick swipe
of denatured alcohol or
an art gum eraser. When
you glue up, the joint will
overlap the finish by
1/16 in. That's enough for a
great glue bond, but good
insurance that no unfin-
ished wood will show.

TAKE YOUR PICK

Seal the Back

It is not absolutely necessary to seal the back of wainscoting or paneling, since it will be affixed to the wall. The amount of air movement, and hence the amount of change in relative humidity, is far less between the wainscoting and the wall than it is on the front. However, if you are prefinishing anyway, it helps to at least seal the back of the wood with a coat or two of the same finish before installing it. If there is some moisture coming through the walls, sealing the back adds stability to the panel. You can also seal the edges if you are not planning to tack them with glue, but that doesn't have much effect one way or the other. What's more important is to seal the end grain at the bottom of tongue-and-groove paneling to prevent cracking due to moisture coming up through the floor.

The panel on this door shrank enough to show a line of unstained wood where the panel meets the frame.

frames or tacked with a spot of glue on just one edge. Prefinishing the panels before they are framed lets you apply color and an even finish right up to the edge of the panel. Even the section underneath the frame will be colored, so that when the panel shrinks, no white line of wood will show.

I like to stain and seal the panels before assembling them, but I leave the final coat until after the frames are in place. The first coat or two of finish keeps the panels clean. Then, after assembling the panels in their frames, I sand and stain the frames, making sure that they match the panels. Next, I seal the frames and add a final coat to the entire piece for a uniform look and sheen.

Stains and Color

Whether your walls are lined with large built-in bookcases and corner cupboards or paneling and wainscoting, you may be dealing with a lot of wood surface in one room. It is important to

select a color that gives the room the effect you want. Applying a light or dark finish has a serious impact on the room's appearance and ambience. Choose a stain that won't fade in areas hit by direct sunlight. Finally, make sure that you can color such a large area uniformly. That's easy with paint, but stains can be more challenging.

The right color

Picking a color to stain one piece of furniture is pretty straightforward. You can go with a color that tickles your fancy, match something else in the room, or let the wood decide. Built-in bookshelves, wainscoting, and wall paneling are another issue altogether. For one thing, you can't easily move them to another room if they don't quite fit in. But more important, you're selecting a color that will affect the look and feel of the entire room, simply because there is so much of it.

Light or dark. Light colors can open up a room and make it more airy. Dark paneling can make a room feel small and somber. Some people may see it as calm and intimate, while others may view it as foreboding and claustrophobic. Since dark colors tend to eat up light, such finishes may demand a change in your lighting scheme as well.

Complementary colors. Take a good look at the other colors in the room. If wainscoting or paneling covers the bottom half of the wall, think about how the finish will work with the paint or wallpaper above it. White and light colors may give too stark a contrast to a fairly dark wood

"Applying a light or dark finish has a serious impact on the room's appearance and ambience."

TRADE SECRET

This may sound like a travesty to die-hard wood fanciers, but some people may opt to paint built-ins or paneling. Unfortunately, some woods contain resins that bleed color into paint. You could end up with a surprise, especially if you use white or light-colored paint. To avoid this problem, use a primer that seals the wood and creates a good base for painting. My favorite product for indoor work is shellac-based BIN made by Zinsser. It sticks well; dries fast; seals in stains, resin, and knots; and provides an ideal base for either oil- or water-based paint.

and vice versa. Colors like forest green may bring out more red in the adjacent wood, while a rust color may make brown wood appear greenish. Try to imagine how your carpet, drapes, and upholstery will be showcased against the wood. Consider making a stained sample board of the same wood and placing it near the pieces it will live among. Remember to view wall panel samples vertically, since most wood looks considerably darker in its vertical format than in its horizontal one.

The effect of lighting. It's important to preview colors in the lighting they will live in. Seeing a color under strong fluorescent or halogen lighting at the paint store does not tell you how it will look in your room. You may have incandescent or natural light that will affect the color. Check the color at least twice—once in the daylight and again at night, when it is illuminated by the room's electric lights.

Sun exposure

Just as the sun can fade upholstery, it can also affect wood. Sunlight darkens some woods, lightens others, and bleaches out dye stains. If the woodwork will be bathed in strong sunlight and you want to maintain a constant color, you need to be careful about which stain you choose. Most of the stains on the market contain both pigments and dyes. The pigment portion won't fade, but the dye portion may. Buy yourself some

Make up a stained sample board and set it in place to predict how the color will complement your furniture and carpet.

Repainting Old Wood Paneling

Sometimes the best thing you can do for old, dark plywood paneling is to paint it a solid color. Make sure the new paint will adhere well by going through a good preparation routine. First, clean the wood of accumulated grease and dirt by scrubbing it with TSP or detergent in water. Rinse and wipe off the wood. When it is dry, sand it lightly with 220-grit paper. Prime the wood with at least one coat of BIN primer. Add a second coat if the wood absorbs a lot of the first one. On grooved plywood paneling, the vertical reveals cut into the surface absorb a lot of finish. Give them an extra coat of sealer with a small brush. Let the primer dry overnight before you paint.

The reveal grooves in cheap wall paneling absorb lots of paint, so brush an extra coat of primer into them first.

IN DETAIL
What Makes the Color in Stain?

Wood colorants are either dyes or pigments or a combination of the two. Dyes are colors that dissolve in liquid. Because dye particles are so small—the size of a molecule—they're absorbed into wood. Pigments are ground-up particles of colored dirt. They do not dissolve in liquid but remain suspended. Eventually, pigment particles settle to the bottom of a container. Since most commercial stains contain both types of colorants, remember to stir a stain very well before you apply it.

Dye stain dissolves in hot water.

WHAT CAN GO WRONG

Oops, Metamerism!

Colors change dramatically when they are viewed under different light sources. This characteristic is called *metamerism*. Natural sunlight provides the standard of what we call true colors, and we compare everything to those. Incandescent lighting, for instance, makes colors look more reddish than sunlight does, while fluorescent light makes items look more bluish or greenish. Make sure you look at the wood sample in the lighting that the room provides or you may be in for a big shock once the finish is on.

Changing the light source can affect how we see the colors of an object.

> *"In most cases, solid wood absorbs more stain than veneered panels, especially on exposed end grain."*

Strong sunlight can fade stains and wood as well as fabrics.

insurance by carefully reading the label and choosing an all-pigment stain. Incidentally, using an all-pigment stain also diminishes the sun's fading effect on the wood itself.

Uniformity

Bookcases, cabinets, and wainscoting are often made of a combination of woods that each take stain differently. You may have veneered panels and solid wood moldings or frames; veneer absorbs stain at a different rate than solid wood does. In some cases, the moldings may be made from an entirely different species of wood than the panels or the veneered stock.

Here's a strategy to make sure all the wood ends up looking the same. Start by testing each of the elements separately to see how the stain reacts on it. In most cases, solid wood absorbs more stain than veneered panels, especially on exposed end grain. Certain areas of solid wood may take in more

color than others do (see top left photo, facing page). By testing stain samples on scrap wood first, you will know what you are up against.

Secondary staining. Choose a stain based on what looks right on the darkest piece of your test scraps. But be careful: The wood that is the darkest of the group before you stain will not necessarily be the darkest of the group after you stain. This method provides you with a color that is not too dark on any of the wood but is too light in several areas. Apply the stain uniformly over the entire piece. The easiest way to get it even is to flood it on liberally, then wipe it all off while it is still wet. You'll end up with the entire unit stained, with some areas just right, some too light, but none too dark. From here on, each step adjusts the light areas by making them darker.

Let the stain dry completely. Set up the piece as close as possible to the way it will be viewed and look at the color. Then use the same stain to

Exterior and interior/exterior stains won't fade in sunlight, but interior stains may.

TRADE SECRET

Create a perfect fit for your prefinished cabinet or bookcase by using prefinished scribed molding strips. Flat molding strips can be used as an interface where the cabinet or bookcase meets the wall or ceiling. When the unit is installed, scribe the moldings to snugly fit the contours of the wall and hide the seam where it meets the unit.

Make plenty of extra molding strips and finish them when you do the rest of the piece. This gives you several shots at scribing them accurately, just in case. Attach them to the cabinet with a few spots of hot glue or fine headless finishing nails. Plug the nail holes with a wax touch-up crayon or colored finishing putty that stays flexible.

The same stain may come out lighter on a veneered panel than it does on a solid wood frame.

You may have to restain some areas with the same or a different color to get all the parts to match.

go back over only the areas that are too light. Work carefully with a small cloth pad, a small trim brush, or a cotton swab so you can control exactly where you apply the stain. Let the stain dry and check it again. Get the color as even as possible, then seal it and check it again once the sealer has dried.

Glazing. You can still alter the color after the sealer is on, but only to make it darker. The same stain that you used on the raw wood can go over the finish too, but now it's called glaze instead of stain. You'll find that while the glaze is still wet it can wipe off the more slippery finish. This makes it easier to "erase" an area that is too dark. Apply the stain with a rag or brush, then use a dry brush to blend it exactly where you need it.

Top Coats

Almost any finish will do for bookshelves, paneling, and the like. Durability is not a big issue, since there won't be hot pots, scratchy china, or wet glasses to cause problems. Still, you'll want to

Custom Pickling Stains

I want to put a pickled finish on my bookshelves that will match the colors in the room. How do I mix a custom pickling stain?

Start by making a sample board or two, then go to the store and find a paint chip from the color rack that looks right to you. Have the clerk mix a quart of paint. Both latex and oil-based

You can change the tint of pickling stain by stirring in small amounts of universal tinting colors, such as the Tints-All brand used here.

paint will work, but the latter gives you more working time, since it dries much slower. Pour a small amount into a tray and reduce it with solvent by one-third (use water for latex paint and mineral spirits for oil-based paint). Test the sample on the wood to make sure it looks the way you want it. If not, you can add more solvent or more paint, or even alter the color slightly by adding small amounts of concentrated UTC stains. (For more on pickling, see pp. 28–29.)

IN DETAIL
Dealing with Knots

Sadly, knots are prone to bleeding their sap through finishes. Spot seal them first, letting them dry before you apply primer or clear finish. For clear finishes, use Bull's Eye SealCoat or another wax-free shellac. Under paint, use B-I-N.

Before adding a clear finish, preseal knots with Bull's Eye SealCoat or wax-free shellac.

TAKE YOUR PICK
Satin vs. Gloss

Whether you choose a satin or a gloss finish is entirely up to you; however, for this type of work, I would steer you away from gloss. A high-gloss finish demands many coats, which must be sanded in between for an ultra-smooth surface, then buffed out. For low-wear pieces and vertical wall panels, satin or low-luster finishes look better and hide more defects to boot.

TOOLS AND MATERIALS
Glazing Brushes

The brush you use to blend out glaze color must be springy enough to move the glaze around yet soft enough not to leave brush marks. The easiest glazes to control are the oil-based ones, for which a natural bristle brush works best. China bristle will do in a pinch, but softer fitch or ox-hair blends are better. The best of both worlds may be a hybrid, such as a China bristle/ox-hair brush.

These brushes are blends of China bristle and ox hair, making them ideal for glazing.

Use a dry brush to move the glaze where you want it, blend it, and remove it, wiping the bristles frequently as you work.

choose a finish that tolerates being cleaned and looks consistent over the years.

Preparation

Whenever you finish built-ins, mask all the areas adjacent to it. Rosin paper is great for protecting tile, linoleum, and hardwood floors. It is not slippery and is thick enough to block splashes and the occasional minor spill. If you can't lift carpets and turn them back, mask them with a border of duct tape. Mask walls with blue painter's tape and plastic sheeting. Rubberized canvas or plastic drop cloths complete the picture. (For stripping existing paint, see pp. 16–19.)

Putty any defects or open knots, matching the putty to the color of the wood if you plan to use a clear or stained finish. You can use any light-colored putty under paint. There is a range of solvent- and water-based putties to choose from at the store; if they dry hard they will work. Put the putty on slightly proud, let it dry until it does

not take a fingernail impression, and then sand it flush with 180-grit paper on a sanding block. Sanding should have been done before installation, but if it hasn't, sand all the surfaces uniformly to 180 grit.

Painted surfaces

Not all wood is worthy of being showcased. Wall paneling, built-ins, fireplaces, and wainscoting may be made from paint-grade lumber, or wood that is not attractive enough to warrant a clear finish. Such pieces are designed for paint, and that is exactly what you should do with them.

Seal any wood you intend to paint with a good primer-sealer or stain killer. My favorite for indoor work is fast-drying, shellac-based B-I-N by Zinsser. It provides an excellent working base for paint to adhere to and hides the color beneath it. It is also excellent for sealing in knots that tend to bleed through paint and create brown shadows. B-I-N comes in white, which is adequate under any paint, and in tintable bases that can be colored to match the paint.

Both oil- and water-based paints are fine for interior work and go over primer nicely. Opt for either trim paint or washable kitchen/bathroom paint. Though they are more expensive, these paints have better wear resistance and can be cleaned more easily. Apply the paint however you prefer—with brushes, rollers, paint pads, or a spray gun. If you use a spray gun, install a ventilation fan and mask the entire room, as overspray has a tendency to get on everything. Plan on at least one coat of primer and two coats of paint.

> "Seal any wood you intend to paint with a good primer-sealer or stain killer."

WHAT CAN GO WRONG

The Heat Factor

Depending on its design, a fireplace may be the one area in a room where high temperature could be a problem. If the wood surrounding the fireplace is likely to get hot, your finish options are limited. Oil-based varnishes and polyurethanes are both up to the task, since they are not particularly sensitive to moderate heat. The same goes for thin, oil-based, wipe-on finishes, such as boiled linseed oil, tung oil, and Danish oil. Avoid shellac and lacquer, though, since they both start to soften at temperatures as low as 160°F.

Pull back the carpet or mask the edges with duct tape before you paint built-ins.

Putty color doesn't matter if you are planning to paint the wood.

Clear coatings

Since walls and built-ins tend to be undemanding, virtually any finish is adequate. Now you just need to decide which one you prefer. Here's the cornucopia that awaits you.

Oils and Danish oil are the simplest of the clear finishes. Choose boiled (not raw) linseed oil, tung oil, or Danish oil mixtures like Watco and Waterlox. Brush or wipe the oil fairly liberally onto the raw wood or, better yet, scrub it into the pores of the wood with a very fine nylon abrasive pad. Let it sit about 10 minutes, then wipe off whatever has not been absorbed. Allow the wood to dry overnight, then add another coat. You can keep adding one coat per day until you get the look you want. Two coats are the minimum required for some protection and a

Create a temporary "room" for spray finishing. This Zip Wall system includes thin plastic sheeting and spring-loaded poles that can be assembled and disassembled in minutes.

TRADE SECRET

After the first staining, it's a good idea to check your bookcase or cabinet setup before you move on. This may mean propping it up or clamping it in place. You may find that under normal lighting, the interior areas, such as the inside back of the case, looks decidedly darker. Checking the piece partway through the staining process gives you the option of leaving certain areas a bit lighter, so that it looks attractive when it is finally finished and assembled. To lighten a stain, thin a portion of it with a bit of its solvent (mineral spirits for oil-based stains, water for water-based stains). You many decide to use a lighter mix for interior parts and a darker mix elsewhere.

TOOLS AND MATERIALS
One-Coat Paint?

I think not. The assurance that you can cover dark wood with one coat of light-colored paint is, to quote Mary Poppins, "a piecrust promise—easily made, easily broken." Even with a coat of primer first, the odds are you will need two coats of paint to get good coverage and uniform color. Plan for it when you decide how much paint to buy and how much time to schedule for the task.

Plan for one coat of primer and two coats of paint if you want to hide dark wood.

"Shellac looks beautiful, dries very fast, and lends an old-world charm to your woodwork."

natural, woody look. Add a few extra coats for better durability on places like fireplace mantels that may be subjected to water or dripped wax from holiday decorations. Each coat adds more depth and gloss.

Shellac looks beautiful, dries very fast, and lends an old-world charm to your woodwork. If you can find it, use Bull's Eye SealCoat, a wax-free shellac. SealCoat should be used as is, without thinning. Otherwise, use any clear shellac thinned with one part denatured alcohol to two parts shellac. Apply the first coat by flooding it on with a brush or rag and following behind with a clean cloth or shop towel to wipe off whatever is not absorbed immediately. Give a sealer coat about an hour or two to dry, then sand it very lightly with 320-grit sandpaper to smooth out the raised grain.

Add at least two more coats of shellac with a brush or spray gun. Use a natural bristle brush and apply the shellac in thin coats. Do not go back and rebrush—it dries too fast for that. Apply it once as evenly as possible and move on. Don't bother to sand between coats unless you get dirt or drips in the finish. You can apply two coats per day if the room temperature is average. Cooler temperatures mean slower drying time. When you are finished, give the shellac two days to dry, then go over the piece with a thin coat of paste wax. One warning with shellac: Don't clean it with anything that contains ammonia, which eats into the finish.

Brushing lacquers and spray-on lacquers are still used for a large portion of high-end wood

furniture and they work for these projects, too. Use a lacquer thinner as the solvent, but otherwise follow the rules for shellac as described above. Seal the wood with a thin coat of either SealCoat or lacquer sanding sealer, let it dry for about two hours, and then sand it lightly. Use the same brushing technique as for shellac, adding two coats per day. Don't bother to sand between coats unless you get dirt in the finish.

Oil-based polyurethanes and varnishes don't need sealer and can be brushed or wiped on. Try wiping them on for an easy, fairly durable finish that looks great and is applied with a minimum of fuss. Dip a piece of nylon abrasive pad into the polyurethane or varnish and scrub it into the wood. Now wipe off all the excess with a clean rag or shop towel. Let it dry overnight, then wipe on a second coat. Repeat the process for a third coat. This method nets you a thin, low-luster finish that is more than adequate. If you prefer the finish to be a bit thicker or shinier, add the second and third coats with a brush instead of with a nylon pad, as a brush applies a thicker coat in one pass. In any case, keep it to one coat per day. The wipe-on version is fine as is, but you may

Shellac and Ammonia Don't Mix
After applying shellac, give it two days to dry, then go over the piece with a thin coat of paste wax. One warning with shellac: Don't clean it with anything that contains ammonia, as that will eat into the finish.

IN DETAIL
Brushing the Inside of a Cabinet or Bookshelf

First, remove all the adjustable and nonpermanent shelves and finish them separately. Brush the inside top by placing the bristle tips about 1 in. away from the corner. Brush toward the center of the panel; then, with the bristles partially unloaded, brush again from the corner, this time placing the bristles against the corner's edges. Don't load the brush too much or you'll end up

with drips. Move on to the left side panel. Brush the sides vertically from the top down, starting from the upper corner where it meets the inside lid. Stop short of the bottom corner, then reverse the brush and go upward from there to meet the wet area on the side. Use this same technique from the first side around to the back, then on the other side. Save the bottom panel for last.

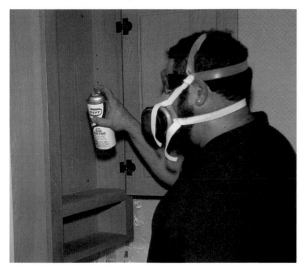

Aerosol cans are an easy way to apply spray lacquer, but don't forget to wear a respirator.

Scrub polyurethane into the wood with fine Scotch-brite, then wipe off the excess before it dries.

want to rub out brushed varnish. (See Rubbing Out, p. 30.)

Water-based polyurethanes and acrylics look different than other finishes because they are clear rather than amber. They also dry much faster than oils and smell less. Use them on white and light-colored woods to keep the wood as blond as possible. Water-based polyurethanes are about as tough as the oil-based varieties, while water-based acrylics are equivalent to lacquers. Start with a coat of water-based sanding sealer on the raw wood, or use SealCoat as described in the shellac technique. For flat surfaces, I like to apply water-based finishes with a paint pad. I find it gives a smoother finish, is easier to control than a brush, and is about as fast as a spray gun. For areas that a pad won't get into, use a nylon bristle brush. It is the softest of the synthetic bristles and works best with water-based materials. Let the first coat dry overnight before you sand it very lightly with 400-grit or finer paper to smooth the raised grain. Add two more coats of water-based polyurethane or acrylic for the top coat. If you decide to wax this finish, wait several weeks. Water-based finishes dry to the touch very quickly but take four weeks to fully cure.

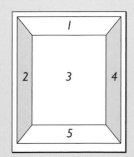

Painting Sequence
Paint the inside of a bookcase or cabinet in the following sequence: 1) top, 2) left side, 3) back, 4) right side, 5) bottom.

SAFETY FIRST

Rags soaked with drying oils, such as linseed oil, can spontaneously combust if they are left in a pile for even a couple of hours. If you've been using oil finishes or fillers, put the rags out to dry on a work-bench, a clothesline, or the edge of a trash can—but make sure they are only one layer thick. By the next day the rags will be hard, crusty, and dry, at which time it is safe to add them to the household trash.

Trim

Just as exterior trim lends character to the outside of your home, so the doors, windows, and moldings add appeal to the interior. They can be painted to blend into the walls or set off with contrasting colors to give definition to a room. In many homes, the trim and doors are the one place where natural or stained wood provides a strong contrast to painted or papered walls. Still other homes have painted trim, hiding the fact that these utilitarian wood items are often made of lumber too coarse to show.

No matter what the finish, interior doors, trim, and molding get lots of wear from regular use and need good, durable coatings that can take the stress of constant use. Whether you are working on chair rails, doors, windows, or moldings, the methods and materials are the same. So, while I usually refer throughout this chapter to moldings, you can assume that the rules apply to all these items.

TOOLS AND MATERIALS

What You'll Need: Stripping Tools

- Brushes, paint pads, spray gun
- Masking materials
- Drop cloths, resin paper, plastic sheeting
- Polyurethane, trim paint
- Nylon abrasive pads, steel wool
- Sandpaper
- Rags or shop towels
- Ladders
- Sawhorses or worktable
- Mineral spirits, naphtha
- Stripper, scrapers

Professional estimate

- One hour per window or door, painted
- Four hours per door, stripped and refinished

> "The first step in achieving a fine finish is preparing the surface properly."

New- and Old-Wood Preparation

As always, the first step in achieving a fine finish is preparing the surface properly. If you're installing new molding, doors, or windows, all you really have to do is putty and sand (and usually very little sanding at that). Frequently, though, we find ourselves facing the arduous task of stripping old varnish—or worse, old paint—in an attempt to find a diamond in the rough. That is not always possible, since old trim, doors, and windows are frequently made with paint-grade wood. In any case, when you work in place, you'll need to mask the area, then sand and putty the wood before you finish it.

First, you mask

Whether you are stripping or finishing, mask off the area thoroughly any time you work on installed pieces. Be especially careful if you mask around the walls, since some types of masking tape tear wallpaper when you try to remove it. Opt for the special low-tack masking tapes made for that purpose. Pair the tape with large rolls of one- or two-mil. plastic sheeting and you have an inexpensive, lightweight masking team. As thin as it is, the plastic protects surfaces from stripper, solvents, stains, and paint.

Prefinishing is the best alternative to masking. It is much easier, and there is no chance of slopping stains onto adjacent walls and floors. You are also more likely to get a uniform color. New molding or chair rails can be stained and finished

This white tape is made with a low-tack adhesive that can be used on wallpaper without harming it.

in long strips, then later cut to fit during the installation. To stain molding, lay all the pieces on a worktable so you can make sure they match in color. When it comes time to install them, you will most likely attach them with headless finishing nails. Countersink them so they are slightly below the surface of the wood, and then hide the small holes with nondrying wax sticks.

Prefinishing isn't just for natural wood. You can also prime and paint colored moldings before you put them up. The problem is that nail hole putty comes in white, which is fine if your trim is white but problematic if your trim is another color. However, you may find your custom trim

TRADE SECRET

Wondering if the paint on that molding is hiding some beautiful wood? With older homes, the odds are in your favor. To find out, scrape a small, out-of-the-way area. If you find hardwood, it is almost certainly something that can be restored to stained wood and still look good. If one section of molding is a good grade of hardwood, chances are the rest of the molding in the house is, too. If you aren't sure, take the plunge and scrape another section of molding, a window, or the edge of a door. You just may find something worth restoring. The worst that can happen is that you'll end up having to spot-prime and repaint the scraped areas.

You can buy inexpensive plastic sheeting, perfect for masking, in 10-ft. × 100-ft. rolls.

color in your child's box of crayons, a perfectly legitimate substitute for commercial wax sticks. If not, you still have two other options. One is to fill the holes with garden-variety white painter's putty and hide them with a dab of paint the next

Countersink finish nails with a nail set, then fill the holes with drying putty before you paint. Alternatively, fill the holes with wax sticks or painter's putty after you paint.

Paint-Grade Lumber

Even on old homes, all too often the painted moldings and windows were designed to be just that— painted. That means they were made with paint-grade lumber. While the prospect of stripping off old paint and resurrecting beautiful natural wood underneath may be enticing, it is not always practical. Before you commit to a large project, scrape a small area to find out what is underneath. You may find finger-jointed, pieced-together

sections of mismatched softwoods that won't stain evenly or be attractive in a clear finish, no matter how much you may want it to.

day. The other option is for the perfectionists among you. Prime the molding, but hold off on the last coat of paint. Fill the nail holes with putty, and then paint the last coat after the molding is installed.

Prepping new wood

New wood is fairly easy to work with. For moldings that are installed before finishing, you'll need to putty nail holes, chips, and defects. Under clear finishes, choose a putty that is as close as possible to the unstained wood. If you plan to stain the wood, select putty that colors the same as the wood under the stain. Fill the spot so that the putty is just slightly proud. When it is dry, sand it

TRADE SECRET

Putty often absorbs stain differently than wood does. Some putties absorb more stain, some less, and some just the right amount. To find out what your putty will do, gouge a scrap of the wood you will be using and fill it with putty. Let it dry, sand it flush, then stain the area. See what you've ended up with, then adjust

the putty color so that it will hide well after staining. You can color it by stirring in small amounts of universal tinting colors (UTCs). This is a trial-and-error process, so you may have to do a few samples before you hit it just right.

Some putties absorb more stain than the surrounding wood does, resulting in dark spots.

TOOLS AND MATERIALS
Sanding Shapes

There's no need to tear up your fingers with sandpaper on surfaces that aren't flat and easy. Sanding blocks come in all sorts of shapes for use by hand and as replaceable pads for electric detail sanders. Shaped rubber "tadpoles" help you get into grooves easily. They're usually sold as a set of several shapes or as one flexible module that can be reconfigured for both coves and grooves. You can also make your own sanding block for coves by wrapping a piece of sandpaper around a dowel or shaping an art gum eraser with a razor knife.

Wrap some duct tape around a dowel and cover it with a piece of sandpaper to make a cushioned sanding block for getting into coves.

flush with the surrounding wood. In some cases, the putty may discolor softwoods, such as pine. You can avoid this by sealing pine with a first coat of clear finish before filling the holes.

Even though moldings, window frames, and doors are new, they still need to be sanded, though not aggressively. Often planed wood is too smooth and has shiny mill glaze on the surface that makes it difficult for stains and finishes to penetrate. You'll need to sand only once, fairly lightly, with 180-grit paper. That's smooth enough for stain and clear finish to penetrate it, yet rough enough for primer and paint to adhere to it.

Stripping old wood

There comes a time in the life of every window, door, and molding when it begs for a second chance. It may be clad with an old, alligatored, or pebbly varnish or shellac finish that has long since turned dark and dismal, or it may be hidden under far too many layers of paint. That's when you haul out the stripping gear. There are three basic stripping methods: chemicals, scrapers, and heat guns. The technique you use depends on the finish on the wood.

Thin, clear finishes. Thin, clear finishes, such as varnish and shellac, are best removed with chemical strippers. Mask the area generously; you'd be surprised at how far errant stripper can splash. Use a thick-bodied, semipaste stripper so that it stays where you put it. Daub it on thickly with a large brush, and then cover it with plastic film to keep the active ingredients from evaporat-

Sand new molding just once with 180-grit paper to remove the shiny mill glaze that can repel finishes.

ing too fast. Leave it alone and let the chemicals do the work. Check it in about 15 minutes and see if the finish has completely softened. If it has, it should come off easily right down to the raw wood. If the old finish is stubborn, rewet it with stripper, recover it, and give it more time.

When the finish has fully softened, scrape it off with a scraper, a coarse nylon stripping pad, or steel wool. Get the wood as clean as possible. Go back over it with more stripper if you need to, keeping the wood wet with stripper until it is clean. Don't stop and let it dry or it will be worse when you come back, so strip it all in one shot. When the wood is clean, wash it down with naphtha, mineral spirits, or the stripper's recommended solvent. Scrub the wood clean with solvent and a fine nylon abrasive pad, and then wipe

"There comes a time in the life of every window, door, and molding when it begs for a second chance."

Layers of paint behind a hinge can alter the fit of a door. Keep the hinge mortise clean by masking it before you finish.

TRADE SECRET

Windows and moldings pretty much have to be finished in situ, but doors come off easily and can be finished in your workshop. If it is a new door, fit it first, allowing for seasonal swelling and the thickness of your finish, which is typically $1/16$ in. or less. If you have to plane the

Cover wet stripper with plastic film to keep the active ingredients from evaporating too quickly.

it dry with shop towels. Let the wood dry at least overnight before you refinish it.

Thick paints. I prefer to combine techniques when stripping thick paint, especially if there are many built-up layers. Start by dry-scraping whatever lifts easily off the wood. Be careful not to gouge the wood and don't worry if the old paint

Once the finish gunk is off, scrub the wood with a nylon abrasive pad soaked in naphtha or a special paint remover afterwash.

door to make it fit, do that before you apply the finish. Pull the hinge pins, lift out the door, and set it on a pair of sawhorses. Now you can remove the handle, locks, hinges, and other hardware. I keep finish out of the hinge mortises by masking them first.

Nail Holes on Prefinished Molding

Got holes? Fill them with wax crayons. There's a wide array of colored wax sticks in common wood stain colors. They are designed to fill the small holes left by finish nails in moldings that are already finished. Simply rub the wax across the hole until it is filled. Remove the excess by using the edge of a credit card as a scraper, and then rub a brown paper bag over it for a smooth finish. And yes, you can use one of your kid's crayons if it is the right color.

doesn't all pop right off. We still have some more tools in our arsenal. (Be sure to see p. 111 for lead paint precautions.)

Next, switch to a heat gun. Put it on the high setting and move it back and forth in a small area about 4 in. from the surface. As soon as the paint lifts and bubbles, scrape it off with a metal scraper, then move on to the next area. The heat gun removes most but not all of the paint. The little that is left will be easier to remove with paint stripper (see Thin, clear finishes, pp. 56–57).

If you're planning to paint, or if you find that what you've uncovered is simply not good enough for a stained or clear finish, you can usually stop after the heat gun. Those last bits of

SAFETY FIRST

Planning to use paint remover? Before you start, open the windows for ventilation and get a fan going to remove the fumes. Make sure the fan blows outward so you work in clean air. Suit up with neoprene gloves, an organic vapor respirator, and goggles. Wear old clothes, an apron to catch splashes, and long sleeves to protect your arms.

IN DETAIL
Wood Conditioner

Wood conditioner is a thin, oily liquid that works *only* with oil-based stains and should never be used with water-based ones. Apply it after the wood has been sanded and is ready for staining. Flood it onto the wood liberally with a rag or brush, then wipe off the excess. The wood should be fully wet but not puddled or dripping. Wood conditioner works only while it is wet, so stain the wood right after you have applied the conditioner. The stain will go on much more evenly, but will not be as dark. For a deeper color, use a darker stain or let the stain dry overnight, then apply a second coat. There is no need to reapply conditioner before the second coat of stain.

Both sides were coated with the same stain, but the right side was first treated with wood conditioner, which made the finish lighter and more uniform.

"*The most common types of stains are the oil-based ones and, for work like this, they are probably the best choice.*"

Scraping is a quick way to remove multiple layers of paint.

paint lodged in the pores and crevices can stay there. Let the wood cool, then sand it with 100-grit paper, followed by 150- or 180-grit paper, making sure you feather any paint still sticking to the wood. When the surface is smooth, prime and paint it.

A heat gun and a wide spackle knife make a potent stripping combo.

Stains under Clear Top Coats

All types of interior trim share a similar set of characteristics: They get a lot of wear and they're very visible. As a result, the same finishes are best for all of them. They are often constructed from the same woods as well, so they present similar staining and finishing problems, like the inclination to absorb stain unevenly. Fortunately, there are some ways around that problem.

Choosing and applying stain

When the trim has been stripped (if necessary) and both the new and the old wood have been properly sanded, they are ready to be stained, once you have masked off adequately. The most common types of stains are the oil-based ones and, for work like this, they are probably the best choice. You'll find some water-based stains on the shelves as well, and they have the advantage of smelling less than their oil-based cousins do. However, they tend to dry much faster, and when you have lots of wood surface to cover at once, a slower drying stain is a big help.

Several woods, including resinous hardwoods like cherry, and virtually all softwoods, such as pine, fir, and hemlock, can become cranky around oil-based stains. Instead of the uniform coloring you get with most hardwoods, these woods can produce uneven and splotchy coats.

Wood conditioner. While you may think that uneven staining is a fairly rare situation, in truth it is fairly common. A lot of molding is

SAFETY FIRST

Heat guns are efficient tools for removing lots of paint quickly, but they can do damage just as fast. Watch where you aim the gun when it is not heating finish. It's easy to forget where you are pointing it when you pull it away from the paint surface in order to scrape. At best, it will quickly melt a hole in your plastic sheeting. At worst, it may burn you, hurt someone else, or even start a fire.

Stain often comes out splotchy and uneven on soft-wood molding.

made of softwoods, which can be finicky when it comes to oil-based stains, the most predominant stains on the market. Therefore, when it comes to windows and moldings, you'll probably need wood conditioner more often than not. Think of it as stain insurance that guarantees even coloration. It adds very little time and effort to the job and saves you from a staining disaster. Simply flood wood conditioner onto raw wood, wipe it off, and then stain.

Not all woods require conditioner, but that piece of information is not really helpful all by itself. If you are not sure whether or not the wood you are staining needs to be preconditioned, err on the safe side and use it. You won't mess up by applying it to wood that does not need it. The worst that will happen is that the stain will come out a bit lighter than you expected and you will have paid, in time and money, for some insurance that you didn't absolutely need. In any case, you can always add a second coat of stain to make the wood darker once the first coat has dried.

Wood presealer. Another strategy to get softwoods to stain evenly is to preseal the wood. It's fairly simple and quite effective. Simply soak the wood with a very thin coat of finish, and then wipe it off immediately. There should not be enough finish to sit on top of the wood, just enough to seal it slightly. Under oil-based polyurethane, use a thin coat of the same polyurethane cut 50/50 with mineral spirits, or apply a single coat of boiled linseed oil. Under water-based polyurethane, use thinned wax-free shellac or Bull's Eye SealCoat right out of the can. The key is to keep that first coat thin. The surface should still feel like wood, not like plastic, when you are done.

As with conditioner, the stain comes out lighter on sealed wood than it does on unsealed wood. Make sure you test the color on a sealed piece of scrap wood so you know what to expect. You can always add a second coat of stain after the first one dries or seal the first coat and glaze a second coat. (See p. 28 and pp. 44–47 for more on staining and glazing.)

Matching existing molding

Matching an existing stain color is often harder than it looks. If you are going to attempt it, make sure you have plenty of sample boards on hand, and don't get discouraged after the first few attempts. Of course, you may get lucky and hit the color right off the bat with the first stain you try, but don't count on it.

Sample boards. Set aside several lengths of extra molding to make sample boards, and test

| TAKE YOUR PICK |

Liquid vs. Gel

Traditionally, oil-based stains came in liquid form. While they work great, they have the disadvantage of being rather drippy and runny. That's not a problem on horizontal surfaces, but it can be very messy on vertical ones. Some stores now carry lines of similar stains in a thicker gel form. The gels don't drip or run and tend to stain more uniformly than many of the liquids do. Use a nylon abrasive pad instead of a brush to apply them. The pad holds more stain than a brush and stays wet longer. For vertical surfaces, gels really can't be beat.

TRADE SECRET

How you sand wood greatly influences how it responds to stain. Consistent, uniform sanding translates into a more uniform stain color. Make sure you sand all areas and all parts with the same type and grit of sandpaper. Don't sand some areas and skip others because you think they are smooth enough. In addition, sanded wood reacts to stain differently than machined (but unsanded) wood does. Furthermore, don't sand part of the piece to 100 grit and part to 180 grit, or you will end up with two different intensities of stain color.

This board was sanded with two different grits of sandpaper; when one stain was applied, two colors emerged.

"Polyurethane is about the best thing you can use to coat windows, doors, and moldings."

Wood conditioner is easy to use. Flood it on, wipe it off, and then stain.

the back of one with the stain to see if it absorbs evenly. If it's splotchy, use wood conditioner or preseal all the molding, and do the same to all the sample boards as well. Buy a half-pint of the stain you think looks closest to what you want, as well as two or three other colors to mix and match. It's best to use the same types of stain from the same manufacturer. Choose at least one

A single layer of boiled linseed oil acts as a presealer coat under oil-based stains and finishes.

IN DETAIL

Stain and Wood Conditioner Compatibility

How do you know if your stain is compatible with wood conditioner? It is really quite simple. Look on the store shelf where you bought the stain. If the stain needs or could benefit from wood conditioner, the manufacturer of the stain also offers wood conditioner. When a brand of stain does not offer a conditioner to go with it, you most likely don't need it.

stain that is a bit redder than you think it should be, one that is a bit too green or yellow, and one that is darker than you think you want. These are your mixing colors. Stain a small section of one of the boards with each of the stains so you have reference colors.

Mix to match. Take a look at the samples you have and compare them under the same lighting to the moldings already in place. Your first color choice may need to be a bit more reddish or yellowish, or a bit darker or lighter. Now start to play. Mix two or more of the stains in a plastic dish or paper cup, then put the mixed stain on one of the sample boards to see what it looks like. Measure the mixing amounts with a measuring spoon and have a notebook and pencil at hand to keep track of your mixtures. After all, you want to be able to reproduce it accurately once you hit the magic combination. You can make stains lighter and weaker by adding mineral spirits. Each mixture either gets you closer to or farther away from the color you need. With a few tries and about 15 minutes of time, you'll undoubtedly find a winner.

Your notebook should tell you what colors you need and in what proportions. Figure out how much stain you'll need to do the whole job (stain covers about 300 sq. ft. per gallon), and buy the right amounts of each color to create a large enough batch of custom stain. When you get the stains home, remix your formula and check it again on a sample board just to make sure (this is the finisher's version of "measure twice, cut once"). Plan to keep a bit extra for future touch

WHAT CAN GO WRONG

Water over Oil Peels

Oil-based polyurethane can be applied over water-based stain, but not necessarily the other way around. Some water-based polyurethanes don't adhere very well to oil-based ones. You can increase the odds by making sure the stain is completely dry before you apply the top coat. Better yet, use a tie coat of SealCoat or another wax-free shellac.

The best way to see how a stain will look on your molding is to make a sample board.

Oil-based polyurethane. Oil-based polyurethane enjoys great popularity among woodworkers, and for good reason. It is very durable and easy to apply, and adds a warm amber tint to wood that gives it a deep, rich appearance. It dries much slower and smells more than water-based polyurethane. The slow drying time means you can go back over it to smooth out drips or blend areas together, but it also means there is more time for dust to settle into it. Polyurethane is self-sealing, so you won't need to apply a sealer coat, and it doesn't raise the grain of the wood.

Some folks like to use those gray foam-on-a-stick brushes for oil-based polyurethane, but I prefer a good, natural bristle brush. For brushing,

ups. Store the mixture in a jar or container with a tight-fitting lid and label it with the mixture's brands, colors, and proportions. You may want to mix another batch some day.

Applying sealers and top coats

Polyurethane is about the best thing you can use to coat windows, doors, and moldings. It is tough and moderately flexible, and can withstand the abuses that windows and doors often receive. Polyurethane comes in oil- and water-based versions. Both are durable enough but after that the two part ways. Whichever one you use, two to three coats should be enough.

When you make custom-color stains, measure accurately and keep notes so you can mix a larger amount of that "perfect color" once you find it.

IN DETAIL

Presealing before Staining

Whether you use SealCoat, thinned polyurethane, or boiled linseed oil, the technique of presealing is the same. The only difference is the speed at which you need to work. SealCoat dries very fast, thinned polyurethane dries much slower, and boiled linseed oil dries the slowest. To preseal wood, flood the surface by wiping or brushing on the sealer, then wipe it off immediately. Don't leave any extra sitting on top of the wood. You want only what penetrates the wood to remain. Let the wood dry overnight before you stain it. As with wood conditioner, presealing minimizes the amount of stain the wood absorbs, so stain appears lighter on presealed wood than it does on raw wood.

TAKE YOUR PICK

Double Stain vs. Mixture

Custom mixing a stain with several off-the-shelf varieties is one way to match a color. Another way is to stain two or three times. First apply one color, let it dry thoroughly overnight, then restain it with the same or a different color. Make sure you try out this technique with samples first. With multilayer staining, it is best to start with a lighter color and restain with a darker one. Trying it the other way around can make the stain look very muddy.

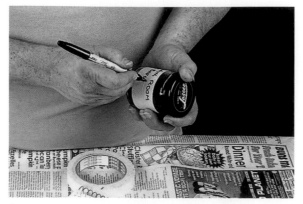

Store excess custom stain in a jar with a tight-fitting lid and record the brands, colors, and formulation ratio on the label.

I like to thin polyurethane about 10% with mineral spirits and apply multiple light coats.

Oil-based polyurethane needs a lot of time to dry, so apply only one coat per day. Sand lightly between coats if you wait more than a week, or if you need to smooth out any dust that has gotten into the finish. After the last coat, give it a week to dry completely, then smooth any nibs or dust in the last coat by applying paste wax with 0000 steel wool.

Water-based polyurethane. Water-based polyurethane dries fast and smells very little. Although it is milky white in the can, it cures completely clear and doesn't add any color to wood. While manufacturers recommend using a sanding sealer first with some polyurethanes, this isn't absolutely necessary. The first coat on raw wood raises the grain, leaving it feeling slightly rough to the touch. After the first coat has dried, sand it lightly with 320-grit paper to knock down the roughness. If you wait more than a week

between coats, sand the surface lightly with 320-grit paper or a nylon abrasive pad. Otherwise, sand only if you need to smooth the surface or remove drips and dust nibs. Don't use steel wool between coats of water-based polyurethane or you may end up with tiny bits of rusted metal in the finish.

I apply polyurethane with either a nylon brush or a paint pad. Pads work particularly well with water-based materials. Flexible paint pads, which are mounted on foam, give you the advantages of a pad without restricting you to flat surfaces. Apply a very thin coat. If you build up too much wet material at once, you will trap water in the finish, making it cloudy and soft for a long time. You can put on two coats per day in dry weather, but give it more drying time if the humidity is high. Don't work the material—simply brush it on and let it be. Trying to brush it to even it out makes it worse.

Primed and Painted Trim

Painting doors, windows, and moldings is not a whole lot different than painting anything else. You still have to clean old surfaces and sand old paint to get better adhesion, and raw wood needs to be primed before it is painted. The main difference with trim is that you're working on smaller surfaces. Rollers and paint pads, which are ideal for large areas, give way to the more detailed control of brushes. At times, technique is just as important as choosing the right material or applicator.

"In most cases, you won't know which type of finish is on the trim, so play it safe and seal it first with a coat of primer to guarantee good adhesion."

TRADE SECRET

Air-dry finishes form a skin when exposed to oxygen, which is how they coat wood. It doesn't matter whether you leave a can open or reseal it with some space left inside. Either way, there is enough oxygen to turn at least some of the liquid into a solid polyurethane film. The only way to avoid this dilemma is to lay a sheet of plastic sandwich wrap directly on top of the finish before you close the lid. Press the film onto the surface of the polyurethane, making sure the entire area is covered. When it is time to use the finish again, take off the lid and discard the plastic wrap.

Cleaning to repaint

There's usually no need to strip off old paint if you are merely going to repaint, but you do have to prepare the surface. Clean the old paint by scrubbing it with TSP in water, using a nylon abrasive pad or a scrub brush to dislodge grease and dirt. Sponge off the surface with clean water and wipe it dry with rags or paper towels. Make sure the old paint is solid, with no raised or cracked areas.

Sand the surface with 220-grit paper to roughen it up before you paint. This makes the next coat adhere better. Soften sharp edges by sanding them lightly, too. If you sand through to bare wood, spot-prime those areas. Otherwise, you can simply paint over what is there. If you find nicks or defects, patch them with fast-drying putty or spackle. Let the patch dry, then sand it flush with 220-grit sandpaper.

Treat stained and varnished wood the same way. If you are painting over wood with a clear finish, clean it thoroughly with TSP in water. Rinse it off with clean water and let the wood dry. Sand the surface with 220-grit paper before you paint. In most cases, you won't know which type of finish is on the trim, so play it safe and seal it first with a coat of primer to guarantee good adhesion.

Some interior flush doors and sliding closet doors may be stained but not sealed. They require a primer that also stops stain bleeding. To cover all the bases, use a bleed-sealing primer, such as B-I-N.

I thin oil-based polyurethane about 10% with mineral spirits before I apply it with a natural bristle brush.

A flexible paint pad is the ideal application tool for water-based polyurethane.

IN DETAIL
Final Smoothing

After the last coat of oil-based polyurethane is on, smooth it out and get rid of embedded dust with steel wool and wax. Dip a pad of 0000 steel wool into paste wax and rub the finish smooth. Wipe off the wax immediately with clean rags or shop towels. This simple step makes the wood look and feel silky smooth. Do it on a chair rail and your houseguests will walk around the room running their hands along the satiny wood.

Don't paint over cracked or peeling paint. This windowsill needs to be stripped before being painted.

Primers and paints

Whether it is new or stripped wood, all raw wood needs to be primed before being painted. Sand new wood lightly with 100-grit paper to remove mill glaze, those shiny areas resulting from planer blades. This is especially common on molding. Use painter's caulk or putty, such as Dap 33, to fill seams, gouges, and nail holes. If the wood is clean and free of knots, prime it with latex primer. For resinous and knotty woods, use a bleed-sealing primer, such as BIN or SealCoat. You can use either one under both oil- and water-based trim paints.

For interior work, both oil- and water-based coatings are appropriate. Use interior latex trim paint, washable kitchen or bathroom paint, or oil-based trim paint. All are durable and appropriate for painted trim, windows, and doors. Oil-based

paints smell more and dry slower, but they are very durable and offer good abrasion resistance. Water-based paints dry quickly and require less ventilation. The glossier versions tend to resist wear better than the low-luster offerings.

Painting techniques

Walls and paneling can be painted the same way as drywall surfaces. Paint the corners first with a pad or a brush, and then paint the main areas with a roller. Doors, windows, and trim are too small for rollers, so use brushes and small paint pads for those areas.

Double-hung windows. Before you start, remove the locks, handles, and other hardware. Most window hardware is attached with only two screws; it is easier to remove the hardware than it is to mask around it. Some types of windows can easily be removed from their jambs. If you have the type that come out easily, remove them and lay them on sawhorses to paint. For those that don't come out, open the window and reverse the two sections, with the inner sash raised and the outer sash lowered. Paint the inner sash first, then the exposed section of the outer sash. Reverse their positions and paint the remainder of the outer sash. Paint the edges, frame, and sill last. (See drawings, facing page.)

After the paint is dry, move the window up and down a few times to make sure it does not stick. Push both sashes all the way to the bottom and paint the upper half of the jamb. Let it dry completely before you move the sashes up to paint the lower portion of the jamb. By painting

> *"Whether it is new or stripped wood, all raw wood needs to be primed before being painted."*

TOOLS AND MATERIALS

The Right Stain for Window Trim

Windows and sills that are subjected to strong sunlight are also prone to intense fading. For these areas, choose an all-pigment stain. Most common interior stains contain dyes as well as pigments, and the dye portion can fade over time. Look for products that are labeled as interior/exterior or that contain pigment as the only colorant. These materials hold their color without fading.

SAFETY FIRST

Before you finish a project, make sure you have good ventilation in the room—open windows and a fan—especially when using oil-based paints. That's for you. For the paint, don't let it get too cold or it won't adhere properly. Keep the room above 55°F for latex paints and above 45°F for oil-based paints.

the jambs after the window is completely dry, you are less likely to paint the window shut. However, you should still take great care to avoid applying paint that is too thick or getting paint drips in the corners, two surefire ways of unintentionally painting windows shut.

Painting windows also presents the problem of how to keep paint off the glass. In some cases, the wood may go right up to the glass, or there may be a bead of caulking between the two. Depending on your skill with a brush, you can either mask the glass or paint carefully and clean up errors later with a flat razor blade. (For more

information on painting windows and doors, see Chapter 8.)

Chair rails and baseboards. While you could probably remove chair rails and baseboards, it is far easier to paint them in place, masking them off with 2-in.-wide tape. Use blue painter's tape for wood and painted surfaces, low-tack tape for wallpaper. Even with low-tack tape, test it first in a hidden area to make sure it does not pull up the wallpaper. On the bottom side of chair rails, attach some light plastic sheeting that extends down the wall and out into the room at least a foot. This protects against drips on the walls and

Painting a Double-Hung Window

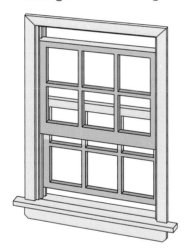
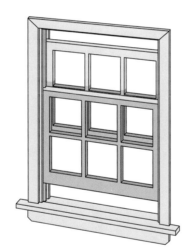
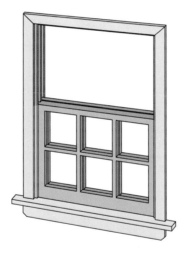

Open the window with the two sections overlapped—inner sash raised, outer sash lowered. First paint the entire inner sash, and then paint the exposed area of the outer sash.

Reverse the positions of the windows and paint the remainder of the outer sash.

Push both sashes all the way to the bottom and paint the upper half of the jamb to the edge of the face of the frame. Let it dry completely before you raise the sashes to paint the lower half of the jamb, the frame face, and the windowsill.

TOOLS AND MATERIALS
The Right Applicator

Use a synthetic bristle brush for latex paints, since water makes natural bristles splay. For oils, you can use either synthetic or natural bristles, but I prefer natural China bristle brushes. There are also different paint pads for oil-based and water-based paints. Pads designed for water-based paints may come apart in the solvents used in oil-based paints, but pads designed for oil-based paints will work for both. Make sure you

read the fine print before you buy an applicator. Some brands color code their products to make it easier, with yellow backing foam for oil-and-water pads and blue foam for water-only pads.

Some companies color code their paint pads to let you know whether they should be used with oil- or water-based materials.

TOOLS AND MATERIALS
Portable Paint Trays

Don't drag a whole can of paint around as you walk along painting chair rails. Instead, pour some into a small paint tray. You'll find inexpensive plastic ones at the paint store complete with indents for your thumb and fingers. They are small enough to hold in one hand while you walk around painting with the other.

Inexpensive, portable paint trays are a lot more convenient to carry around than full cans of paint.

"Whenever possible—and it almost always is—remove the door from its hinges and paint it separately."

floor. Check for any obvious gaps or joints, especially where sections of the rail or baseboard meet, and fill them with paintable caulk or putty.

Once everything has been masked, painting is a simple job. Use a comfortable 2-in. or 2½-in. brush with fairly long bristles. Use natural bristles for oil-based paints and varnishes, synthetic bristles for latex and water-based paints. Start from one end of the room (probably at a door) and paint the full width of the rail or baseboard as you move along. As long as you are working from a wet edge onto unpainted wood, you won't get overlap marks. Don't stop until you get to a break in the rail (probably at another door). Hold the brush parallel to the rail or molding edge of the baseboard to get the bristles down into the coves or grooves in the design.

Two-sided door and frame. Each side of an interior door may face a different room with a different color scheme. Somewhere along the way you have to divide the color in half. Obviously, you want the face to match the frame when it is closed, but what do you do when it is open? Conventional wisdom decrees that the hinge edge of the door should match the adjacent color when the door is open. (See drawings, facing page.) The opposite (or latch) edge should match the color on the other side.

Whenever possible—and it almost always is—remove the door from its hinges and paint it separately. Remember to remove the hinges, doorknob, and locks before you start painting. Just in case they ever show, paint the top and bottom edges of the door, too.

When you paint the frame, split the color at the doorstop, painting the lighter color of the frame first. After it is dry, mask it and paint the darker side. Because darker colors hide better, you'll need to mask only once.

Sliding closet doors. Many sliding doors lift off their tracks with very little effort. If yours do, take them down and paint them horizontally on sawhorses. If they don't, here's a good strategy for painting them. (See drawings, facing page.) First, move the doors until they overlap a small amount. Paint the door that is fully exposed first, but leave the edges until later. Next, paint the door that is three-quarters exposed, starting from the outer edge and moving toward the overlap. Then immediately switch the position of the doors and paint the remaining area. Since you ended your last strokes just before you switched the door positions, that last edge will still be wet enough to blend without creating an overlap

A long bristle brush held parallel to a chair rail lets the bristles get down into the molding's coves and grooves.

WHAT CAN GO WRONG

Failing Caulk

Sometimes it isn't the paint that is coming loose around windowpanes but the caulk beneath it. If this happens, remove the caulk by scraping, chiseling, or employing a caulk remover that attaches to a portable drill. Then sand the area, making certain you feather the existing paint edge. Also, sand the old paint that is still holding firm. Recaulk the windowpanes with paintable caulking, then spot-prime the new or bare areas with latex or shellac-based primer before you repaint.

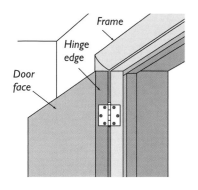

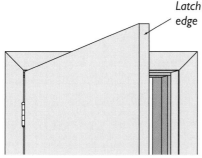

Painting Doors and Door Frames
Paint the hinge edge the same color as the adjacent door face. Paint the latch edge the same color as the opposite side of the door.

get drips or lap marks, it is best to keep both sides wet with paint at the same time. Work with a fairly dry brush, since runs are hard to avoid, and check for drips on both sides before you move on to the next section. After the louvers are done, pull back the masking tape and paint the frames. Do the rails first, then the stiles and edges. If you took the doors out of their tracks, you can paint the top and bottom edges; otherwise, hit only what you can reach of the top edge and don't lose any sleep over it.

line. Do the inside of the closet doors the same way, assuming you think it's important (after all, it's dark in there, so who's going to see it?). Later, overlap the doors fully and do all four edges at the same time.

Bifold louvered doors. As with sliding closet doors, bifold doors usually come off easily. Whether you decide to paint them in place or remove them and lay them on sawhorses, here's a tip for doors with louvered panels. Mask the frame so that you can paint both sides of the louvers first. If the doors have two louvered sections divided by a rail, do both the front and the back of one louvered section first, then both sides of the other section. Since you see through louvers, it is next to impossible to define the right side versus the wrong side. To make sure you don't

Painting Sliding Doors

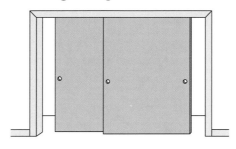

For sliding doors, paint the fully exposed door first. Paint the other door starting from the outer edge, moving toward where it overlaps with the front door.

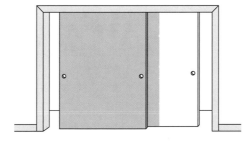

Immediately switch door positions and paint the remaining area.

TRADE SECRET

To reduce the aggressiveness of tape, stick it to your clothing, let it sit for a few seconds, then peel it off. Now use it for masking. The adhesive on the tape picks up some lint from your clothing, making it slightly less tacky.

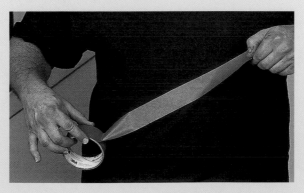

You can reduce the tack of masking tape by applying it to your clothing first.

Floors, Stairs, and

CHAPTER FIVE
Balustrades

Beautiful wood floors evoke an elegance that it is hard to surpass. Part of their beauty relies on the floor's finish to bring out the depth and richness of the wood. Like a fine piece of furniture, we go to great lengths to smooth the floor, apply clear coatings, buff them out, and recoat them until they fairly shine with luster. And then, after all that effort, we walk on them. To make matters worse, floors suffer from a considerable amount of wood movement due to moisture in the form of spills or water vapor rising from damp basements. The bottom line is that floor finishes, in addition to looking beautiful, must be flexible enough to tolerate lots of movement and tough enough to take shoe traffic, dings, and dents without chipping, scuffing, or peeling.

TOOLS AND MATERIALS

What You'll Need: Finishing a Floor

- Drum sander (rent)
- Edger or spinner (rent)
- Buffer (rent)
- Belt sander
- Sandpaper
- Screens and pad
- Scrapers
- Floor brushes
- Lamb's wool or synthetic applicator pads
- Shellac, wax, oil, polyurethane, or Danish Finish
- Trowel filler and pore filler
- Large putty knife, trowel, or squeegee
- Towels and wiping rags
- Sheets and tacks for doorways
- Masking tape and paper
- Kneepads

Professional estimate
300-sq.-ft. floor,
15 hours

Stripping and Rough Sanding

Each finish has its own application strategy; however, the first preparation steps are always the same. In fact, unlike other woodworking chores, there is not much preparation difference between new and refinished floors. The first operation is rough sanding to either level a new floor or to remove the finish on an old one.

Knowing when to strip

The life of a floor's coating can be extended by lightly sanding it for adhesion, and then adding another coat of finish. For very thin finishes, such as shellac or oil and wax, you may have to do this every year. For thicker film finishes, you should do it every three years or so. A lot depends on

You'll need to rent (from left to right) a drum sander, an edger, and a buffer, and buy sanding strips or belts, discs, a pad, and buffer screens.

the amount of traffic and wear the floor gets. But even with great maintenance, you may eventually have to strip off the old finish and go back to bare wood. Here are some of the conditions that indicate when you need to remove an old finish rather than recoat it.

- Water and other stains that will not come out with washing. These stains are generally down in the wood. The only way to remove them is to sand the floor, which means removing the finish.
- Cupped boards, caused by moisture on or beneath the flooring, which usually require sanding to flatten them.
- Bare spots where the finish has worn through, or a finish that is just too scarred and shabby to save. It is very difficult to repair a patch in the floor and have it look good.
- Surface contamination that prevents a recoat from sticking, making it impossible to rejuvenate the floor.
- A change of color, which means you'll have to stain raw wood rather than recoat what is there.

Using the right equipment

The way to get old finish off is to sand it off. The way to get a new floor flat and level enough to be finished is to sand it flat. In most cases, you'll find that old floors have some uneven boards due to wood movement. Sanding flattens them as it takes off the finish. You'll need three tools for sanding a floor, all of which are too expensive to buy for one job. Fortunately, you can rent them.

"You'll need three tools for sanding a floor, all of which are all too expensive to buy for one job. Fortunately, you can rent them."

IN DETAIL

Rug Damage

Putting rugs on top of finished wood floors can cause premature damage to the coating. It's not really the rug itself that is the problem but the pad beneath it. Rubber pads and rubber-backed jute pads trap moisture underneath them, leading to delamination and early degradation of the finish. If you must put a rug down, put a pad beneath it that has air spaces to let the floor breathe.

Have the rental agent show you how to change paper grits and make adjustments before you take the tools home.

Rent a drum sander for the main sanding, an edger or spinner for the borders of the room, and a buffer for finely sanding both raw wood and between coats. You'll also need abrasives for each of the sanders. For the drum sander and the edger, get 36-, 60-, and 100-grit media. You can substitute 80 for 60 and 120 for 100 if that is what is available. For the buffer, get a nylon backer pad and 100- and 220-grit screens. Buy plenty of paper. It gets used up more quickly than you'd expect.

Renting Tools

Some flooring companies run specials for weekend rentals. You can often get a deal renting all three sanding tools as a package. Barring that, consider renting just the drum and edge sanders for one day, and get all the rough sanding done. Then rent the buffer for several days for the final raw wood and between-coat sandings. Don't forget to arm yourself with plenty of sandpaper. Better rental houses let you stock up on the various grits you may need, just in case, then charge you only for what you used when you later return the machine and any unused disks, belts, and screens.

Changing the abrasive on these sanders can be tricky. Before you leave the rental establishment, have the clerk show you how to change the belts, strips, or disks on all the machines you rent. If there are other adjustments you'll need to make, such as the height of the wheels on the edger or the angle of the disk or drum, learn how to do those, too.

Sanding blocks help with hand sanding; scrapers, along with a file to sharpen them, let you get into tight corners.

WHAT CAN GO WRONG
Make Sure It's Solid

While it may look like solid wood flooring, some flooring is built like plywood, with a core covered by a thin veneer of wood. These can't be sanded down with a drum or you'll go through the veneer. Before you tackle the job, pull up some edge molding or a transition threshold and look at the edge of the flooring to make sure it is thick enough to refinish. Even with solid wood floors, make sure there is enough wood left so that you won't sand through to the tongue-and-groove joint, or you'll end up with ever-widening gaps between the boards.

IN DETAIL

Durability of Floor Finishes

The durability of a floor finish depends on the type of finish, the type of floor, and the regularity of maintenance. Let's assume you have an oak floor, properly finished and stable, with no moisture problems and only moderate traffic. Coat it with a waxed-oil or shellac finish and it typically lasts a year. With regular maintenance, it can last indefinitely. That's because those finishes are the easiest to recoat. Oil-based and water-based polyurethanes last from 3 to 5 years, while Danish Finish lasts from 5 to 10 years. Regular maintenance, which means light sanding and periodic recoating, can significantly extend the life of those finishes, as well.

If you don't already have them, get some good floor scrapers and a file to sharpen them (or extra blades if you'd rather just replace them). You'll need scrapers for getting into the corners where the power sanders won't reach. Make or buy a comfortable sanding block to use for final hand sanding to blend in the edges, and get some sheets of regular 100-grit sandpaper for that job. Make sure you have good kneepads, too. Once you get past the big drum sander, most of the other operations require you to kneel on the floor.

Drape a sheet over an open doorway to block dust, and tape a rolled-up towel onto the threshold to wipe your feet.

A dust mask and ear protection are must-have gear for machine sanding.

Prepping the room

Sanding is a dusty, messy, noisy experience, so resign yourself early to a major cleanup job afterward. Remove everything from the room that you can, such as drapes, furniture, and items on shelves, and cover or bag everything else. Vibration-sensitive electronic equipment and breakables that could jiggle off shelves or fall off walls in adjacent rooms should be removed. Seal closed doors with blue painter's tape, and cover open doorways with sheets held up with push pins stuck into the casing. This leaves you an entryway, but still blocks the lion's share of the dust. A rolled-up towel at the base of the door-way or on the bottom of the sheet helps create a good seal and does double duty as a mat for wiping your feet.

> **"Sanding is a dusty, messy, noisy experience, so resign yourself early to a major cleanup job afterward."**

SAFETY FIRST

Whichever finish you choose, plan to have everyone in the house spend the night elsewhere. You should wear an organic vapor respirator, goggles, and gloves for all finishes, though it is particularly important with shellac and oil-based coatings. Make sure all pilot lights and spark-producing items are off—even a light switch can produce a spark when it is turned on or off. Don't forget things that come on automatically, such as water heaters and furnaces. Close the windows to keep out dust, but as soon as the finish is dry to the touch, open up the room to air it out. Leave as soon as you are done working and breathe some clean air.

Block the return air vents of your heating system or they will get filled with dust. Look for wires close to the floor and get them out of the way. Tie up hanging lamps so you don't bang into them. Remove the baseboards if you can. Otherwise, you are likely to damage them with the sanders. In any case, plan on repainting them. While you are at it, mask yourself, too. Wear a good dust mask and ear protection. Those sanding machines are noisy. And, if the weather is warm enough, open the windows to ventilate the room as you work.

Before you even plug in the sander, walk around the room and check for protruding nails, especially near the perimeter. Drop them below the surface with a nail set and hammer. If the sander hits a nail, at best it will destroy the sanding disk, strip, or belt; at worst, the drum.

Protruding nails can wreak havoc with a machine, so set them before you sand the floor.

Power Requirements

Some of the heavy drum sanders have hefty power requirements that may require a 220-volt line (like an electric clothes dryer does). Even those designed for a 110-volt line require a 20-amp circuit, and many house circuits are only 15 amps. Check before you plug it in. If you don't have a heavy-duty extension cord and think you'll

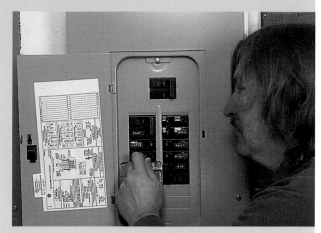

Most rental machines must be plugged into a circuit with a 20-amp breaker; some need 220-volt lines.

need one (most floor sanders have extra-long power cords so that you won't), rent one when you get the sander. And while you work, keep the sander's cord out of the way. Running over a cord with the sander will instantly destroy it. One more thing: None of the big machines have dead man's switches. If you do trip a circuit breaker, be sure to turn off the machine before you reset it, or you will return to find the drum sander eating its way into your floor.

Following the right sequence

Drum sander. Start with the drum sander. It's a good idea to practice with it first on scrap flooring or a large board, as it can be difficult to control if you haven't worked with one before. Push the sander forward while you gradually lower the drum to make contact with the floor. The sander must be moving when the drum touches down or it will leave a deep groove. You'll find the sander cuts more aggressively

WHAT CAN GO WRONG

Silicone Contamination

Sometimes the decision between recoating and stripping has more to do with what is on the finish than with how much of it has worn off. Some aerosol cans contain small amounts of silicone oil to keep the tips from clogging. That oil becomes airborne when you use

Strip the old finish completely if sandpaper is gummy.

a spray can indoors and eventually settles onto the floor. It builds up a layer of almost invisible oil that prevents a new coat of finish from sticking to the existing one. Before deciding to recoat or strip, scrape your nail across the floor. If any sticky stuff collects on it, or if your sandpaper gets gummy when you start to sand for recoating, you need to strip the old finish completely.

IN DETAIL

The Limit on Sanding

Each time you sand a floor you remove a good bit of wood, so there is a limit to how many times you can completely refinish it. Sand too deep and you are likely to start cutting into the tongue-and-groove joints, at which point the gaps between the boards become more noticeable. How many times can you refinish a solid wood floor? At least four or five times; however, if you are very judicious when sanding, you may be able to do several more.

It takes only a second of inattention for a drum sander to cut a hefty groove in the floor.

it by holding it back. Oh, yes: Make sure you memorize exactly where the on/off switch is before you start grinding wood. It is easy to let the drum sander get away from you and ruin the floor in short order. Trust me, this machine is difficult to master.

When flattening a floor, removing any thick, old paint. When working on parquet flooring, steer the sander diagonally. Once the floor is flat, switch to sanding with the grain using the same grit. Overlap each pass by two-thirds, starting at one side and moving toward the other (see left drawing, below). When you work inside four walls, you'll have to sand from a transition line to one end of the room. Then reverse the direction to get the area from the transition line to the other wall. Overlap the transition line with each pass (see right drawing, below).

when it's pushed forward and feathers a bit better when it's pulled backward. Once it touches the floor, it pulls itself along, so you'll need to control

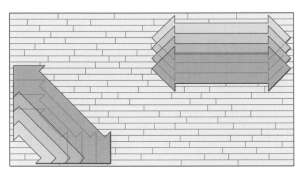

Floor Sanding Patterns
Whether you're sanding diagonally or with the grain, always overlap each pass by two-thirds, starting at one side and working toward the other.

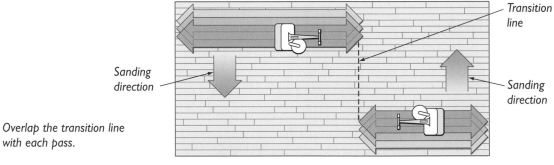

Transition line

Sanding direction

Sanding direction

Overlap the transition line with each pass.

> "The sander must be moving when the drum touches down or it will leave a deep groove."

WHAT CAN GO WRONG

Like Herding Cats

Handling a powerful drum sander or edger is a bit like trying to herd cats. These machines sand very fast and aggressively and have a rather small area of contact. That means they can gouge out a divot in the floor faster than a hot knife through butter. No matter how unnecessary it may seem, try them out on scrap wood first, even if it means buying a big sheet of ¾-in. plywood just to make a test floor.

Floor Sanding Patterns

Wall

Use the edger in small areas where the drum sander doesn't fit. Move it in an overlapping, zigzag pattern.

Move the edger from left to right in small, circular motions heading into the wall.

Don't sand with anything coarser than what you absolutely need. No matter what you use, you'll eventually have to remove the sanding scratches, and coarser papers leave bigger scratches. On flat, new floors or those with thin finishes, try sanding first with 60-grit paper. If the paper clogs up too fast or is too slow in cutting, drop down to the coarser 36-grit paper. For flattening a floor or removing old paint or thick finish, you'll probably have to use 36, but it never hurts to try 60 first. You may save yourself some work and some expensive sanding media. When you are finished with each grit, stop and vacuum or sweep up the dust before you change papers and move on. Sand up to 60-grit paper with the drum.

Edger. The drum sander can only get to within 6 in. of the edge of the room, so you'll need to switch to the edger to sand the perimeter. Like the drum, it tilts forward to make contact with the floor, and it should be moving when it touches down. In all likelihood, you'll need to start with the same grit paper on the edger as you did on the drum. Once again, practice with this machine first on scrap wood. It is also a tough one to master.

The edger picks up where the drum sander left off, letting you sand right up to the wall.

SAFETY FIRST

Sanding dust can catch fire or explode if there are sufficient amounts of it and a spark is present. Ventilate the room as you work, clean up sanding dust frequently, and avoid sparks and flames. Extinguish pilot lights in the area and don't smoke. Empty the dust bags outside, preferably in a noncombustible container away from buildings, and don't leave a full bag of dust on a sanding machine overnight. And of course, wear a dust mask.

Ventilation, a dust mask, and frequent cleanup keep dust dangers in check.

TOOLS AND MATERIALS

What You'll Need: Filling Holes

Pads, screens, trowels, and filler

From left to right:
- Pore filler with plastic applicator
- Trowel filler with squeegee
- Spot filler with putty knife
- Buffer with screen and two nylon pads.

Move the edger from left to right in small, circular motions, heading into the wall. Use the edger for small areas the drum can't reach, moving in a zigzag pattern (see drawings, previous page). Keep the edger moving at all times when it is sanding or it will quickly cut a half-moon groove in the floor. Go up through the grits just as you did with the drum.

Scrapers and hand sanding. The edger gets close along the wall, but it can't get into the corners. For that you must resort to scrapers and some hand sanding. Pull the scrapers outward from the corner in the direction of the grain. Try to level the corners with the sanded area.

Use scrapers to get into the corners, pulling outward in the direction of the grain.

After scraping, feather all the areas in toward the center of the room using a block and some sandpaper. You'll definitely have to sand the corners by hand and you may need to feather in all the edges, as well. As before, work up to 60-grit sandpaper.

Filling and Second Sanding

Once you've finished the primary sanding with the drum, edger, and scrapers, you can take a deep breath. But don't get too comfortable, because there's lots more sanding to do. First, you need to fill all the holes, cracks, and openings between the boards. That means spot filling the obvious holes and troweling on floor filler for the minor cracks and seams. Once the filler is dry, resand it and get ready to finish.

Filling cracks and holes

There are two steps to filling cracks and holes and two different materials for the job: spot filler and trowel filler. Spot filler is nothing more than standard wood putty. You can buy specialty spot filler from a flooring outlet or use the same putty that you would for other woodworking jobs. As with all putties, spot filler comes in a variety of wood tones. If you buy it from a flooring outlet, you can get a color-matched set of spot putty and trowel filler.

Trowel filler is a thinner version of wood putty and it does a similar job. In this case, it's used to fill narrow openings between boards and

> *"There are two steps to filling cracks and holes and two different materials for the job: spot filler and trowel filler."*

TRADE SECRET

While you can't use belt sanders and random-orbit sanders to sand an entire floor, they come in very handy for blending one sanded section into another. For example, the edger may leave the perimeter of the floor looking different from the main part that was done with the drum sander. A belt sander or a random-orbit sander does a good job of blending the two areas. They are also great for correcting irregularities and slipups, such as washboards and divots where you started and stopped the larger machines.

seams that often get enlarged during the sanding process. As with all putties, trowel filler comes in solvent- and water-based versions. I strongly recommend the water-based ones. They dry fast enough, are nonflammable, and create far fewer fumes. Trowel filler is also available in a range of colors to match most woods used for flooring. Choose the color that best matches your flooring as well as your spot filler. It comes in at least 1-gallon cans, which is the bare minimum you'll need, even for a small floor.

Now, check the floor for wide cracks and nail holes, particularly near the walls where the last plank may have been nailed in place. Press spot filler into the void, making it flush with the surrounding wood. Next, apply trowel filler to the entire floor to fill openings whether they are clearly visible or not. While these seams may not be obvious in a dust-laden raw wood floor, they will certainly show up once the finish has been applied. This step makes a big difference later, even if it doesn't seem necessary now.

Pour a large dollop of filler onto the floor and trowel it into the wood. Start from one corner and work toward the center of the room, spreading it with a large squeegee. Try to scrape off whatever does not go into the voids. A dried puddle of filler is very hard to sand and may deflect the sander, causing it to gouge the floor. Before sanding, let the filler dry for at least two hours, more if you used a slower drying variety. The label provides guidelines.

Once it is dry, sand the spot putty and trowel filler at the same time with the drum sander. The

Spot filler, the floor finisher's version of wood putty, seals obvious nail holes and gouges.

patterns are the same, but you'll be using 100-grit paper. When you are done sanding, there shouldn't be any filler sitting on top of the boards, just down in between them and in nail holes and cracks. Do the perimeter of the room and any narrow hallways with the edger and

Squeegee the trowel filler into the wood, covering the entire floor.

IN DETAIL
Dents

In the course of filling an older floor, you may come across some dents and gouges. You'll probably be tempted to plug them with filler or putty. Don't. Odds are that they will be more visible when filled than as depressions that look exactly like the rest of the wood. It is one thing to look at thin lines of filler between the cracks of the boards and quite another to see grainless patches in the middle of a board. Instead, scrape out the old finish, sand the dents by hand as smooth as you can, and try to forget they're there.

TRADE SECRET

Use a new 100-grit screen on the buffer for the last sanding of raw wood and filler before finishing. Then reuse the same screen, now worn, for the first sanding of the finish or for the sanding after the pore filler is applied. The used 100-grit screen will be less aggressive than when it was new and you'll get double the life from it.

IN DETAIL

Floor Sanding Sequence

1. Sand with drum and edger at 36 grit.
2. Sand with drum and edger at 60 grit.
3. Scrape and hand sand corners and edges to 60 grit.
4. Apply trowel filler.
5. Sand with drum and edger at 100 grit.
6. Scrape and hand sand corners and edges to 100 grit.
7. Vacuum or sweep the floor.
8. Pop the grain.
9. Sand with buffer with new 100-grit screen.
10. Vacuum and tack the floor.

"After all that sanding and scraping, you'll be pleased to know that applying the actual finish is the easy part."

100-grit disks. As before, you'll need to switch to scrapers and hand sanding to get into the corners.

Popping the grain

This step is not absolutely necessary unless you are planning to coat the floor with a water-based product, but it does provide a better finish. To pop the grain of the wood, sponge clean water onto the floor, and then wipe off whatever remains. Don't leave any puddles. You want the wood fully wet but not flooded. The water raises the grain of the wood and, once it is dry, the surface feels rougher.

Let the wood dry completely, usually overnight, then sand it again. This time just use the buffer and screens. The pros call this *screening*. The

The buffer head drives a nylon pad faced with a grit-laden screen.

Using its own weight for sanding, the buffer just needs to be guided across the floor.

buffer sits on a thick, nylon pad that spins concentrically. Below it, held on mostly by friction, is what looks like a disk made of window screen. However, this screen has abrasive grit attached to it, just like sandpaper. Go over the entire floor with the 100-grit screen, moving the buffer slowly from side to side as you progress forward. The buffer can get right up to the wall, leaving only a few inside corners for you to do by hand.

Cleaning up

After you've finished sanding and screening, you'll need to vacuum or sweep as thoroughly as you can. In addition to the floor, there will be dust on everything in the room—windows, walls, shelves, ceiling, you name it. And all of it

IN DETAIL

Oily Stain Rags

Make sure you have plenty of rags handy for wiping off stain, as you will go through lots of them. Keep a large plastic bag beside you to dispose of the soiled ones, so they don't mar the unstained floor. As soon as you are done staining, take the rags out of the bag and lay them out singly to dry. When they are dry and crusty, they are landfill safe and no longer in danger of spontaneously igniting.

WHAT CAN GO WRONG

Don't Paint Yourself into a Corner

Although application methods may vary, one finishing technique remains constant. On your last application, make sure you are going toward the doorway, so that you don't paint yourself into a corner. This may sound like some classic cartoon situation, but nevertheless it does happen frequently. It may take a little planning to ensure that you don't end up in a corner or with a corner that you just can't reach.

will be just waiting to drop back onto your newly wet floor when you least expect it. Vacuum the floor last. Afterward, lift off whatever dust remains on the floor with a tack cloth, but don't bother with the ones available at the store—use an old towel or soft cotton cloth. Wet it and wring it out thoroughly. It should be damp but not wet. Use this as your tack cloth, working from one corner and ending up at the doorway where you exit. Place the damp towel in the doorway and use it to wipe your feet when you enter and leave the room.

Applying Stain and Finish

After all that sanding and scraping, you'll be pleased to know that applying the actual finish is the easy part. Now all that remains is to choose the color, pick an appropriate finish and applicator, and go at it. Each finish is a bit different in cost, application method, drying time, durability, and appearance. Read through the thumbnail sketch of each one before you decide. But first, I have a few words about stains.

Applying stains

Most wood floors look great with nothing more than the color of the wood, so there is no need to stain. But, as with furniture, you do have a wide range of options for changing the color. A floor is a large, permanent wooden object that you see a lot of every day, so make sure you get the color you want before you commit to stain-

ing it. Make up samples on sections of scrap flooring. Apply both the stain and your intended top coat, since that will affect the color. This test sample also warns you if there are any compatibility problems.

You can use standard furniture stain or ones designed just for floors. Stains are available in both oil- and water-based versions. Technically, you can use either, but oil-based stains generally dry much more slowly than water-based ones, and you need all the time you can get to apply the stain and make sure it is even. For that reason, I stick to oil-based stains. At best, it is a contest to see whether the stain is faster at drying

It's wise to make up a large sample before you commit to staining the entire floor.

IN DETAIL
Finish Preparation Checklist

- Close up the room to keep dirt out.
- Tie up hanging lamps and drapes.
- Remove or tie up eletrical cords.
- Tape a rolled-up towel to the bottom of the doors to wipe your feet.
- Mask cement or mortar, such as a fireplace, so it doesn't shed masonry dust into the finish.

- Mask the bottom of the wall and the baseboards or plan to repaint them.
- Block traffic by taping off doors and posting detour signs. Even the mail slot in the door should be taped up lest someone drop a letter onto the newly coated vestibule floor, bringing new meaning to the term junk mail.
- Arrange for the rooms above to be vacant. People walking around upstairs can make dust and debris rain down on the fresh finish.

TOOLS AND MATERIALS
Nordic Confusion

Nowhere is there more confusion about terms than in floor finishing. Floor finishers use entirely different nomenclature than the rest of the wood-finishing world. The term *Swedish Finish,* for example, refers to a two-part, acid-cured, solvent-based coating, the equivalent to what furniture folks call *conversion varnish.* In furniture jargon, *Danish oil* refers to a thin, wipe-on, oil-varnish mixture; in the flooring world, *Danish Finish* is a one-package, self-crosslinking, water-based finish for floors.

Play it safe. Describe the finish you want to your vendors in generic terms and don't just toss buzzwords around. If you tell them you want a one-package, self-crosslinking, water-based finish, you will probably get just that, no matter what it is called in the store.

than you are at applying it. Oil-based stains contain lots of solvent, so wear a respirator, ventilate the room, and leave as soon as you are done.

During your test phase, observe how much time you have to manipulate the stain before it dries. That will tip you off to how fast you have to work. Staining is best done as a two-person job, with one person flooding the stain on continuously while the other follows behind to wipe it off. Don't leave puddles or areas with excess stain. Wipe off as much as you can with soft cloths or towels.

If you must do it alone, work in small sections, starting from one corner. Wet a manageable area and then wipe it off, trying to make sure that the stain always stays on the same amount of time before it is wiped off. This helps keep the color uniform. It's a good idea to apply the stain along a plank or strip line so that it is easier to blend the unstained section into the stained one. Overlapping an already dried area with wet stain creates a dark lap mark. Work from the most recently wet edge out into the new wood so that you are always overlapping an area that is still wet.

Applying other floor finishes

There are lots of floor finishes available, depending upon the look you want, the durability you need, and the ease of application you require. Think about how you use your floor, what it is subjected to, and the maintenance schedule you're willing to follow. There aren't better or worse finishes, only those that are more or less appropriate for your particular situation.

Each of the thumbnails below has guidelines for applying the finish, but there is one step that is common to all of them—edging. Start by going around the room with a controllable applicator, either a brush or a paint pad, and coat about 6 in. to 8 in. out from the wall. The larger floor applicator can't get snug up to the wall, so this step allows you to apply finish right against the edges and corners. You'll overlap this edge when you do the main floor, blending the finish so there are no lines.

Finish: Penetrating oil

Best applicators: Lamb's wool pad, natural bristle brush

Cleaning solvent: Mineral spirits

Cost: $25 per gallon

Pros: Easy to apply and repair, natural look, good chatoyance

Cons: Slow drying, oily odor for weeks, may stay tacky for weeks, low stain and scratch resistance

Maintenance schedule: Should be recoated once a year

Staining a Floor

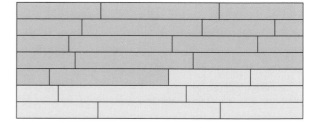

Apply stain along a plank or strip line to avoid overlap marks.

"There aren't better or worse finishes, only those that are more or less appropriate for your particular situation."

TRADE SECRET

Rags and brushes are satisfactory for applying stain, but I've found that the very best applicator is a fine, nylon abrasive pad. For whatever reason, it holds more stain and stays wet longer. The result is a more uniform color and less aggravation.

Scotch-Brite works great as a stain applicator, staying wet much longer than rags.

Penetrating oils include boiled linseed oil, tung oil, and Danish oil mixtures like Watco. The former two dry slowly and give you plenty of time to work, but the latter sets up faster. Test it first to find out how much working time you'll have. Use a lamb's wool pad or a floor brush to flood it onto the wood. Allow it to soak in by keeping the floor wet for up to an hour. You'll find that some areas absorb quicker than others do, so go back and redistribute the oil from the wet areas to the dry ones and keep all the wood equally wet. Wipe off the excess when the oil stops soaking in and before it gets tacky. Make sure you dispose of the oily rags properly.

The fact that you have to keep wiping means you will be walking back and forth on the wet floor for a while. Make sure your shoe soles are clean before you enter the room. As you wipe off the floor, work from the far wall to the doorway. Leave an old towel at the doorway to act as a mat and wipe your feet on it when you come and go.

Let the oil dry overnight and do a second coat the same way the next day. It should not take any more than two coats. Give the floor a couple of days to dry, then wax it. Use very fine steel wool, fine nylon abrasive pads, or a stiff bristle scrub brush to apply paste wax to the floor, then wipe it off with rags. If you still have the rented buffer, use a lamb's wool pad to buff the wax. An old

The first step is to coat about 8 in. around the edges of the room with a brush or pad.

Chatoyance

The word *chatoyance* (shay-toy-ants), which is French for "like a cat's eye," comes to us courtesy of the jewelry trade. It's used to describe shimmering stones, such as Tiger's Eye, which has great depth and shimmers with light and dark bands when viewed from different angles. Some woods do that too, including ribbon mahogany and quilted maple. Shellac and oil-based finishes bring out the chatoyance in wood, but water-based coatings do not.

Chatoyance is the color-flipping shimmer evident in both this oiled, curly maple and the Tiger's Eye gemstone that inspired the term.

IN DETAIL
Pore Filler

Woods with large, open pores, such as oak and mahogany, show their woody textures under a finish. However, if you prefer, you can fill the pores for a smoother appearance. Water-based pore filler, which works for both oil- and water-based coatings, is applied pretty much like trowel filler. The difference is that it is less coarse, so it fills small pores more easily.

Buy a color that matches the wood and apply it after the first coat of finish is dry but has not yet been screen sanded. Squeegee the pore filler on and off the wood, removing whatever does not soak into the pores. Let it dry for several hours (the drying time is on the label), and then sand it at the same time you screen sand the first coat of finish.

TAKE YOUR PICK

Oil-Based vs. Water-Based Finishes

Oil-based coatings look and wear differently than their water-based counterparts. Oil-based finishes generally have an amber tone; water-based coatings are completely colorless. Oil-based materials dry much slower and smell more, but they are usually cheaper. Water-based coatings are less prone to delamination but a bit more prone to scuffing.

Oil-based polyurethane (right) adds an amber color to wood, whereas water-based polyurethane (left) does not change the wood's color.

Penetrating oils.

wool army blanket also works well. Cut a disk of the wool the size of the nylon pad that backs up the sanding screens. Friction holds it onto the pad as you work.

Finish: Shellac

Best applicator: Natural bristle brush, lamb's wool pad

Cleaning solvent: Denatured alcohol

Cost: $20 per gallon

Pros: Fast drying, adheres well to anything, easy to apply and repair, good chatoyance

Cons: Flammable; alcohol odor until it dries; low abrasion resistance; breaks down in the presence of alcohol or strong alkaline cleansers, such as ammonia

Maintenance schedule: Should be recoated once a year

Shellac is flammable, so be extra cautious about sparks and make sure all pilot lights are off. Brush on a coat of shellac as evenly as you can with a natural bristle brush or lamb's wool applicator. Put it down once and move on. Don't try

to go back over it or brush it out, and for heaven's sake, don't walk on it. It dries way too fast for that. Start from a corner and work out toward the doorway. If the floor still looks "hungry," as though it absorbed the finish and still wants more, you can apply a second coat after sanding the floor with a 220-grit screen. Let it dry overnight, then apply a coat of wax the same way as described for the penetrating oil finish.

Finish: Oil-based polyurethane

Best applicator: Natural bristle brush, round solvent-resistant applicator pad

Cleaning solvent: Mineral spirits

Cost: $25 per gallon

Pros: Low maintenance, easy to apply, moderate scratch resistance, good stain and water resistance

Cons: Solvent odor during application and drying time; fairly slow drying

Maintenance schedule: Recoat every 3 to 5 years

Shellac.

"Shellac is flammable, so be extra cautious about sparks and make sure all pilot lights are off."

TRADE SECRET

Not sure if some contamination will wreak havoc with a sensitive, water-based finish? Or perhaps you are worried that your water-based finish may not stick well to an oil-based stain. In either case, one tie coat of shellac acts as a bridge, sealing in contamination and insuring that the water-based coating adheres well. Apply it as described for a shellac finish, and then let it dry for several hours before applying the water-based finish.

Wax-free shellac acts as a tie coat, allowing water-based polyurethane to adhere to oil-based stain.

coat just as you did the first, then reapply the polyurethane the same way. The third coat takes about a week to dry before you can walk on it. If you use a synthetic applicator pad, make sure it is solvent-resistant. There are paint pads for solvent- and water-based materials, and they are often color coded to let you know which is which. The pad in the top photo on p. 84 shows a yellow foam edge, indicating it is for solvent-based use.

Use a rented buffer to finish off the waxed floor.

Apply an even coat of polyurethane with a pad or a brush. Try to brush it out so that all areas are evenly coated. Let the first coat dry overnight. Sand the first coat lightly with a 180- or 220-grit screen on the buffer. Vacuum up the sanding dust and tack off the floor with a damp cloth. Apply a second coat the same way as the first and give it about three days to dry. Two coats are adequate, but three are better. If you choose to add a third coat, screen the second

WHAT CAN GO WRONG
Shiny Spots from Oil Finish

Oil finishes should penetrate the wood, and whatever does not soak in should be wiped off. If excess oil is left on the surface, it may create shiny spots. You can usually remove them by scrubbing them as soon as they show up (usually the next morning) with steel wool and mineral spirits.

The Cat Urine Situation

I love cats and have two of them, but if there is one devilment of a problem for hardwood floors, it's cat urine. Its strong alkaline nature makes oil-based finishes saponify, or break down chemically, turning them white and soft. It even attacks some waterborne coatings that contain uncrosslinked acrylic resins. What's worse is that once the urine soaks into the wood, it can prevent new oil-based finishes from curing over it. It leaves stains that won't sand out

Cat urine odor? SealCoat, a wax-free shellac, seals it in.

and smells that won't come out. In extreme cases, you may have to replace sections of stained flooring or restain the entire floor in a darker color. Sealing in the odor is a bit easier. A coat of wax-free shellac should go under all floor finishes to seal in the odor and allow the new finish to cure properly.

WHAT CAN GO WRONG

No Damp Mop or Cleansers for a Month

Dry to the touch is not the same thing as cured. Water-based finishes dry to the touch very quickly. In fact, you can usually walk on them the next day. But that does not mean they are fully cured. Ditto for oil-based coatings. A full cure for both of these finishes can take up to a month, and the last characteristic to develop is the coating's chemical resistance. For that reason, it is best not to wet mop or wipe the floor with cleansers for at least a month after the finish has been applied.

Oil-based polyurethane.

Finish: Water-based polyurethane

Best applicator: Synthetic floor brush, synthetic floor pad, synthetic round pad

Cleaning solvent: Soap and water, ammoniated cleanser

Cost: $35 per gallon

Pros: Fast drying, low odor, nonflammable, fewer dangerous solvents, good stain and scratch resistance

Cons: More expensive, more difficult to apply

Maintenance schedule: Recoat every 3 to 5 years

and

Finish: Danish Finish

Best applicator: Synthetic floor brush, synthetic floor pad, synthetic round pad

Cleaning solvent: Soap and water, ammoniated cleanser

Cost: $75 per gallon

Pros: Fast drying, low odor, nonflammable, fewer dangerous solvents, excellent stain and scratch resistance

Cons: More expensive, more difficult to apply

Maintenance schedule: Recoat every 5 to 10 years

Both water-based polyurethane and Danish Finish are water-based coatings that are applied exactly the same way. Danish Finish is self-crosslinking, meaning that after it is applied, it *crosslinks* (or cures) over the next week or so into a much more durable material. In general, Danish Finish is more expensive—though much tougher and longer lasting—than water-based polyurethane. Since these finishes don't create an amber tone the way oil-based polyurethanes do, they are good choices for applying over a painted decorative pattern on a hardwood floor.

Popping the grain prior to the last sanding is preferable on all finishes, but it is absolutely

Water-based polyurethane.

> *"Popping the grain prior to the last sanding is preferable on all finishes, but it is absolutely necessary with water-based ones."*

TRADE SECRET

Paint pads and 12-in. floor brushes are too big to fit into a can of finish. Instead, use a deep-sided pan to hold the finish as you work. Slip it into a plastic bag first and fill it only partway so that the finish won't slosh out when you move it. This also makes cleanup easier.

A high-sided pan lined with a plastic bag holds finish and provides easy cleanup.

Danish Finish.

necessary with these water-based ones. Stir the finish gently before you use it, but don't shake the can or you will create air bubbles. Don't thin the material, but do strain it. Use a standard paint strainer, available free or cheap at paint stores, or a clean, retired nylon stocking.

A round, synthetic pad is a perfect applicator for water-based coatings. Notice the blue foam backing, which indicates water-based use only.

Apply a thin coat of finish quickly and smoothly with a synthetic pad or a synthetic brush. Don't use a lamb's wool applicator; you'll find that instead of laying the finish on smoothly the way it does with oil-based coatings, it creates bubbles and foam on the surface. Also, don't go back and rebrush or work the finish. In this case, thinner is better.

Let it dry for at least six hours. Sand with a 220-grit screen after it is dry, tack off any dust with a damp cloth, and then add a second coat. Let that one dry overnight before you screen and tack, then add a third coat. Let the finish set up for at least three days before you walk on it, and keep damp mops and cleansers off it for a month.

Finishing Stairs and Balustrades

Wooden stairways and their balustrades (the posts and handrails) are finished pretty much the same way as floors. The problems are that the big rental sanders won't fit in areas that small and the balustrades and risers get in the way. Clearly, they require a different approach, even if the finishing materials and coating sequences are the same.

Some stairways and many balustrades can be dismantled. However, that is a fairly major job, and it probably does not make sense to tackle it just to refinish. What makes more sense is to avoid total refinishing with regular maintenance, or to approach stripping as you would any complex piece of furniture.

WHAT CAN GO WRONG
Oil-Stain Bleed

Some oil stains can bleed back out of the pores of large-grained woods, such as oak and ash. Even though the stain was uniform when you applied it, the bleeding can later leave nubs at the mouth of the pores and create dark areas. You can usually fix this by scrubbing those areas the next day with steel wool dipped in a mixture of one part stain to four parts mineral spirits. Scrub the darker areas, and then wipe them off immediately to pick up the excess stain.

IN DETAIL
Protect Risers
and Baseboards

It's quite easy to dent and gouge wood when trying to use a sander in tight corners or up against balusters. You may want to mask risers and baseboards with pieces of cardboard. Use low-tack tape if you are working near wallpaper, painter's tape if you are working near other coatings. You'll find that you can make one perfect-fitting cardboard mask and move it with you as you go from step to step—chances are that each step is exactly the same.

Recoating

Stairs present a particular challenge to finishing. Not only are there a myriad of separate treads acting like discrete, tiny floors, but there also vertical risers. At least with treads you have gravity working with you. But then again, the balusters intersect the treads in many cases. The prospect of trying to sand off finish in between closely placed posts is daunting.

Rather than fight it, approach the stairs by recoating. First clean the surface with TSP in water to remove dirt and grease, then rinse the steps by sponging them off with clean water. Dry them and sand the parts you plan to recoat with 120- or 150-grit paper for better adhesion. Mask off the wall or baseboards, balusters, risers, and anything else you do not want to finish, and add another coat of the finish that is already on there.

Using alternative stripping methods

If it comes to stripping the old finish, brace yourself for a tough job. This is truly a case of trying to choose between the lesser of two evils.

Sand and scrape. Here's where a good belt sander or an aggressive random-orbit sander comes in handy. Use either one to remove the finish on the bulk of the tread. Be careful around the risers, baseboard strip, and balusters, as it is easy to damage them. A fairly aggressive 60-grit belt or disk will take the finish off pretty quickly. Follow that by hand scraping the areas you could not reach with the sander. Resand with 100-grit paper and sand the scraped areas by hand. Go

through the same finishing application steps as for floors, though you may be able to skip the trowel filler step if there are no open seams on the treads.

Chemical strippers. Stripping the stairs with chemicals means you can do the risers and balustrade at the same time. But make no mistake about it—this is a messy, smelly, complicated job. It is bad enough stripping moldings and furniture. This process fills the stairwell with fumes and gunk and makes you wish you had carpeted stairs. (For more on stripping, see pp. 16–19.)

First, mask everything you don't want stripper to touch with plastic sheeting and ventilate the stairwell as best you can. Suit up with goggles, neoprene gloves, old clothes with long sleeves,

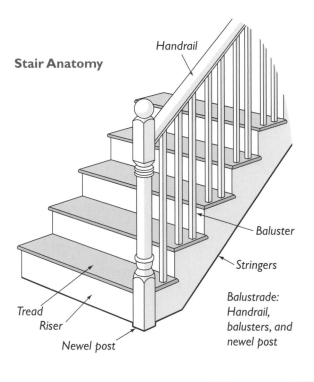

Stair Anatomy

Handrail

Baluster

Stringers

Balustrade: Handrail, balusters, and newel post

Tread

Riser

Newel post

"Stripping the stairs with chemicals means you can do the risers and balustrade at the same time. But make no mistake about it—this is a messy, smelly, complicated job."

IN DETAIL
Adding a Decorative Motif to Stairs

If you have a bit of artistry in your soul, painting something on stair risers can be a delightful yet subtle decorating technique. Use artist's acrylic paints for creating a design. You can find them at craft and art supply stores in every color of the rainbow. To protect your work, seal it after it is dry with the same finish

you use for the natural treads. One word of warning, though: Oil-based finishes are amber and may discolor your work, so stick with water-based ones if you can. By the way, you can use the same techniques and materials to add a decorative edging or a center rose to the floor, as well.

and an organic vapor respirator. Work one section at a time. If you are stripping the balustrade, do that first, starting with the handrail, then several balusters at a time. If you use a slow evaporating stripper, you can probably do all the balusters at once. Daub the stripper on, cover it with plastic to keep the active solvents on the wood, and let it sit until the finish is completely softened. Take off the gunk with coarse nylon abrasive pads. You can use handfuls of coarse wood shavings to get the gunk out of turned grooves and beads. Twine is also great for cleaning out narrow grooves.

When the balusters are clean, move on to the treads and risers. I prefer a fast-acting stripper on treads, since you have to wait to get the tread clean before you can move on. Plus, a stripper-coated tread is much too slippery to walk on. Start at the top of the stairs and do one or two at a time. Daub on the stripper, cover it with plastic bags or sheeting and, when it is soft, scrape it off with a putty knife or wooden scraper. Put the gunk onto newspapers and set them out to dry. Once the gunk is dry, it is landfill safe. Keep the wood wet with stripper, reapplying it as needed, until *all* the finish is off. Leaving the job halfway done makes it far worse when you come back.

When the finish is off, scrub the wood with mineral spirits and nylon abrasive pads to remove any wax or silicone. Let it dry, and then sand with 100-grit paper. You can put on the finish as soon as everything is clean and evenly sanded.

To get in between closely placed balusters, switch to a 1-in. trim or sash brush.

Narrow scrapers fit between balusters.

IN DETAIL

Masking Balusters

Turned balusters present a problem all their own. They are easy to nick during sanding and hard to protect in a way that lets you get around them on the tread. Here's a solution. Tape them with low-tack masking tape, then cover that with several layers of duct tape or foam-core tape. The strong adhesive on duct tape and foam-core tape may pull off paint, but this way they provide cushioning without risk.

Furniture

CHAPTER SIX

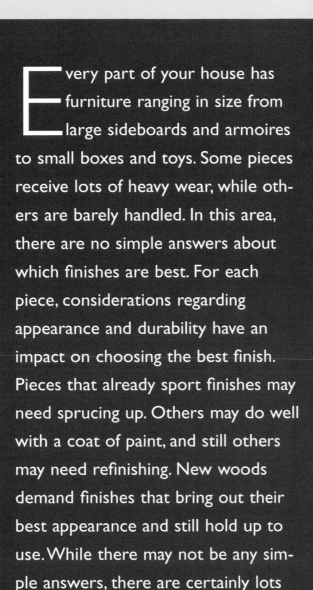

Every part of your house has furniture ranging in size from large sideboards and armoires to small boxes and toys. Some pieces receive lots of heavy wear, while others are barely handled. In this area, there are no simple answers about which finishes are best. For each piece, considerations regarding appearance and durability have an impact on choosing the best finish. Pieces that already sport finishes may need sprucing up. Others may do well with a coat of paint, and still others may need refinishing. New woods demand finishes that bring out their best appearance and still hold up to use. While there may not be any simple answers, there are certainly lots of choices. Let's dive in.

TRADE SECRET

You can't lighten a dark stain, but you can make a light finish darker. First, clean the piece by scrubbing it with 0000 steel wool and naphtha. When it's dry, sand the surface lightly with 400-grit paper. Use a commercial oil-based stain, such as Minwax or Olympic. Wipe or brush it on according to the directions, then wipe off any excess, taking care to keep the color uniform. You can't add a lot of color, just a little, because you are coloring on top of finish, not on raw wood. When the stain is dry, apply at least one or two coats of shellac, oil-based varnish, or oil-based polyurethane.

You can darken an already finished piece by adding another coat of stain.

"The first line of defense is cleaning. A good scrub often shows you what is dirt and what is damage as it removes invisible surface grease and oil."

Touching Up and Renewing

Look around your house. Chances are, there are some lovely pieces of furniture that are starting to show some wear. Before you leap to the ambitious—and possibly unnecessary—task of refinishing, take a good look at what ails them. In many cases, some simple repair work can give new life to an old acquisition. You may even find that some garage-sale specials need only be spruced up rather than totally overhauled.

Cleaning an old finish

The first line of defense is cleaning. A good scrub often shows you what is dirt and what is damage as it removes invisible surface grease and oil. That's no small issue. Surface contamination can undo any meaningful finish repairs by preventing good adhesion.

TSP in water is a good cleaning agent and removes most grease, oils, and dirt. For situations where you would rather not get too much water on the piece, scrubbing with mineral spirits or naphtha and fine 0000 steel wool removes dirt and oils fast, and dries quickly as well. Unlike the TSP wash, there is no need to rinse it off and no chance of leaving a soapy residue. Simply wipe off the furniture with a dry cloth after the solvent evaporates. Naphtha and mineral spirits are especially good at removing old wax and furniture polish. Since these solvents stain fabric, do this operation in the garage or basement shop,

First, you clean. Scrubbing wood with naphtha and steel wool removes dirt, oil, and grease.

not on carpeting. The steel wool may dull the finish a bit, but don't worry about that. You can fix it by rubbing out the finish later (see Rubbing Out, p. 30).

Making minor repairs

A few minor furniture repairs may save you from refinishing a cherished piece. Most have little or no risk of damaging your pieces any further; at worst, you can still fall back on refinishing them if they don't come out to your liking. Here are three of the more common furniture problems and the things you can do to correct them.

Watermarks and stains. Cleaning does not remove stains that go into the finish or the wood, nor does it get rid of water rings. As it turns out, most stains that don't come out with simple cleaning can't be removed. Things like ink spills don't

WHAT CAN GO WRONG

When Disaster Strikes

You take a chance when you try to remove water rings, sand out surface scratches, or add a coat of extra finish. Sometimes the unthinkable happens and the piece looks far worse than when you started. Don't panic. You still have the option of stripping and refinishing the piece entirely. Before you knew that there were possible repair methods, you probably had planned to strip it anyway. There is always some risk in tackling repair work, but your odds of success are pretty good. Take a chance. You have little to lose and much to gain.

usually come out unless you strip. If they go down into the wood, they may not come out at all.

White water rings, on the other hand, can often be removed. Start with a dry surface. If there is still water on the surface, wipe it up and let it dry overnight. Some rings come out by themselves as the water dries. If they don't, wipe them gently once or twice with a clean cloth dampened with denatured alcohol. Don't get the cloth too wet or the alcohol may dissolve or etch shellac and lacquer finishes. What do I mean by a damp cloth? Damp means about as wet as a healthy dog's nose. The white rings should disappear as quickly as you wipe, but may come out only halfway on the first pass. If you need to, wipe a second time.

Worn edges and nicks. Stop by the furniture finishing section of your hardware or home store and you are bound to see some touch-up materials. They usually come in the form of felt-tipped pens, wood-colored wax pencils, and

White water rings come out with an alcohol-dampened rag.

Preventing Water Rings

There are a couple of simple ways to prevent water rings. The most obvious solution is to use coasters. White water rings are caused by water sitting on a lacquer or shellac surface for too long. Keep sweating glasses off the finish and you avoid the problem. Routine paste wax also helps somewhat. Applying wax about twice a year leaves thin film that makes water bead up instead of penetrating into the finish. The wax itself may take a white ring, but that comes out immediately with rewaxing.

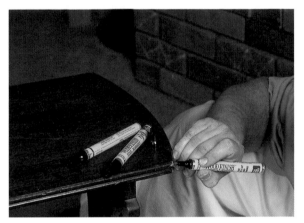

Replacing color on a worn corner is easy with a felt-tip furniture repair marker.

crayons. The felt-tipped pens hide scratches that have gone through the stain and show up as light-colored lines. Most commonly, these occur on sharp edges that have worn through or on the legs and feet of furniture that are scratched during cleaning and use.

Use the felt-tip pens just as you would any marker, "coloring in" the light areas. Test them first on a brown paper bag to make sure you have the right color to match your finish. Once they are on, you can't undo them. For deeper scratches, nicks,

IN DETAIL
White and Dark Watermarks

When you set a wet glass on wood long enough to leave a stain, it makes either a white or a dark ring. White rings are usually in the finish itself and are caused by moisture trapped in the coating. These can usually be taken out quite easily without harming the finish. Dark rings, on the other hand, typically indicate that the water went through the finish and stained the wood. These can rarely be removed, and never without harming the finish, though they sometimes lighten by themselves when the source of the damaging water is removed.

Dark rings are usually impossible to remove.

TOOLS AND MATERIALS
Touch-Up Pens Do Double Duty

After you've fixed the minor scratches around the living room, keep those touch-up pens in the workshop. They are great for when you've sanded through the color on the edge of a new project. Run them along a sharp edge that sanded through before you add the next coat of finish. But leave the wax crayons in the kitchen junk drawer. They are fine for after the finish is on, but not between coats. Finishes don't stick to wax.

When Crayons Don't Work
It is fine to use crayons after the finish is on but not between coats. Finishes don't stick to wax.

Fill voids with a furniture repair crayon.

Level the wax by rubbing it with a brown paper bag.

and gouges that need to be filled as well as colored, use the wax pencils. Simply rub them over the depression until it is filled. Remove excess wax on the surrounding surface by rubbing it with a brown paper bag until the fill is flush (see photos above). You can also use your children's crayons if you have the right color.

Minor surface scratches. Look down the length of a tabletop and you may see a profusion of small, light-colored surface scratches that aren't deep enough to affect the color but which alter the sheen of the finish by breaking up the smooth reflection on the surface. You can often sand these out if the finish is thick enough. Use very fine 600- or 800-grit sandpaper lubricated with a bit of mineral spirits or soapy water. Don't sand too much, just enough to take out the scratches. After sanding, wipe off the surface and rub it back up to satin or gloss, whichever it was originally.

Adding another coat of finish

You can give your favorite piece of furniture a new lease on life by applying another coat or two of clear finish over the old one. If you know what the existing finish is, simply add another coat of the same thing. If you don't know, play it safe by using one of the three things that can go

Sanding with 600-grit paper removes minor scratches on a thick finish.

> *"You can give your favorite piece of furniture a new lease on life by applying another coat or two of clear finish over the old one."*

TRADE SECRET

The new, thick clear finishes showing up on some modern furniture are almost bullet-proof, but they still get minor chips and are hard to repair. You can fill a small chip in a clear finish with a drop or two of fast-drying, cyanoacrylate adhesive (commonly called Super Glue). Let it dry completely, usually overnight. If you need to,

add another drop until the filled void is just barely proud of the surrounding surface. Mask around the fill, and then sand it flush with 600-grit sandpaper on a hard block. Once it is level, bring up the sheen by rubbing it with a small amount of automotive rubbing or polishing compound on the tip of your finger or the palm of your hand.

over any finish: shellac, oil varnish, or oil-based polyurethane. You can add water-based polyurethane to that list only if you seal the old finish first with wax-free shellac.

Whatever you use, the preparation process is always the same. Thoroughly clean and dewax the piece by scrubbing it with naphtha or mineral spirits and 0000 steel wool or a fine nylon abrasive pad. Touch it up with felt-tip furniture repair markers, and then let it dry before you recoat. Brush on at least two thin coats of clear finish, letting each coat dry overnight. If you plan to rub out the finish, add a third coat and let it dry for at least a week or two before rubbing.

Shellac, oil varnish, and oil-based polyurethane are safe to go over any existing finish.

Thick Enough to Sand

How can you tell if a finish with minor scratches is thick enough to sand? Our eyes are pretty good at depth perception. Finishes that look like a smooth layer of plastic atop wood are usually thick enough to sand. On the other hand, finishes that look natural and woody are generally too thin to sand. Unfortunately, you can't really test this on a hidden area. The aprons and legs of tables generally have less finish on them than the top.

Finishes that look thick enough to sand, like this one, generally are.

Stripping Old Finishes

Restoring and maintaining your furniture is all well and good, but there are times when nothing will do but to strip it off and start over again. Perhaps your heart is set on a lighter color or the finish is just too far gone to save. Stripping is a messy, tedious, smelly job, but not a particularly difficult one.

Refinishing

The most obvious reason to remove old finish is to change the color of a piece. As I mentioned previously, you can darken wood by restaining it,

TRADE SECRET

Drawers run on either metal glides or wooden rails. The metal glides rarely stick, but if they do, a shot of silicone spray usually fixes them right up. For wood-to-wood surfaces, try rubbing the wooden rails with a white wax candle or some canning paraffin. Just a bit of wax often makes them slide more easily.

Sticking wooden drawers glide easier if you rub the rails with a wax candle or some canning paraffin.

TRADE SECRET

For those yard sale treasures that come clad in a dozen coats of paint, a good strategy for stripping is to use two different methods. Start by getting the bulk of the paint off with a heat gun, and then switch to chemical stripper for whatever remains. It is almost impossible to get all the paint off with just a heat gun, but the combination is faster and less messy than using only chemicals. One word of warning: Don't use a heat gun unless you know the piece is solid wood. Older furniture was often veneered using hide glue, and the veneer comes off with heat.

A heat gun followed by chemical stripper is often the best one-two punch for removing multiple layers of paint.

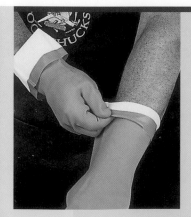

> *"Thin coatings come off quickly and easily with paint remover, making it a better choice than scrapers."*

Glazing, or applying stain over finish, makes wood darker, but too much hides the grain.

but this results in a loss of depth and clarity. Coating a finish with a *glaze*—the term for stain applied over finish—hides some of the wood below. The more color that is applied, the worse it gets. You'll also need to strip off an old finish that has started to peel or crack. At those times, bite the bullet and haul out the stripper.

Shellac and lacquer finishes come off easily when rubbed with refinisher and a nylon abrasive pad.

Interior furniture frequently has a fairly thin finish on it. Thin coatings come off quickly and easily with paint remover, making it a better choice than scrapers. It is too easy to gouge wood while scraping; if you intend to refinish in a clear coating (as opposed to paint), gouges can be a nightmare. Besides, most furniture is veneered rather than solid wood. Veneer is too thin to allow much leeway for sanding out scraper gouges.

Lacquer and shellac finishes come off easily with a thin solvent called *refinisher*. You'll find refinisher in the same section of the store where other paint removers are sold. You can also cobble up your own refinisher by mixing equal parts of denatured alcohol and lacquer thinner. After a light scrub with steel wool and refinisher, the piece is usually ready for a new finish with no other washing or sanding required. If that doesn't take off the finish, though, you'll have to resort to more heavy-duty stripping methods. (For guidelines on choosing and using strippers, see pp. 16–17.)

Bleaching

Frequently, the original wood stain comes off with the old finish, but not always. At times you'll find that, even though you've gotten down to raw wood, there is still too much color in the wood. The wood may be discolored from the stripper or the old stain left by the last finisher, or it may simply be darker than what you wanted. In cases such as these, you can bleach wood to lighten its color. There are three general tech-

SAFETY FIRST

Wear a dust mask when you work with dry oxalic acid powder and put on a pair of gloves before you handle laundry bleach. Wood bleach requires more care—add an apron and goggles to the gloves. Buy long gloves and turn the ends into cuffs so that if you lift your hand, the bleach gets trapped in the cuff instead of running down your arm.

Mix 1 tablespoon of oxalic acid in 1 cup of warm water to make a wood bleach solution.

niques and they do three different jobs. The one common denominator is that they work only on raw wood—none of them will work through finish. So, before using bleach, make sure all the old finish is off and sand the surface lightly with 180-grit paper.

This board was finished with pigment stain on the left and dye stain on the right. A swipe of chlorine removed the dye (right) but left the pigment and the natural wood relatively unchanged.

Not All Wood Is Wood

I remember the time I stripped the highly figured top of an admittedly cheap coffee table, only to stare in horror as the wood grain came off with the finish. What started out as figured walnut burl soon looked like totally featureless white gumwood. Be aware that many pieces of furniture are made with plain wood

What appears to be finished wood may be nothing more than a thin vinyl "photo" of wood on pressboard.

(or even fiberboard) with a picture of fancy wood printed on top. This is particularly common with television and stereo speaker cabinets. So look carefully before you strip one of those pieces, because the stripper takes off everything. Printed finishes have a two-dimensional quality that betrays their true nature. If you are not sure, test a tiny hidden area first. But don't panic if you find yourself in the same situation as I did. Instead, go back and reread the section on painting furniture. I'll bet you can make a beautiful accent piece out of that sow's ear.

Oxalic acid. Some strippers leave certain high-tannin woods, such as oak, with a light-gray cast. These same woods may also develop blue-black stains where they came in contact with iron handles or hinges. A 6% solution of oxalic acid in warm water (1 tablespoon of powder to 1 cup of warm water) removes both of these conditions. Brush or sponge it on and let it dry overnight. There will be a light crystal coating on the wood in the morning. Sponge it off with

SAFETY FIRST

Now and again, you'll run across an old finishing tome that suggests you can make quick, easy-to-use scrapers from a piece of glass. The idea is that the ultrasharp edge of a broken piece of glass makes scrapers that cut with ease and are dirt cheap to boot. But this is a terrible idea. Finishing is dangerous enough without adding the prospect of a handful of broken glass and a puddle of blood on your furniture. If you must scrape, use metal scrapers. They're already sharp when you buy them, and you can sharpen them simply by running a fine mill file in one direction across the edge.

IN DETAIL
The Right Bleach

The chemical reactions produced by different types of bleach cause different effects. Make sure you choose the right bleach for the job.

Two-part bleach

lightens or removes the natural color of wood. Chemically it is a base, so neutralize it with a solution of 10% distilled white vinegar in water.

Chlorine beach

removes dye and certain types of discoloration, such as grape juice and tea. Use laundry bleach or swimming pool shock treatment. Chlorine bleach is neutralized with distilled water.

Oxalic acid

removes black iron stains, lightens stripped wood, and removes water stains. Being an acid, it is neutralized with a base, such as baking soda dissolved in water.

"*Neither oxalic acid nor chlorine bleach changes the color of wood; they just remove discoloration and stains.*"

These maple, walnut, and mahogany boards (left to right) were rendered white with a two-part wood bleach solution.

plenty of clean water and let the wood dry. Make sure you wear a dust mask when you mix the solution and when you sand, as oxalic acid is toxic and irritating to mucous membranes.

Chlorine (laundry bleach). Pigment stains that are down in the wood don't come out easily. You pretty much have to sand them out. But dye stains, which are quite common in commercial furniture finishes, often come out with a quick wash of full-strength laundry bleach. Buy a fresh bottle, since bleach starts to lose its "oomph" after it has been opened. The stain will come out almost immediately, but let the wood dry overnight. Chlorine reduces to salt and water, so you don't need to neutralize it or wash it off. Simply brush or sand off any salt residue the next morning.

Wood bleach. Neither oxalic acid nor chlorine bleach changes the color of wood; they just remove discoloration and stains. Wood bleach,

which is a two-part mixture, lightens the top surface of the wood itself. You won't be able to sand afterward because you'll cut through to unbleached wood, so make sure you do that first. This chemical is particularly nasty and quickly burns skin, so wear goggles and gloves. The bleach is sold as a pair of separate bottled solutions. Some manufacturers have you mix them together, others require that you apply one first, then the other, so read the label's directions carefully. Either way, both solutions have to contact the wood at the same time. The bleach usually bubbles and foams as it is working; by morning it leaves the wood looking pale or white, no matter what color it was originally. Wood bleach sometimes leaves the surface of the furniture slightly alkaline, so I like to wash it off the next day. Lots of clean water will do the job, but if you prefer, you can add about 10% white vinegar to the wash water.

Sealing with shellac

Paint removers often contain wax to slow down their drying time. Furniture that has been polished over the years may also contain silicone oil and other contaminants. Stripping may remove some of this, but it can also drive waxes and oils deeper into the wood. Some of it may sand out and some of it may not. These contaminants don't affect the stain you use, but they may prevent lacquer or water-based finishes from flowing out smoothly. If you plan on using either of those finishes, you need to seal the wood with a coat of wax-free shellac after you've stained it. It's a cheap insurance policy.

WHAT CAN GO WRONG

Refinishing Antiques

Those of you who have been watching *Antiques Road Show* know what I am about to tell you. If you're thinking about refinishing an antique, think twice. It may be worth a whole lot more as it is, and you run the risk of destroying much of its value with a new finish. If you're not sure what an antique is worth, check with a conservator or antique specialist. In most cases, your piece is simply old and can be refinished to make it more useful and attractive. But those rare exceptions make it worth checking first.

Dent

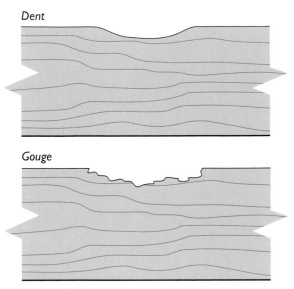

Gouge

Dents vs. Gouges
A dent is an indentation in the wood surface where the grain has been crushed or deflected. A gouge is an indentation in the wood surface where the grain has been torn or broken.

Sanding, Staining, and Sealing

The preparation steps for finishing are quite similar for both new wood and stripped pieces. The main difference is that new wood requires a bit more sanding. After all, stripped wood was properly prepared when the original finish was applied. We can assume it was sanded well at that time. Still, it is not a bad idea to add just the last steps of the preparation process when you're dealing with refinished pieces. Sanding lightly with 180-grit garnet paper ensures that the old is as fit as the new when it comes time to stain.

Finish Firewood

What can go wrong? Almost everything. The color can be wrong, the materials can be incompatible, the coating may not dry—and that's just the beginning. The best advice I can give you is to "finish firewood." That is, before you do any finishing with new materials, test the putty, stain, and finish—in fact, the entire finishing process—on scrap wood. Use the same wood as your project. Testing the finishing process tells you more than three hours of reading about it will, and just may save your bacon. If you know the scrap wood is going to be firewood anyway, you won't be afraid to try things, and you won't be disappointed if the whole experiment goes south. Of course, you don't actually have to burn the samples when you are done. You can toss them out with the trash or run them through the planer (if you have one) to salvage for another day of testing.

To steam out a dent, place several drops of water into the dent.

Cover the spot with a slightly damp cloth and place a hot iron or knife directly over the drop. Hold it there, checking frequently, until the spot is dry. If the dent is not completely out, repeat the process.

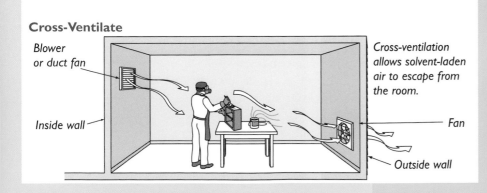

Cross-Ventilate

Blower or duct fan

Cross-ventilation allows solvent-laden air to escape from the room.

Inside wall

Fan

Outside wall

SAFETY FIRST

Good cross-ventilation is a must for moving solvent-laden air out of the room while you use paint remover. Bear in mind that the fumes are heavier than the air, so the best place for the exhaust fan is at floor level. Mine sits on the floor in front of my partially opened garage door.

TRADE SECRET

Finish doesn't stick to very sharp edges and even if it does, it quickly wears off with use. Avoid the problem by "breaking the edges" of very sharp corners. On the final sanding, go along the edges with just a few strokes of 180-grit sandpaper. Don't go hog wild and round it over, just take off the sharpness. The edges should still look crisp, but they will feel less sharp and hold finish better.

Gently sand a sharp edge to soften it but not enough to round it.

Mix two or three colors of the same brand of putty to get just the tint you need.

Fixing dents and gouges

It's inevitable that during the course of refinishing old furniture, making new furniture, or simply transporting furniture from point A to point B, you'll end up with some random dings. Basically, these dings fall into two categories: dents and gouges. Often, dents can be plumped up with a hot iron and a few drops of water. (See photos,

The original shape of a puttied spot should show up distinctly after sanding, like the filled nail hole in this birdhouse roof.

previous page.) Gouges have to be filled with putty. If you are not sure what kind of ding you're dealing with, try steaming it first. If the dent does not level, you can always fill it with putty afterward.

There are a number of putties on the market in a wide range of colors. They all work, though some dry a bit faster than others do. Try to find one that is close to the color of the wood, or buy several colors and mix them to form a custom color. Just be sure you stick to one type and one brand of putty if you mix them. One word of warning about color: Putty does not absorb stain the same way wood does. Some putties absorb more stain, some less. A putty that was the perfect color before staining may stick out like a sore thumb after staining. Test it first by applying putty to a sample board or a hidden area and staining it. This gives you an opportunity to readjust the putty color before you put it where it matters.

Press the putty into the gouge so that it is just slightly proud of the wood's surface. When it is dry, sand it flush with 120-grit sandpaper. Don't leave any extra putty on the surface around the gouge. The original shape of the gouge should show up after you sand it.

Sanding

Always sand all surfaces with the same grit and type of paper. This ensures that the stain colors more evenly and that the top coat looks and feels uniform. Start with 80-grit open-coat aluminum oxide sandpaper to smooth everything and remove machine marks. Follow that with

"Always sand all surfaces with the same grit and type of paper."

WHAT CAN GO WRONG

One Wrong Putty

There are two categories of putty: one that dries and one that doesn't. Oil putty (sometimes called painter's putty) usually comes in transparent jars and looks the same in the container, but it stays soft indefinitely. It is good for filling nail holes in prefinished molding, but it should not be used under a finish. If you are not sure which kind of putty you have, smear a bit of it on some scrap wood. A thin layer of drying putty should be hard in less than two hours.

For the last sanding, go with the grain using 180-grit garnet paper.

excess so there are no puddles, and let the wood dry overnight. In the morning it feels rough to the touch. Sand it very lightly—just enough to remove the roughness—with 220-grit paper before you stain.

Staining

Naturally, staining is optional. If you like the color of the wood as it is, leave it alone and go on to the finish. Stain is for when you want to change the color. Store shelves are amply stocked with every wood color you could conceivably want. . .or so it would seem. Yet, once you start

120-grit paper, then 180-grit paper. Use an electric sander, if you have one, for all but the very last grit. I like to do the last sanding with 180- or 220-grit garnet paper, sanding with the grain. Garnet paper leaves the surface a bit nicer than aluminum oxide and is perfect for the final sanding. When refinishing, you can usually skip directly to this last sanding step.

Raising the grain

Raising the grain is optional but it does offer some benefits, especially with water-based coatings. Besides leaving the wood smoother, the process also acts as an early warning system for problems. Glue squeeze-out, which resists stain and leaves a light-colored patch, shows up when wet, as does oil and wax contamination. Raising the grain is fast and easy. Simply sponge lots of clean water onto the entire surface, wipe off any

Glue Squeeze-Out

Wayward glue on the surface of wood prevents stain from biting in, leaving a light-colored patch. If you spot squeeze-out during grain raising or while sanding, make sure you get it off before you stain. Cabinet scrapers, a single-edge razor blade, or sandpaper can take it off no matter what type of glue it is. Scrape or sand with the

Remove glue squeeze-out with scrapers or a sanding block.

grain to prevent cross-grain marks, and always resand the spot with the same final-grit paper so it acts the like the rest of the surface.

TRADE SECRET

Not sure if the putty in that gouge is dry enough to sand? Test it by pressing your thumbnail in the center. If it is still soft enough to leave an impression, wait a bit longer before you sand it. On a deep gouge, the putty may take overnight to dry all the way through.

Putty will shrink as it hardens, so let it protrude slightly above the surrounding surface. The putty is ready to sand when it will not take an impression from your thumbnail.

IN DETAIL
Dark End Grain

When wood is cut across rather than with the grain, the end grain is exposed. The cut end-grain fibers absorb finish more easily than the surrounding long grain. The result is an uneven appearance. While this can be used to create interesting effects, usually people want wood to have the same degree of color on all sides. One way to make the cross grain and the end grain absorb finish equally is to seal the end grain. Glue size, when used as a sealer, works well to make porous end grain perform like the surrounding wood.

Thinned, custom-colored paint works great as a stain.

using stain, two problems may occur. The first problem is that even with all those colors available, you may not be able to find just the right one. The second issue is that the stain may come out uneven, splotchy, or a different color than the sample you saw at the store. Fortunately, there's a solution or two for each problem.

Finding the right color. Before you stain your furniture, make a sample board of the same wood sanded to the same grit. Colors vary in both hue and intensity on different woods. For example, if you are staining cherry and the color sample in the store was on pine, your stain will come out another color. That's because cherry starts out a different color and absorbs stain differently than pine does. Don't be afraid to buy two or more colors and mix them to get just the right tone, but make sure they are the same type and brand of stain.

Don't try to mix oil-based stains with water-based ones.

If all else fails, you can have the store mix a custom-colored stain. Simply choose a paint chip that is the right color, have them mix a quart in either oil-based or latex paint, and thin it about 50% with the appropriate solvent (use mineral spirits for oil-based paint and water for latex paint). Thinned paint actually works great as a stain.

Applying stain evenly. The keys to even staining are good preparation and good technique. Preparation means sanding all the parts with the same grit of fine sandpaper. You can't just do the tops and doors and let aprons and legs fend for themselves. Sand everything equally. The other key is how you apply the stain. The easiest way to get even coloration is to flood it onto the wood liberally with a brush, nylon pad, sponge,

For uniform color, flood the stain on, then wipe it off while it's still wet.

> *"The easiest way to get even coloration is to flood [the stain] onto the wood. . .then wipe it off while it is still wet."*

TAKE YOUR PICK
Oil-Based vs. Water-Based Stains

Oil-based stains are far more common, but water-based ones are starting to show up in stores with greater frequency. That's because they smell less and dry faster than oil-based stains, and they are not prone to splotching. Drying fast could be a good thing or a bad thing, depending on how large an item you are staining. If it is a large rocking chair or armoire, you may want the longer working time of oil-based stains. Test both on some scrap wood and see which one best fits your style of working.

or foam applicator, then wipe it off while it is still wet. That way, the wood controls how much stain it absorbs. It absorbs what it can, then you wipe off the rest. If you need more color than this method provides, use a darker stain or stain twice. If the wood is prone to splotching, use wood conditioner before you stain. See why making samples first is so important? (For more information on staining and wood conditioners, see pp. 58–59.)

Applying sealer

Sealer is the first coat of finish to form a film. In other words, if you were to put a coat of boiled

While not critical, the right sealer can sometimes save time and material.

linseed oil onto raw wood and let it dry, it would act as a sealer. Stains often act as a sealer coat because they contain resin, form a film, and are applied to raw wood first. However, because we employ stains for their color, we don't often

Sanding Sealer

Sanding sealer is a special type of sealer that was originally developed for lacquer. Softwoods and some porous hardwoods tend to absorb the first few coats of a lacquer finish completely, making it very hard to build up a finish. To solve that problem, formulators made a lacquer laced with zinc stearate, a soft, soapy solid that adds loft for

Sanding sealer powder abrades easily when you sand it, acting as its own sanding lubricant.

quicker build. One or two coats of sanding sealer seals the wood far more quickly than the same amount of top coat lacquer. In addition, the stearate is soft, making the sealer easy to sand. It also acts as a sanding lubricant that makes the material "powder off" instead of forming a sticky film. Its popularity with lacquer has made other finish manufacturers offer similar products for their coatings, but it really does its best work when used with lacquer. You don't have to use it, but it makes lacquer jobs much quicker. Be careful, though. It's a soft coating, so use no more than one or two coats before you switch to a lacquer top coat. If you build up thick coats of sanding sealer and top it with the more brittle lacquer, the finish may chip and crack.

SAFETY FIRST

Remember that oil-soaked rags can spontaneously combust. Dispose of them carefully in an airtight container.

TRADE SECRET

Most people try to scrape off excess paint on the lip of the can. That actually has the effect of removing most of the paint you've just put on the brush. Instead, follow the pro's method. First, dip your brush about 1½ in. into the paint. Let the excess drip for a moment, then lightly slap the brush against the internal sides of the can. Instead of dumping paint back into the can, you're forcing it deeper into the bristles of the brush, and keeping both sides wet in the process.

TOOLS AND MATERIALS
Penetrating Finishes

Drying oils, which are usually nut oils, gather oxygen from the air to convert from a liquid to a solid form. Since they are so thin, the first couple of coats tend to be absorbed into the wood. They cure among the wood fibers near the surface, creating a case-hardened layer of wood. This layer looks and feels natural but is better at repelling water and stains than raw wood, though admittedly not much better. If you continue to add more coats, they sit on the surface and eventually create what looks like a coat of varnish.

"Choose a furniture's finish based on how much use it receives and which look you prefer."

think of them as sealers. A few high-tech commercial finishes require special sealers to go under them, but most of the ones we use don't. Lacquer tends to absorb quickly into certain woods and may benefit from sanding sealer, but it is not critical. Water-based sealers, while not absolutely necessary, are designed to limit the amount of grain raising caused by water-based finishes. Oil-based varnish, polyurethane, Danish oil, and drying oils do not require any special sealers and are considered self-sealing.

Still, there is much that sealers can do. They frequently block contaminants, sand more easily, and help build up a finish faster by limiting absorption. Although many companies offer a dedicated sealer for their products, there is something that could honestly be called a universal sealer. It is none other than our old friend, wax-free shellac. Ironically, shellac does all the jobs of sealers better than any one of the specific prod-

Paste wax is a great finish for things that get little wear, like this keepsake box.

ucts. It seals in all sorts of contamination, from bleeding stains to resinous knots, and does yeoman service blocking silicone oil and waxes. Shellac is easy to sand, dries quickly, and is compatible under all oil-, water-, and solvent-based finishes. If you have just one product to use as a sealer, make it wax-free shellac.

Applying Clear Finishes

For some people, the whole point of using wood for furniture is to show off its beauty. Whether it is stained or left as nature made it, the combination of fine woods and clear finishes is magical. The right finish helps protect heavily used wood surfaces and enhances their beauty. There are plenty of valid choices for furniture, from thin, natural-looking coatings that are very easy to apply to elegant, old-world finishes that require some brushing skill.

Choosing the right finish

Choose a furniture's finish based on how much use it receives and which look you prefer. Heavy use means better durability is required, which means a thicker finish. It goes without saying that a very thin, almost nonexistent finish doesn't protect wood from scratches and stains as well as a thicker coating does.

Dining tables and chairs, nightstands, sideboards, and coffee tables that receive some fairly serious wear, occasional spills, and scratches last longer with a thicker, more durable finish. I prefer

IN DETAIL
Waxed vs. Wax-Free Shellac

In its natural state, shellac contains about 5% wax, which can prevent polyurethane from sticking to it. Waxed shellac should not be used under a polyurethane top coat. However, you can also buy dewaxed (or wax-free) shellac that can go under polyurethane with no problems whatsoever. Until recently, all of the canned, premixed, liquid shellacs contained wax. If you wanted dewaxed shellac, you had to buy it in aerosol cans or mix it yourself with flakes bought from specialty suppliers. Zinsser now offers premixed, wax-free, liquid shellac called SealCoat. As far as I know, this is the only such product on the market.

varnish, brushing lacquer, and oil- or water-based polyurethane for these items. In addition to offering more protection, these finishes can be built up and rubbed out to look deep, rich, and (depending on your preference) shiny or satiny.

Light-duty items, such as armoires, chests, cribs, picture frames, and jewelry boxes, do fine with shellac, wax, or thin, wipe-on finishes, such as drying oils and Danish oil. Of course, it can't hurt to err on the side of the more durable finishes. However, thin, penetrating coatings leave the wood looking very natural. Such finishes provide less protection, but that is not always an issue. The good news is that thin, natural-looking finishes are delightfully easy to apply. In fact, they are almost foolproof.

Applying wipe-on finishes

The easiest way to apply finish is to flood it on and wipe it off immediately. Oddly enough, you can use this technique with almost any finish

After scrubbing oil-based polyurethane onto this teak table with a nylon abrasive pad, I wiped off the excess with shop towels.

except water-based coatings. It even works with brush-on coatings, such as varnish and polyurethane. Some finishes are formulated specifically for this sort of application. Wipe-on finishes are easy to apply, don't stay wet or thick long enough to collect dirt and dust, and look natural.

Wax. Good old paste wax can be a finish all by itself. Rub in an ample amount with a fine nylon abrasive pad or 0000 steel wool, then rub off the excess. Apply two coats to make sure you cover the entire surface, then buff it with a soft cloth or shop towel. Wax offers very little protection; however, it is perfect for certain items.

Drying oils and Danish oil. Apply tung oil, boiled linseed oil, and Danish oil by flooding them onto the wood with a brush or rag. Let them absorb for 10 minutes, then wipe off the excess. Let them dry overnight and apply a second coat the next day. For an added fillip, wax them after they are dry.

Two coats of drying oil or Danish oil bring out the beauty of a lightly used side table.

IN DETAIL
One Section at a Time

If you are wiping on a coating that dries quickly or is fairly thick, finish one section of furniture at a time. For instance, do one leg and a section of the apron, wipe it off, and then continue. On a cabinet, do one side or perhaps just the panel, then move on to the frame. For larger surfaces with no natural breaks, work more quickly or enlist a friend to wipe it off as you scrub it on. It's a great bonding experience.

SAFETY FIRST

Which finishes are safe to use on toys and cribs? All of them. I'd rank shellac as the safest, since it is edible, while boiled linseed oil and oil varnish are probably the least safe, since they have metallic driers in them. But this is really splitting hairs. It would be virtually impossible for a child to ingest enough cured finish by gnawing on toys or crib rails to damage themselves. For the most part, we can't digest cured coatings anyway, so they'd pass through us as if we had swallowed a plastic bead.

TOOLS AND MATERIALS
Danish Oil vs. Lemon Oil

Danish oil, teak oil, rosewood oil, and a host of other similarly named cousins fall into the category of wipe-on finishes. They consist of a drying oil mixed with an oil-modified resin and a good bit of solvent, usually mineral spirits. That makes for a thin, natural-looking, wipe-on varnish that is easy to apply and looks great. Lemon oil is a different matter altogether. It's a nondrying mineral oil with lemon scent added to it. Lemon oil is used for cleaning or polishing already finished pieces, but it is not a finish. Oil-based finishes dry to form a film, albeit a thin one. Lemon oil and other mineral oils do not.

The perfect finish for this cheval mirror is shellac, since it is easy to apply, dries fast, and has a beautiful sheen.

Oil-based varnish and polyurethane.
These finishes are a bit thicker, so apply them with a nylon abrasive pad. Don't bother to thin them, just dip the pad and scrub the finish onto the wood. As soon as you do one area, go back and wipe off the excess. If you want a second coat, let it dry overnight and add another coat the next day. I prefer to use these products as they are packaged, but you can also slow the finishes down if they are drying too fast for you to apply. Just add 1 cup of boiled linseed oil to 1 quart of varnish or polyurethane. This mixture looks the same but offers a bit less protection. You can also wax these finishes after they dry.

Shellac. Watch out—shellac dries very fast. Use it for small pieces or items that allow you to do a small section at a time. Don't worry about overlaps, since shellac dissolves itself if you go back over it. Flood it on with a rag or brush and wipe it off immediately. There's no time to lose and it doesn't need to sink in. Let it dry for at least two hours before you wax it.

Applying brush-on coatings

The problem with building up thicker, more durable coatings is that the only practical way to apply them quickly is with a brush. Rollers aren't appropriate for clear finishes, and wipe-on methods apply so little per coat that it takes multiple coats to build up the finish. Learning to use a brush is not all that difficult, but, like whistling or riding a bike, there is a knack to it that requires a little bit of practice. I'd say it is harder than brushing your teeth but easier than learning to drive a car.

Too often people get bogged down thinking that each finish requires a different brushing method. That's not true. The technique I use is unique in that it works with both fast- and slow-drying brush-on materials, including varnish, polyurethane, lacquer, shellac, and water-based coatings. Oil varnish is applied in the sequence shown in the photos on the facing page. For shellac, lacquer, and water-based finishes, just omit the final step (# 4—tipping off).

Before you start, prepare your brush by soaking it all the way up to the ferrule in the appropriate solvent. Use mineral spirits for oil varnish and polyurethane, water for water-based polyurethane, lacquer thinner for brush-on lacquer, and alcohol for shellac. Squeeze or shake out the excess solvent, then you are ready to go.

> "Learning to use a brush is not all that difficult, but, like whistling or riding a bike, there is a knack to it that requires a little bit of practice."

IN DETAIL
Which Finish Is Best?

A common misconception is that certain woods require certain finishes. The truth is that almost any finish can be applied to any wood. The type of finish you choose should be based on what the piece will endure, not what kind of wood it is. High-wear pieces should get tougher finishes than low-wear pieces. There is, however, at least one exception to this rule.

Members of the *Dalbergia* family of exotic woods (including rosewood, cocobolo, African blackwood, kingwood, and tulipwood) contain an antioxidant that may prevent oil-based coatings from curing. These woods do fine with shellac, lacquer, wax, and water-based finishes, but not with Danish oil, tung oil, linseed oil, oil varnish, and oil-based polyurethane.

Apply at least three coats of finish, letting each one dry overnight. Sand lightly between coats with 320-grit paper to remove any nibs, hairs, or dust that may have settled onto the finish. After the last coat, wait several weeks and rub out the finish for an elegant texture and a flawless appearance (see Rubbing Out, p. 30).

1. Dip only the lower third of the bristles into the varnish.

2. Touch the tips gently to the inside wall of the container to remove excess finish. Don't scrape the brush over the rim; that will unload it.

3. Hold the brush at about 45-degree angle and press down just enough to deflect the tip of the bristles. Move the brush slowly along the grain at about 8 seconds per foot.

4. Go back and tip off the surface by holding the brush at 90-degree angle to the surface. First unload the brush by scraping the bristles on the edge of the container. Then, brushing with the grain, run the tips of the bristles very lightly through the varnish.

TRADE SECRET

In most cases, you can use water-based polyurethane over an oil-based stain, provided the stain has had plenty of time to dry. But there are some water-based finishes that may peel off when applied over oil-based stains. To play it safe, seal the stain with a coat of wax-free shellac before applying a water-based top coat.

ards

Painting, sealing, or staining your house is the single largest finishing job you are ever likely to tackle. It involves a large surface area spread out in an awkward configuration. Since you'll be working outdoors, you'll have to take the weather and the sun's position into account, too. Doing it right can make the difference between a paint job that lasts for a couple of years and one that lasts for a couple of decades.

As is often the case with finishing, preparation is the most important step in the process, and the one that requires the greatest amount of time. Good application technique may make the house look great, but great preparation is what makes it last.

TOOLS AND MATERIALS

What You'll Need: Painting the Surfaces

- Masking tape and plastic
- Extension ladders or scaffolding
- Drop cloths
- Caulk and caulking gun
- Hose or pressure washer
- Putty knife and putty
- Sandpaper
- Wire brushes
- Paint and primer or stain and/or clear sealer
- Rollers and tray, brushes, paint pads, and spray rig
- Water-based exterior primer and paint

Professional estimate

1900-sq.-ft. 2-story house, approximately 90 hours
- Preparation: 16 hours
- Masking: 8 hours
- Spray: 8 hours/ Brush: 20 hours
- Trim: 16 hours
- Windows: 30 hours

Preparing the Surfaces

Good surface preparation makes the difference between a paint job that sticks around for a long time and one that takes a powder way too soon. In fact, the majority of paint problems can be prevented with good preparation. Paint doesn't stick well to a dirty or an oxidized surface, and a job isn't much fun without all the proper gear in place. Good preparation means the surface is clean, the seams and cracks are well caulked, there is no loose material, and all your gear is assembled.

Cleaning the surfaces

Occasionally, you'll coat new wood for the first time. If the new wood has weathered and had a chance to oxidize (this can happen in as little as a couple of weeks), rough it up by sanding it with 80-grit paper to create a clean surface. Don't go any finer than that, since a rough surface holds finish better. Brush the surface afterward with a bristle broom to remove the dust. Use paintable caulk to seal areas where the siding meets molding and windows, as well as other areas where water could enter. If you are planning to paint woods that tend to bleed into paint, such as cedar, redwood, mahogany, cypress, and fir, use a primer specifically designed to prevent bleeding.

More often than not, there is already paint, stain, or clear finish on the siding. You can't really see what you are up against unless you clean the surface first. If you have a pressure washer, now is a great time to use it. Use a wide fan and

Set the pressure washer on a wide fan and aim downward if you are working on lapped siding.

the lowest power setting. A narrow or high-pressure stream can drill right through soft wood and peel off paint and layers of wood fiber. Be gentle with it. Otherwise, brush off what you can while the surface is dry, and then wash it off with a garden hose. Remember to aim downward when you wash so you don't get water under the shingles or lapped siding. If a hose doesn't take off the dirt, mix 1 cup of detergent with 2 gallons of water and have at it with a scrub brush. Rinse it off well with the hose when you are finished.

Use scrapers or a wire brush to dislodge loose paint, peeling sections, or blisters. What remains should be solidly attached to the wood. Wherever paint was removed, feather the edges with a sander so there are no steps or ridges where old

> "Good surface preparation makes the difference between a paint job that sticks around for a long time and one that takes a powder way too soon."

TRADE SECRET

Painting over wet wood is a recipe for disaster. Wet wood can make the new paint blister and peel in a very short time, undoing all your hard work. After you have washed down the house, leave plenty of time for it to dry, especially if water has penetrated any uncoated wood. If possible, leave a week between washing and painting to make sure you don't run into big problems later.

Use scrapers or a wire brush to dislodge loose paint.

Repairing common paint problems

An important part of the preparation process is correctly diagnosing any problems that may exist in a previously painted surface. If you know exactly what kind of problem you are dealing with, it's much easier to remedy. The object is to create a good surface for adhesion.

Alligatoring. Very old, oil-based paints eventually crack and look like the skin of an alligator. This can also happen if oil is put over latex or if the top coat is put on before the undercoat is dry. Unlike most other paint maladies, this one requires that the old finish be completely removed before recoating. Once you are down to bare wood, apply a coat of water-based primer and two coats of paint.

Blistering. Bubbles and blisters in paint are most often the result of moisture pushing out from beneath the coating. This happens when it rains shortly after the paint has been applied,

paint meets raw wood. Ridges make new paint crack prematurely. If you've pressure washed first, let the wood dry for at least 24 hours before scraping so you don't dig into soft, wet wood.

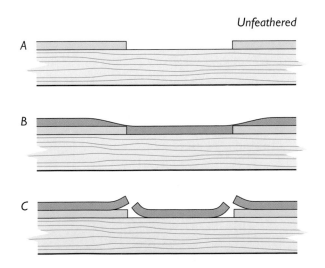

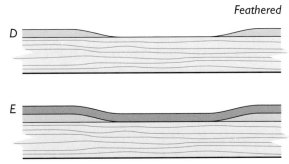

Make the Paint Job Last Longer
Peeling paint can create sharp edges (A) that cause premature paint failure. A new coat of paint is very thin at the sharp, unfeathered edges (B) and cracks after a short time (C). After sanding or feathering peeling paint (D), a new coat of paint can be applied with consistent thickness (E).

TOOLS AND MATERIALS
Pressure Washers

While a pressure washer isn't essential for cleaning your house, it can be a very handy gizmo to have around. You'll find yourself using it to clean the deck, driveway, sidewalks, and even the car. Pressure washers fall into two categories: light-duty electric units and heavy-duty gas-powered ones. The former usually cost less than $300, while the latter typically run from $600 to $1,000. The small ones are fine for cleaning the car and puttering around, but if you really intend to pressure wash your house, you will be a lot happier with a larger unit. Of course, you can always rent a pressure washer, too.

A cheap, electric pressure washer (foreground) is okay for odd jobs like washing the car, but you'll need a good, gas-powered unit (background) to tackle a house.

IN DETAIL
Painting over Old Paint

Whenever paint is peeling, blistering, or cracking, don't attempt to paint over it. That won't stop the peeling but only make the new coat peel off as well. In most cases, peeling is the result of oil-based paint that is simply too old or too thick. The best approach is to remove it. If you plan to repaint, there is no need to get fanatical about cleaning down to bare wood. Use scrapers or a heat gun to get off the lion's share of the paint. Once you get to the point where what little is left sticks stubbornly, switch tactics. Sand the surface with 80-grit paper until it is smooth, even if that means a mixture of feathered paint spots and bare wood. Then prime the entire surface before painting it.

when you paint over a still damp surface, or when you apply coatings in direct sunlight or high humidity. Scrape off the paint blisters, give the wood a chance to dry, and feather the edges with a sander. Prime bare wood and use latex paint. If there is moisture coming from inside the house, either ventilate it or add a vapor barrier before you repaint.

Chalking and fading. As it ages, paint may form a fine surface powder, called *chalk,* or lose color due to sun exposure. This can happen if you use interior paint outside, use cheap paint, or simply wait too long before repainting. Scrub off as much chalk as possible with a stiff bristle brush and a mixture of 1 cup of detergent to 2 gallons of water. Rinse it well with a hose or pressure washer. If you are able to remove all the chalk, you can omit the primer. Otherwise, prime before repainting.

Graying. Natural wood that has been left unsealed (or sealed with a clear sealer that has worn off) turns light gray as a result of oxidation. You can renew the color by washing the surface with a 5% solution of oxalic acid in water or by applying deck and fence brightener. After the treatment dries, rinse off the residue and let the wood dry completely before you recoat it.

Mildew and moss. Although it often looks like black or brown dirt, mildew is actually a fungus that likes to eat paint and stains, especially

On this deck, mildew grows only outside the drip line of the roof.

oil-based ones. It grows in damp areas, particularly under the eaves and on the north side of the house. Both mildew and moss are quite common on oiled or stained natural siding, but they show up on paint, too. Test a spot by dabbing it with full-strength laundry bleach. If it is mildew or moss, the spot will disappear. If it is dirt, it won't.

Remove mildew and moss with a pressure washer, or scrub the surface with a solution of 1 part bleach to 2 parts water. You can also use mildew removers, which are sold in the deck coating area of hardware and paint stores. Afterward, rinse the area thoroughly and prime any bare wood. When you recoat, make sure you use paint that contains mildewcide or add mildewcide to the paint yourself.

> *"Peeling is usually the result of moisture making its way up through the wood, especially when the wood has been coated with oil-based paint."*

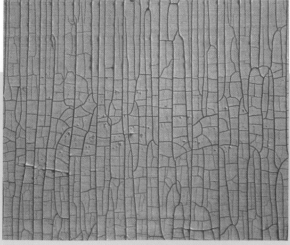

Alligatoring (courtesy Behr/Rohm & Haas).

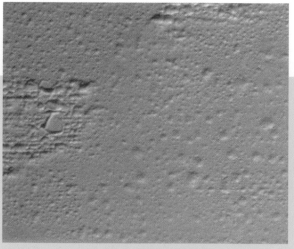

Blistering (courtesy Behr/Rohm & Haas).

Exposure to weather causes graying.

Bleach removes mildew quickly.

Peeling and cracking. Peeling is usually the result of moisture making its way up through the wood, especially when the wood has been coated with oil-based paint. It is often the next step after blistering. Cracking occurs when wood moves underneath dried paint. Causes include poor preparation; lack of a primer coat; painting in cold, windy, or very hot conditions; and applying an excessively thick top coat. If the condition is mild, scrape off what is loose and sand the surface. If it's severe and goes down to the wood, remove the old paint completely, then apply primer and a top coat.

Rusted nail heads. Exposed iron nails rust, even under a coat of paint. To fix the problem, sand the nail heads down to bright metal, then

countersink them. Fill the countersunk holes with acrylic caulk, prime the area, and then repaint.

Tannin stains. This brown or tan discoloration is due to tannins bleeding up through the paint. It shows up in woods that contain water-soluble extractives, such as cedar, redwood, mahogany, cypress, and fir. The fix is pretty easy. Clean the surface well, and then coat it with a primer designed to prevent bleeding, like Bull's Eye 1-2-3 or Parks' Kilz.

Wrinkling. A number of things can make paint wrinkle, such as applying paint too thickly; painting on a surface that is too hot, too cold, or contaminated with dirt or wax; painting before the first coat has completely dried; or leaving uncured paint exposed to rain or high humidity. Scrape the surface, sand or wire brush the wrinkles, and feather uneven areas. Prime any bare wood before you repaint.

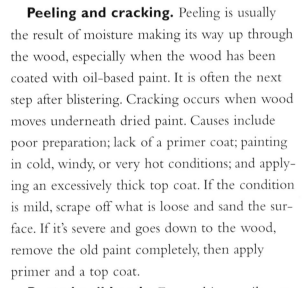

Chalking and color fading (courtesy Behr/Rohm and Haas).

SAFETY FIRST

Any paint made before 1978 is likely to contain lead; paint made before 1950 contains a lot of lead. Do not sand, grind, or heat lead-based paint without learning all the precautions you need to take. Don't even hire a contractor to do it before you read up on the topic. Get the HUD publication *Lead Paint Safety: A Field Guide for Painting, Home Maintenance, and Renovation Work* online (http://www.hud.gov/lea/leahome.html), or contact HUD at: Office of Lead Hazard Control, 451 Seventh St. SW, Room P-3206, Washington, DC 20410, 202-755-1785.

IN DETAIL
Removing Old Paint

Removing many layers of old paint from wood siding is hard work. While you can remove it with scrapers, a sander, or a heat gun, you may want to consider renting or buying a power paint remover. A power stripper is an aggressive disk sander configured just for this purpose and is able to chew through many layers of old, cracked paint in one pass. You can set the depth of cut so that it quickly grinds off paint without going through the wood. Don't go any finer than 80-grit paper, though, since paint adheres better to a slightly rough surface. The job is still messy, so tarp the ground, wear goggles and a dust mask, and plan for cleanup as part of the task. Even with the best equipment, removing paint is a big job and one you may want to farm out to a pro.

Peeling (courtesy Behr/Rohm and Haas).

Removing old finish

Stripping exterior paint is just like stripping interior paint but on a larger scale. Fortunately, it is only necessary in rare cases. If you have to strip, start from the top and work down, using scaffolding and ladders to get to the upper reaches. Spread tarps or drop cloths at least 10 ft. out from the house to catch the chips. Scrape what comes off easily, and then follow up with a heat gun, sandpaper, or a power sander. If you are planning to repaint, don't worry too much about those really stubborn areas that just won't budge. If they are that tenacious, they won't be a problem when you recoat. Just make sure you feather them well.

If you are planning to apply a clear finish or a penetrating stain, remove the old finish or stain with a chemical stripper designed for decks. Make sure you wear safety gear as you roll, brush,

A garden sprayer is a cheap, portable way to apply stripper to shingle siding.

or spray on the stripper. Leave the stripper on for the recommended amount of time, and then wash it off with plenty of water. If you are planning to paint over a stained surface, there is no need to strip off the old finish. Simply wash the surface well and seal it with a primer designed for oil stains.

Spot-sanding and spot-cleaning

Now is the time to check for rough spots, dirty areas, or tree sap. Sand any rough spots with

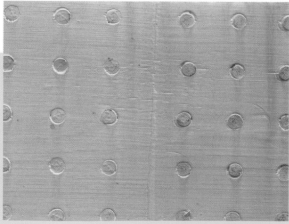

Rusted nail heads (courtesy Behr/Rohm and Haas).

Tannin stain (courtesy Behr/Rohm and Haas).

> *"Stripping exterior paint is just like stripping interior paint but on a larger scale."*

3M makes a special light-green sandpaper specifically designed for latex paint.

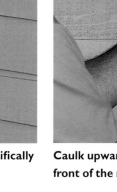

Caulk upward, pushing a bead of paintable caulk in front of the nozzle as you work.

80-grit paper. If you go through to raw wood, spot-prime the area. Clean especially dirty areas with detergent in warm water and a nylon abrasive pad. Remove tree sap with an abrasive pad and mineral spirits.

Caulking and spot-priming

Chip or scrape off old, brittle, or peeling caulk from around windows, edges, and seams. If you have to, sand a bit to get to a clean surface. You don't need to go down to raw wood, but you don't want to caulk over anything that is loose. Recaulk areas where water can enter with exterior paintable acrylic, multipolymer, or polyurethane caulk. If you've added new moldings or windows, make sure you caulk around new wood, as well. One of the primary causes of paint

failure is water seeping under the paint, often through the end grain. Thorough caulking can prevent this and make a paint job last longer. (For more on caulking, see pp. 132–135.)

If you have scraped and sanded some areas down to raw wood, you need to prime them before repainting. It is tempting to ignore a small area, but that may well be the start of a new

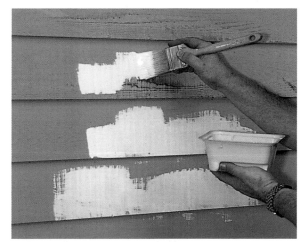

Spot-prime areas of raw wood before you paint.

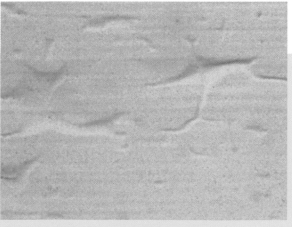

Wrinkling (courtesy Behr/Rohm and Haas).

WHAT CAN GO WRONG

Spray Down, not Up

If you have shingles or lapped siding on your house, make sure you only wash downward. Don't spray water upward or you will get water behind the siding. This is especially important if you are using a pressure washer. You could soak the insulation, cause leaks, and drench the unfinished back of the siding. Wet siding may take weeks to dry. Don't paint while it is still wet or the finish will peel and blister prematurely.

TOOLS AND MATERIALS
The Right Brush

Natural bristle brushes are great for oil-based paints, but use synthetic ones for water-based coatings. You'll find both nylon and polyester bristle brushes, as well as combinations of the two filaments. Buy better quality brushes even though they cost more. You'll really see the difference when you start to paint. And always presoak the brush in the appropriate solvent (mineral spirits for oil, water for latex) before you start.

Synthetic bristles (left) work with all paints, but natural bristles (right) don't work well with water-based coatings.

round of peeling. Use a stain-sealing primer, such as 1-2-3 or Kilz, on bleeding woods, like redwood, cedar, fir, and mahogany. For other woods, use high-quality, exterior latex primer.

Masking and tarping

Mask off what you don't want to paint. Window frames, concrete footings, natural wood soffits, adjacent decks, shrubbery, and sidewalks are candidates for masking. Use plastic or canvas drop cloths or tarps for ground coverage, and paper or plastic media for vertical sites. Bear in mind that masking tape gets harder to remove the longer it remains, so mask right before you are ready to paint and remove the tape as soon as the paint dries. Some specialty tapes, such as 3M 2090 Long Mask, are designed to stay on longer and peel off easier without tearing or leaving adhesive residue.

Using ladders and scaffolding

While I'm sure you've heard this before, it bears repeating: Make certain your ladder or scaffold is

There are a wealth of masking and taping products that make painting clean lines easier.

It's a whole lot easier to paint a line if you mask what you want to keep clean.

set up securely. If the ground is uneven, use leveler feet. Once you get on the ladder or scaffolding, work only the areas you can get to easily, and don't try to overreach. Instead, stop and reposition the ladder. While it may take extra time to move the ladder just for that one little spot you can almost reach, you'll be safer and happier (and healthier) if you make sure your ladder is properly positioned. If you have hung anything on the ladder, such as a roller pan, scraping tool, or bucket of paint, take it down with you before you move the ladder. It may seem like you could balance the whole thing while sliding the ladder over just a foot or two, but it will look different when you are standing there with a bucket of paint cascading down your head.

> "Make certain your ladder or scaffold is set up securely."

TOOLS AND MATERIALS
Colors Galore

Your home store can mix any color you want—designer colors, bright colors, pastels. Just take in an item in the color you want. In some cases, they'll simply find the closest color chip that matches. But more and more stores are turning to color-matching computers that read the sample and instantly match a paint color to it. Even in the seemingly low-tech arena of painting, computers have their place.

Choosing the Finish

Oil- or water-based finish? Actually, modern chemistry has all but eliminated that classic tough decision. Today's water-based coatings are easier to use and superior to oils in almost every way. In fact, you'll find that many home stores now carry water-based exterior paints almost exclusively. You'll still need to make some choices about stains and coatings, types of primers, quality grades of paint, and of course, colors. This section should help you make the right choice before you start applying a finish.

Sealing and staining wood

Wood siding doesn't have to be painted. You can leave it raw or coat it with clear sealer or stain. Here you have a wide variety of options.

The raw wood option. For simplicity and low cost, nothing beats the raw wood option. Cedar and redwood siding can be left entirely

Waterproofing deck sealers work on house siding.

uncoated because they have a natural resistance to decay. The surface oxidizes in a year or two, turning a nice silver-gray and offering a bit of protection. If you go for the gray, wash the siding every year or so when it becomes dirty and treat it if mildew develops.

Clear coatings. The same clear sealers and "rainproofers" applied to decks work on wood siding, too. Typically, these oil-based, clear sealers

Cedar and redwood siding can be left uncoated to turn an attractive, rustic gray as it ages.

Solid color stains look like paint from the street and hold up longer than clear coatings.

SAFETY FIRST

Rags soaked with drying oils, such as linseed oil, can spontaneously combust if they are left in a pile for even a couple of hours. If you've been using oil finishes or fillers, put the rags out to dry on a workbench, a clothesline, or the edge of a trash can—but make sure they are only one layer thick. By the next day the rags will be hard, crusty, and dry, at which time it is safe to add them to the household trash.

IN DETAIL

Opacity Equals Longevity

Do you like the look of un-painted wood? Me too. But the sad truth is that paint lasts longer and protects better than clear finishes do. That's because opaque paint blocks the ultraviolet (UV) range, the most damaging element of sunlight. Generally speaking, the more opaque a sealer or a stain is, the longer it lasts.

contain wax to help shed water. Deck coatings must be reapplied every few years, but at least the thin finish helps the wood stay the same color as when it was new. Bear in mind that this is a high-maintenance coating. If you aren't prepared to reapply the finish often, consider using something more durable.

Semitransparent stain/sealers. Adding a modest amount of pigment to a sealer not only introduces color, but also blocks some of the sun's destructive rays. Semitransparent sealers come in various wood tones, such as cedar, redwood, and dark and light driftwood. Use them to match the color of your siding or to change it to

something more appealing. Sometimes called stains, they typically last at least two or three times longer than clear coatings before they need to be rejuvenated. One or two coats alter the wood color, but still allow the grain to show through. Three or more coats make the wood look like it has been painted rather than stained.

Opaque stains and sealers. Opaque stains are the modern version of whitewash. In essence, they are cheaper, less durable versions of paint. They coat and color wood completely but show more of the grain than heavier-bodied paint does. While they last the longest of the stains, they aren't as durable as good paint.

Applying primers

Priming the surface is the first step in any paint job. While it may seem easier simply to add another coat of paint, it is always better to prime first. Primer hides old colors and bleeding wood stains underneath the paint. At the same time, it adheres well to both old paint and raw wood and provides a good base for new coatings.

Types of primer. There are three common types of primer: water-based, alcohol-reduced, and oil-based primer. Water-based primer is your best bet for 90% of all situations. Alcohol-reduced primer is based on shellac. While it is great for interior work, it is too heat-sensitive for exterior jobs because direct sun can make it soften and move. Oil-based primer is used only to seal in water-soluble bleeding problems. Raw cedar and redwood, for example, contain water-soluble extractives that may bleed through

Semitransparent sealer adds protection and uniform color, yet still allows the siding to look like wood.

"Priming the surface is the first step in any paint job."

WHAT CAN GO WRONG

Water or Oil but not Shellac

Shellac-based primers (like BIN) are great for interior work but not appropriate for exterior priming. Shellac softens in the hot sun, even under a coat of latex paint. Use either oil- or water-based primers for exterior work and save the shellac-based ones for projects inside the house.

The local paint store has a variety of specialty primers to meet your every need.

water-based primer. Ironically, though, water-based primer will still do the job. In most cases, water-based primer actually stops the bleeding, even though the primer becomes discolored in the process. However, it is then harder to hide discolored primer, especially with white or light-colored paint.

Some companies offer primers that can be tinted at the store, or you can do it yourself with tubes of universal tinting colors.

The Right Color

It can be frustrating to choose what you think is the perfect color of paint in the store, only to find that it looks entirely different on the wide expanse of your house. That's because store lighting is a different color than sunlight, and surrounding vegetation may add unanticipated contrast. Besides, it is quite difficult to really see a color based on a sample chip on a paint chart. Here's a fairly cheap way to prevent a disaster. Buy a 4-ft. by 8-ft. sheet of ¼-in. plywood, some primer, and a quart of the color you think you want to use. Prime and paint the entire sheet and stand it up against a wall of the house. Step back and look at it. Not exactly right? Paint the other side a different color. Still not right? Repaint both sides until the color is exactly what you want.

A 4 ft. × 8 ft. paint sample gives you a much better idea of how your house will look in your favorite color. On the other hand, a 2-in. paint chip isn't much help.

Tinted primer. Just as you can tint paint, you can also tint primer. It is not necessary, but tinted primer makes the paint look more uniform. Likewise, it is not critical to perfectly match the primer to the top coat, but being close helps. Some companies, especially those specializing in primers, now offer tintable base primers for custom coloring.

IN DETAIL
Priming Vinyl, Aluminum, and Masonry

Vinyl siding and masonry should be primed with only acrylic, latex, and water-based primers. Oil-based primers may break down over masonry and do not adhere well to vinyl. However, aluminum siding and gutters do better with oil/alkyd primers. Any paint will work over any primer, so you are free to switch to latex paint once the primer is on and dry, no matter what material is underneath.

TOOLS AND MATERIALS
Semiopaque Stain on Steroids

Colored deck stain/sealers work on wood siding, but they are not all equal. The best of the lot are the newest all-acrylic formulas, such as Wolman Extreme. Like the oil-based sealers they replace, these new acrylic stains come in a range of colors. They smell less and have fewer cleanup problems. They also adhere well to fairly wet wood, something oil-based sealers don't do, and they outlast even the best of the oils.

TOOLS AND MATERIALS
Power-Feed Rollers

For large jobs, dipping a roller back into a tray for each pass can quickly get tedious, especially if you are working on a ladder. Power rollers pair a fluid pump with a special roller so that paint is constantly fed from a large tank or bucket to the roller. They let you work much faster without stopping to reload the roller or refill the tray, but they add to cleanup time. For a big job, the trade-off is well worth it.

A power-feed roller is a fairly inexpensive tool and can save you lots of time on a big job.

Applying paint

Walk into any paint or home store and you will see what appears to be the same exterior house paint in several price ranges. Is there really a difference between cheap paint and expensive paint beyond the fancy label? In almost all cases, the answer is yes. Better quality (and more expensive) paint contains ingredients that make the paint flow more easily while hiding the layers beneath, and it really does last longer. Since there is far more labor than materials involved in a paint job, buy the best paint you can afford. A good-quality paint can significantly prolong the life of a finish.

Water vs. oil. It is hard to imagine a situation where I would prefer an oil-based paint to a water-based one. This wasn't always the case. But modern, high-quality, water-based paints (often mixtures of both latex and acrylic resins) outperform oil-based paints in virtually every arena. On top of that, they don't smell as bad, don't require hazardous cleaning solvents, and are better for the environment. In fact, a representative from one large home-center chain recently informed me that the stores were no longer carrying oil-based paint, since there was no real reason for it and they didn't feel comfortable recommending it to their customers.

Color selection. Color is a personal choice, but it is not always an easy one. It is difficult to imagine what a painted house will look like while viewing a small color chip under indoor lighting at the store. It is not a bad idea to stick with soft, muted colors for the main portion of the house and use stronger tones for trim and accents. A color that looks vibrant on a small sample often translates into overpowering on an entire house. Many paint companies offer color guides that display pairs or trios of colors that work well together as primary and trim house paints.

Regional requirements. Not all regions of the country subject paint to the same rigors. If you live in an extreme climate, choose a paint that specifically addresses the problems faced in your area. In parts of the country where the sun beats down all year long, choose lighter colors that don't fade as easily and look for paints with superior UV resistance. Homeowners lucky enough to have an ocean view should look for paints specifically formulated to resist discoloration due to salt spray. Near

If a product contains mildewcide and UV blockers, it usually says so on the label.

"Is there really a difference between cheap paint and expensive paint beyond the fancy label? In almost all cases, the answer is yes. "

IN DETAIL
When to Omit Primer

The reality is that a coat of primer followed by a coat of paint is always better than two coats of paint, just as two thin coats are better than one thick coat. However, you can eliminate the primer if there is a clean, solid coat of paint. In other words, if you are painting a surface that is in good condition merely to change colors or if you are repainting proactively (before the old paint starts to show signs of wear), then you can get away without primer. But when in doubt, go for primer.

Seattle, where I live, we don't have to worry much about the sun, but we need paint with plenty of mildewcide and fungicide to prevent mildew and fungus growth during the long rainy season.

Applying the Finish

You've chosen the color, bought the right stuff, and are ready to paint. Fortunately, all the application techniques are the same whether you are applying primer or paint. Gather your gear, mask areas that need it, set up ladders or scaffolding, and don some old clothes. Add a painter's cap to keep paint off your hair or, if that's gone already, off your scalp. One more thing before you start—take a close look at the weather report.

Some ladders come with leveling feet to accommodate uneven ground.

Working around the weather

Always check the weather report. If it looks like it may rain, put off the job for another day. Rain can turn your hard work into an instant disaster. Check the temperature and humidity, too. Paint works best between 65°F and 85°F and in moderate humidity. When it is too hot, the paint dries too quickly and shows brush marks. If it is too cold, the paint doesn't cure and remains tacky. You also want to work when the humidity is below 85%, since very high humidity can prevent paint from drying properly. On the other hand, very low humidity makes water-based coatings dry faster, which may result in brush marks. If you can't get ideal conditions, you are better off painting on a hot, dry day than on a cold, wet one.

Setting up the work site

It is inevitable that some areas will be too high to reach and that no matter how careful you are, some paint will go astray. Plan for the former with ladders and scaffolding and for the latter with masking and tarps.

Ladders and scaffolding. Whenever you need to paint beyond your reach, use a ladder. Make certain it is set at the correct angle and is tall enough. A ladder should be at least 3 ft. taller than the height you are painting. Set the bottom on level, sturdy ground that will not let the feet slip or sink. You can buy or rent ladders with leveling feet to adjust for uneven ground. Make sure the ladder is sturdy with clean, solid rungs. A label on the side tells you the ladder's weight rating. This is a good time to be honest about your

TRADE SECRET

Two thin coats of paint look better, last longer, and have fewer application problems than one very thick coat of paint does. Plan to do two coats and follow through with it, even though you'll be tempted to quit if the first one looks fine. If you are coating raw wood or siding that was first scraped, that means one coat of primer and two coats of paint—three coats in all.

TAKE YOUR PICK

Satin vs. Gloss

The sheen of paint is entirely up to you, but bear in mind that it is strictly a matter of appearance, not durability. Although some folks seem convinced that exterior gloss paint is substantially more durable than satin, it simply is not true. However, gloss shows irregularities and defects in the siding much more than satin does. Wood, hardboard, and aluminum siding tend to look better in satin.

TRADE SECRET

Primer and paint cover about 400 sq. ft. per gallon. To estimate what you will need, multiply the width by the height of each wall to get the square footage. For triangular areas, such as gables, multiply half the width times the height. Add up the square footage of all the walls and divide by 400 to get the number of gallons per coat. Figure on one coat of primer and two coats of top coat for a really proper job. The front of this house requires 2.9 gallons per coat of primer and paint.

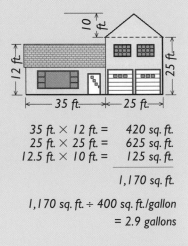

35 ft. × 12 ft. =   420 sq. ft.
25 ft. × 25 ft. =   625 sq. ft.
12.5 ft. × 10 ft. =   125 sq. ft.
_____
1,170 sq. ft.

1,170 sq. ft. ÷ 400 sq. ft./gallon
= 2.9 gallons

"While it is tempting to buy cheap throwaway brushes and budget rollers, they will frustrate you in the long run."

weight—don't climb on a ladder that is too skimpy. Although you are most often better off with an extension ladder, there are situations where a stepladder will work. The same rules apply to a stepladder—make sure all four feet are on firm, level ground, and don't lean or over-reach. Never stand above the third rung from the top. Personally, I like to keep the top of a stepladder at or above my waist.

Masking and tarping. Cover shrubbery, walkways, beauty bark, flowers, and anything else you want to remain unpainted with plastic sheeting or tarps. The most economical way to cover a lot of ground area is with inexpensive half-mil drop cloths. You can also use rolls of plastic film, polyethylene tarps, or canvas drop cloths. Obviously, plants can get overheated if they are left under plastic and in direct sun for too long, so remove the tarps as soon as you are done painting.

For windows, you can either mask the glass before painting or remove mistakes with a single-edge razor blade after painting. Personally, I find it quicker to mask, but a lot depends on how steady your hand is. You can use almost any masking tape if you plan to remove it immediately, but if it is going to stay on for a while, use the blue Long Mask Tape from 3M.

Using the right applicators

Good brushes, rollers, and spray guns apply paint more smoothly. While it is tempting to buy cheap throwaway brushes and budget rollers, they will frustrate you in the long run. Pair up rollers with good paint trays. If you'll be working for several days and don't fancy cleaning up messy trays, invest in one or two good trays that stand by themselves or hook onto a ladder, and use disposable tray liners.

Brushes. Brushes are sold by size, style, and type of bristle. A 4-in. brush, for example, means the body of the brush is 4-in. wide at the ferrule. Width is a matter of comfort—choose one that

Thin, plastic drop cloths keep paint off the plants and beauty bark below it.

IN DETAIL

You Get What You Pay For

Good paint contains little or no barites and other cheap extenders that add weight and volume but don't enhance durability and coverage. High-quality paint contains expensive, durable resins, such as acrylic, rather than the polymethyl methacrylate found in cheaper paints. Good paint also contains pigments that conceal surfaces better, such as TiO2, instead of the zinc white used in second-rate paints.

fits your hand—but wider brushes obviously hold more paint and cover more area in one pass. Use a 3½-in. to 4-in. brush for siding. This size is comfortable to manage and holds a decent amount of paint.

Angled brushes, sometimes called *sash brushes*, are slanted instead of straight. These are often more comfortable for painting around windows and getting into tight corners. A smaller 2-in. to 3-in. trim or sash brush is easier to control than a large siding brush and lets you apply paint in sharp corners and along moldings and gutters.

Natural bristle brushes, which contain real animal hair, are wonderful for oil-based and solvent-based paints, but they tend to splay and become uncontrollable with water-based coatings. For latex paint and other water-based coatings, choose a synthetic bristle brush that is labeled either "for water-based or latex paints" or "for all paints." Nylon is the softest and polyester is the stiffest. Stiffer brushes hold up to thick paints

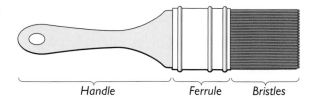

Handle   Ferrule   Bristles

Brush Anatomy

better, but softer ones tend to leave fewer brush marks. Most synthetic brushes are blends of these two fibers and offer the best of both worlds, especially for heavy-body exterior paints.

Rollers—frames, covers, and extension poles. Rollers are more of a problem than a solution on lapped siding and shingles, but they are one of the fastest application methods for large, flat surfaces. Rollers consist of two parts—the frame and the cover—which are sold separately. Choose a frame that has a threaded handle for an extension pole. Most threaded push broom handles also screw into the threads in roller handles. Broom handles add a limited length, but telescoping poles are handy enough to warrant the purchase. Standard rollers are 9 in. long, but you'll also find half-size rollers and covers for getting into smaller spaces, such as between the battens on board-and-batten siding.

There are various types of covers for different coatings, as well as several nap thicknesses for different surfaces. Although lamb's wool is great for oils, synthetic polyester nap is the best choice for the latex and water-based paints you'll probably be using. The nap on the roller also varies, from a short, ⅜-in. nap designed for coating smooth

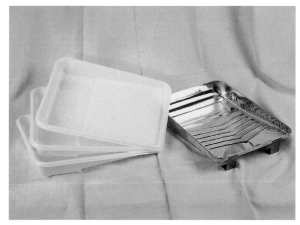

Plastic tray liners are cheap and make cleanup fast and easy.

WHAT CAN GO WRONG

Sudden Rainstorms

If it suddenly looks like rain, pray for sun. Quickly. Rain can destroy wet primer or paint, making sags and runs if it is really fresh, or pockmarks if it is partially set. Once the rain stops, you may have to go back and sand the surface smooth before you repaint. The good news is that water-based paints and primers set up pretty fast, so you are likely to lose only a small portion of the job. In any case, this is a good time to remind you to check the weather report before you open a can of primer or paint.

TOOLS AND MATERIALS

Cold-Weather Paint

If you absolutely must paint in weather below 65°F, don't resolve to just grin and bear it. Visit the paint store and ask about cold-weather paints. These specially formulated paints set up in cold weather, but they have their limits. Read the label and take what it says seriously. An uncured paint job is an unmitigated disaster.

TOOLS AND MATERIALS
Buying Good Brushes

You can tell a lot about a paint-brush by the way it looks and feels. A good brush has plenty of bristles set in ranks so that the ends taper to a round or chiseled edge. When you touch the bristles, they should feel supple and springy, and no hair should come out when you flex them in your hand. As for the bristle configuration, a good general-purpose 4-in. brush has 3½-in.-long bristles in a bundle ⅝ in. to ⅞ in. thick. The smaller 2-in. sash or trim brush is thinner, has 2¾-in.-long bristles, and is ½ in. to ⅝ in. thick. Long, thick bundles of bristles hold more paint and flex more uniformly, providing a smooth delivery of a decent amount of paint in each pass.

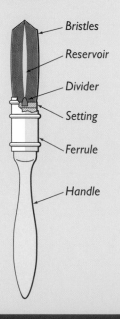

Bristles

Reservoir

Divider

Setting

Ferrule

Handle

A small angled sash brush lets you get into corners and edges more easily; paired with a 4-in. straight brush, the two make a great combination.

surfaces to a thick, 1-in. nap designed for coating textured or rough ones.

Paint pads. Like rollers, paint pads have two components: a replaceable pad and a holder. Better holders have threaded handles that accept extension poles and swivel heads that adjust to a

range of angles. There are also throwaway versions glued onto plastic or Styrofoam mounting blocks. These are often sold as corner and trim pads to be used in conjunction with rollers. Paint pads are not very effective on rough textures, but they can cover a lot of ground quickly on smooth surfaces and don't drip as easily as brushes do. Unlike rollers, paint pads work on some broken surfaces, such as lapped siding, and can get into fairly sharp inside corners.

Spray guns. You can use standard, furniture-type spray guns and small, self-contained pump guns to paint your house, but you may find them more frustrating than helpful. They're often no quicker than a brush. A professional-quality airless spray system, on the other hand, can make quick

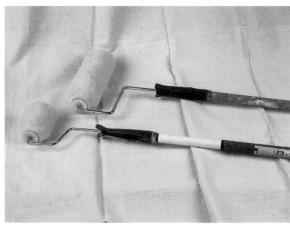

Although a push broom handle fits the threading on a roller frame, multisegment and telescoping extension poles are more versatile.

The roller's cover package tells you whether it has a short nap, for smooth surfaces, or a long nap, for textured ones.

"Warn your neighbors to move their cars if you plan to spray when there is any wind. Even a light breeze can carry paint farther than you would expect."

IN DETAIL
Paint Pads for Water-Based Coatings

There are times when only a brush will get into the various shapes and configurations that some surfaces present. However, when you have large, flat surfaces and are applying water-based coatings, it is quicker and easier to use a paint pad. Try to find one of those nifty paint trays with a roller designed specifically to load paint pads with just enough finish.

A cheap throwaway paint pad (left) and a fancier one with a replaceable pad, threaded handle, and swivel head (right).

How a Spray Gun Works

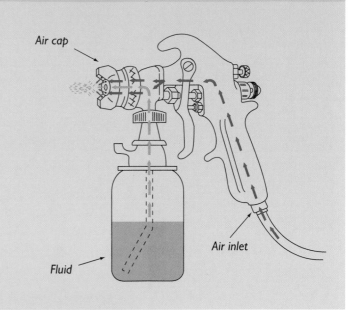

The trigger pulls back the fluid pin and the air plunger, letting fluid and air into the gun. Fluid and air mix just outside the fluid tip. The air cap controls the fan size and shape. The fluid tip controls the rate of flow of the finish.

Air cap

Fluid

Air inlet

work of large areas. It is especially helpful for convoluted surfaces that don't lend themselves to rollers, including lapped or grooved siding. They're also great for applying paint under eaves and overhangs and for coating latticework and other awkward configurations.

An airless spray system is a major investment, but it may be worth it if you plan to use it for more than one job. Otherwise, consider renting one. To keep the price down, get all your masking and tarping done first, have the paint on hand, and make sure everything is ready to go. After the prep work is done, you'll be able to cover a lot of area very quickly, and this keeps the rental fees low. If the house is more than one story, look into a gun extension, which lets you

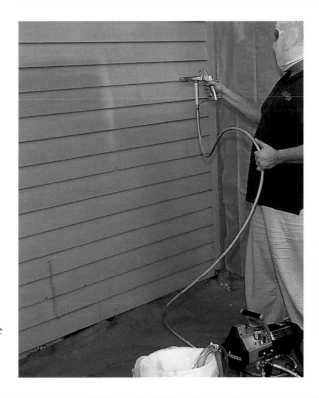

A pump spray rig covers a lot of surface very quickly. The stylish and attractive painter's hood keeps overspray off my head and face.

TRADE SECRET

There is usually some paint left over after a job, and that's good. You may need it to touch up spots that you missed, repair subsequent damage, or paint a matching birdhouse. Mark the lid of the can with the color's name, a dollop of dried paint for reference, the brand (in case the label gets covered with paint), where you bought it, and the date. Seal the lid securely, store it away from extreme heat and cold, and it should last for at least three years, possibly more. If you need to buy more, it will be easy to match the paint from the information on the lid.

TOOLS AND MATERIALS
Spray Equipment

A spray rig for painting the outside of the house may be a good investment. You'll find it is also handy for decks, porches, fences, and any number of projects. Besides, you'll be the most popular homeowner in the neighborhood, provided you are willing to lend it out.

There are two categories of spray painting rigs. Both include all the trimmings—hoses, filters, gun, and tips—but one group is substantially cheaper than the other. The difference is the type of pump used to move the paint. Cheaper units typically use a diaphragm pump, which wears out over time. Replacing the pump is often as difficult and as costly as replacing the entire unit. However, a piston-type pump system provides more power and lasts far longer. As of this writing, these units typically cost from $400 to $800 for the basic setup. Extra tips for the spray gun cost about $25 each.

paint quite high up without ever getting on a ladder. One more thing—make sure you warn your neighbors to move their cars if you plan to spray when there is any wind. Even a light breeze can carry paint farther than you would expect.

Applying the paint

Now that you've done all the preparation, you can get down to the fun part. Open the paint and stir it well. While you are looking at it, make sure it is really the color you chose. Applying the wrong color is hard on marital bliss. Start from the top and paint downward. Do the siding and large walls first and save the windows, doors, trim, and gutters for last.

Horizontal lapped siding. A good brush is the best tool for siding. If the siding is smooth, you can use a paint pad on the flats, but you'll still need a brush for the edges. Start painting from the underside edge first, and then paint the flat surface. That way you will work into a wet edge. Try to finish a whole side or up to a natural break, such as a doorframe or a window. Stopping in the middle of the siding may leave a visible overlap mark.

Flat panels and walls. Flat surfaces are where a roller really shines. However, because it is cylindrical, it won't reach inside corners. Paint the inside edges first with either a brush or a paint pad, painting out far enough to overlap with the roller. Load the roller by running it through a pool of paint and up the ramp of a roller tray. Unload the paint by rolling a large "N" or "Z" in a 2-sq.-ft. area,

and then roll back over it to fill it in. That's the average-size area a loaded roller can cover. Reload, then move on to the adjacent 2-sq.-ft. area, blending into the still wet paint you just applied.

Vertical-grooved and flat-lapped siding. Use a trim or sash brush to paint the recessed grooves and the top and bottom edges first. Work only a few vertical panels at a time so that you can blend the edges while the grooves are still wet. If they are smooth enough, you can coat the flats with a paint pad. Otherwise, use a brush or roller, starting from the top and working down. In this case, run the roller vertically and

Start painting from the underside edge of lapped siding.

"The most important thing about cleaning up is to do it as soon as possible."

IN DETAIL
Spraying Tips

If you've never used a pump sprayer before, practice with it first. Unless it is regulated properly, it creates an uneven spray pattern or applies far too much paint far too fast. To adjust it just right, practice spraying onto a sheet of plywood or a large wall area covered with paper. Adjust both the paint feed and the pump pressure so that you get a moderately thin, even coat while moving the gun at a comfortable rate of speed.

Make sure the fan pattern is uniform. Keep the gun tip about 12 in. away from the surface and move it at a 90-degree angle to the fan (side to side if the fan is vertical). Move the gun smoothly at a consistent speed and keep it parallel to the wood. Make sure the gun is already moving when you pull the trigger, then release the trigger at the end of each stroke.

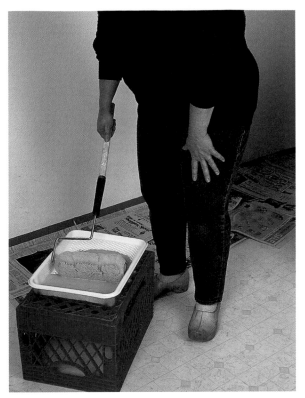

Load the roller by running it through a pool of paint and up the ramp of a roller tray.

Brushes. Clean your brushes the minute you are done painting. I clean mine even during a break for lunch. For latex paint, take them to the sink and wash them with copious amounts of warm water and lots of soap. If the paint does not come out easily, use a cleanser with ammonia in it. The real key to easy cleanup, though, is to keep the brush supple as you go. If paint starts to creep up and dry on the bristles near the ferrule, stop and rinse the brush in warm water before the paint dries. It takes only a minute or two and guarantees that you have a responsive brush all day long and an easy cleanup job that evening.

There is a different strategy for brushes that were not washed out in time and have developed a crust of dried paint. Soak them up to the ferrule in liquid paint remover by suspending them above the container through the hole in the handle. Don't let the brush sit on its bristles or they

don't overload it with too much paint. Doing the "*N*" or "*Z*" trick here will result in drips along the edges of the grooves.

Cleaning up

The most important thing about cleaning up is to do it as soon as possible. Cleaning still wet paint off a brush or out of a gun is fairly easy, but dealing with dried paint on these items is an absolute nightmare. Rollers can be even worse. The one bright spot: Getting rid of empty paint cans is easy. Here are some guidelines for dealing with each of these items.

Roll a 2-sq.-ft. "N," then go back and fill it in.

TRADE SECRET

Some pros spray first, then brush out the sprayed paint. This is called *back brushing* and is usually done only on very rough surfaces. Spraying thick material too heavily can cause *bridging,* a situation where paint bridges over voids and leaves air spaces trapped beneath as it dries. Back brushing alleviates this. It is usually not necessary except when you paint on a very rough, raw wood surface for the first time. Some people also use a brush to blend out areas of uneven spray, but that betrays a lack of spraying ability and is not so much a method of work as a correction of poor skills.

WHAT CAN GO WRONG

Follow the Sun to Avoid Blisters

While you don't want to paint in cold weather, you also don't want to paint in direct sunlight. The sun beating down on a freshly painted surface can make it blister. Paint the west side of the house in the morning and the east side in the afternoon. That way you will always be in the shade and out of direct sunlight.

Don't paint in direct sunlight. Work on the shady side of the house until the sun moves.

will become deformed. Wait until the stripper softens the paint, then comb it out with a brush comb or massage the gunk out with your gloved fingers and some clean stripper. Immediately remove the stripper residue by washing the brush in a pan of lacquer thinner (be sure to wear gloves and a respirator for this operation). Once the brush is clean, remove the thinner by washing the brush in warm soapy water and rinsing it in clear water.

When the soap has been rinsed out, shake the brush to remove the bulk of the water. Wrap the bristles up to the ferrule in a brown paper bag. Feel for the ends of the bristles, and fold the

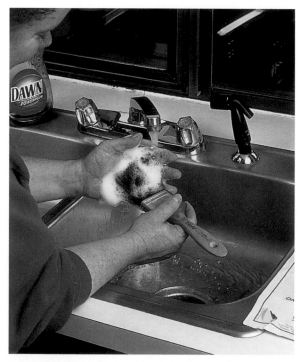

Immediately wash your brush in plenty of soapy water, rewashing and rinsing several times until the water runs clear.

paper over about 1 in. past them. The paper reshapes the bristles as they dry.

Spray guns. For short breaks, seal a spray gun in a plastic bag and cover the open paint can with a layer of plastic film or sandwich wrap. However, as soon as you are finished spraying for the day, clean the system. The method varies from sprayer to sprayer, so read the instructions. In general, you have to run the pump in prime mode with the intake hose removed from the paint but the dump hose still in the bucket. This empties the bulk of the paint from the pump. Next, spray out the remaining paint in the gun line by spraying it into the paint bucket.

Now place the dump hose in an empty bucket and the intake hose in a bucket of clean water. Spray clean water through the lines and into the dump bucket until it runs clear. Run the prime cycle the same way. Take the gun apart and clean that, too. Remove the spray tip and soak it in warm water, then clean out the seating hole with a soft brush or a pipe cleaner.

Rollers. You can wash roller covers in warm soapy water if you do it immediately. However, I can tell you that it takes a lot of time and a lot of water to get them clean. If they are not thoroughly clean—and that means clean enough so that the water runs clear—they will be hard and stiff the next day. Considering the price of roller covers, more often than not I simply let them dry and throw them away. Even if you toss them, remove them and wash the paint off the roller frame or it may not roll smoothly the next day. For short breaks, seal the paint-laden roller in a

"If you have enough paint to save, it is a good idea to label the can and save it for touch-ups later."

TRADE SECRET

Pros do not hold a brush by its handle. In fact, they hold the handle only when cleaning the brush. Hold a brush with your thumb on one side of the ferrule and your fingers on the other, with the base of the handle nestled in the crook of your hand between your thumb and first finger. The bristles should look and act like an extension of your fingers. This way, brushing feels as natural as if you were simply dragging your fingertips across a surface and the bristles are as easy to control as your hand. Proper hand position lets you brush for hours without stressing your wrists or forcing them into awkward positions.

Wrap the brush in a brown paper bag and fold it over about 1 in. past the end of the bristles.

plastic bag. However, a roller left in a plastic bag overnight does not work as well as a new or well-cleaned one.

Paint cans. Remove as much paint as possible from empty paint cans. If there is too little to store, brush it out onto some cardboard and let it dry. Leave the lid off the can until the paint stuck to the sides and bottom is dry. Once it is dry, it is landfill safe and can go out with the household trash. The bottom line is that disposing of paint is a problem only if it is wet.

If you have enough paint to save, it is a good idea to label the can and save it for touch-ups later. Otherwise, take unwanted paint to your

Brush Tricks

Most folks work directly out of a can of paint, but you'll have more control working from a square basin. Start by wetting the bristles all the way to the ferrule in water (for water-based paint) or in mineral spirits (for oil-based paint). Shake or spin off the excess so the bristles are just damp. Dip the bottom third of the bristles into the paint and gently touch the tips to the inside wall of the basin. Don't scrape the loaded brush over the edge or you will unload it again. Touching the tips to the inside edge removes just enough paint so that the brush won't drip.

Dip only the last third of the bristles into the paint.

Touch just the tips to the side of the container. The brush is fully loaded but won't drip.

local hazardous material drop site. Call your local government or trash pickup service for information. Some places have exchange centers where you can drop off or pick up clean solvents and paints at little or no cost.

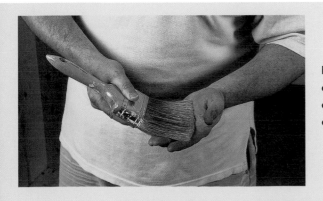

Holding a brush correctly gives you lots of control without causing fatigue.

Windows. Doors.

CHAPTER EIGHT

and Trim

Exterior doors and windows suffer a double whammy. Like exterior walls, they are subject to sun, wind, rain, and variations in humidity. They are also exposed to abrasion and wear in far larger doses than walls. Doors that face direct sunlight suffer from fading and quicker delamination than walls, too. Windows have horizontal surfaces that may allow standing water to rot the wood. As always, good preparation (and sometimes a bit of repair work) is the first defense against premature wear.

When it comes time to select trim coatings, you need to consider the artistic as well as the practical. Contrasting or matching colors affect the appearance of the house in many subtle ways.

TOOLS AND MATERIALS

What You'll Need: Painting Doors and Windows

- Sash brush
- Trim brush
- Paint tray
- Drop cloths or tarps
- Masking shield
- Masking tape
- Plastic masking film
- Ladders
- Rags for wiping
- Cleaning solvent
- Single-edge razor blades and holder

Professional estimate

One hour per window or door

IN DETAIL

Cleaning New Gutters

New, unpainted metal gutters and downspouts sometimes have a thin film of oil on them from the manufacturing process. It is a good idea to remove the oil by wiping the gutters with naphtha before you install them.

Preparing the Surfaces

The sequence for painting a house is as follows: 1) siding, 2) trim, 3) railings, 4) porches, 5) door and window frames, 6) gutters. For the most part, preparation for trim work is the same as for siding, but there are also some extra chores you may need to do. Windowsills and doorsills that stay wet are more prone to rot; if any is present it must be repaired before you paint. Gutters need some special care, and everything that interrupts the siding must be caulked.

Wash and scrape

Window and door frames, gutters, shutters, and contrasting trim need to be prepared just like walls are. Clean them in the same way by rinsing off surface dirt or scrubbing them with a bristle brush and detergent in water. If you use a pressure washer, be very careful about the direction of the spray. It is quite easy to get water behind the frames if the caulking is old, cracked, or missing, and a high-pressure stream can crack glass. Eliminate mildew with mildew remover or a solution of one part laundry bleach to three parts water. Areas below the eaves, overhangs, and windows are particularly prone to mildew because they are often blocked from the sun, which allows moisture to accumulate. Scrape any loose paint and feather the edges with a sander. Spot-prime bare areas with latex primer.

Metal gutters require special attention. In addition to the problems that befall wood, they are also prone to corrosion and rust. Scrape any loose paint or rust with a scraper, wire brush, or coarse

Use a wire brush to scrape loose paint from gutters.

nylon abrasive pad until you see clean metal, then wipe the gutters down with a solution of one part vinegar to three parts water. Make sure you remove rust and foliage stains, since they can bleed through new paint. Most new gutters are already coated, but if you put up unpainted galvanized or aluminum gutters, clean and seal them with a primer designed for metal gutters.

Repair damage

While scraping and washing, you may find rotted sections of window frames or doorways, especially in and around the sills. Ideally, you should remove and replace rotted sections with new wood, but that is often a larger job than is practical. Rotted doorsills or thresholds should be replaced, but window repairs can be a bit more complicated. Although it can be a bit messy, you can repair and reinforce rotted wood if the rotting is not too extensive.

"Although it can be a bit messy, you can repair and reinforce rotted wood if the rotting is not too extensive."

TOOLS AND MATERIALS

Wire Brush on Steroids

Scrubbing with a wire brush is fast and easy on straight, exposed areas. It becomes tougher when you need to work in tight spaces and corners, because there is often no room to move the brush back and forth. To solve this problem, buy a wire cup brush and chuck it into your electric drill. Its rotary action lets you get lots of work done in a small space. Wear goggles, since these brushes tend to fling debris and bits of metal wire as the brush wears. Wheel-mounted nylon abrasive pads do the same sort of job without flinging bits of metal wire.

Repair rotted wood before it gets out of hand. This is a good candidate for repair…

…but this riser board is too far gone and needs to be replaced.

Start by scraping off the paint around the area that is rotted, or remove it with a heat gun or chemical stripper. You'll need to clear away enough paint to expose sound wood. Next, dig out any flaking, crumbling, or severely rotted areas. Soak the remaining wood with hardener. Hardeners come in a one-container form, usually as a milky-looking liquid, and as a two-part thin

Scrape the area and drill a few small holes for penetration, then soak the spongy wood with liquid hardener.

epoxy that you must mix before you apply it. Drill a few holes in the area so the hardener can soak into the old wood. Let it cure according to the instructions. This gives you a solid base to work from, but it won't fill the void where wood is missing. That is next.

Fill the voids with either a two-part epoxy wood-filling compound or auto body polyester filler. I find that the latter works just as well and is generally cheaper if you have a lot of wood to replace, but use it only on areas that will be painted. You may be able to get epoxy wood filler to look convincingly like wood underneath a clear finish, but auto body filler looks like what it is—polyester. Mix the filler and pack the missing wood as tightly as possible. Leave it slightly over-sized to trim back when it is cured. When it is dry, shape it with a wood rasp followed by 80-grit sandpaper wrapped around a sanding block, then prime and paint it as you would for any new wood.

WHAT CAN GO WRONG

Don't Paint Plastic Gutters

Even with primer, it's next to impossible to get paint to stick to plastic gutters. Don't waste your time and money on paint. You're better off buying new gutters. Fortunately, it is not that expensive to replace them.

TRADE SECRET

Doorsills and windowsills are good candidates for rot. A good preventive measure *before* you paint them is to soak the raw wood in preservative. You'll usually find paintable wood preservative solutions where deck coatings are sold. Make sure you get the right type, as there are also nonpaintable wood preservatives. Saturate the wood and let the preservative dry thoroughly before priming and painting. A pretreated, painted frame or sill staves off peeling paint long after its untreated counterpart has failed.

WHAT CAN GO WRONG

Anchor Repair Patches

At times you may need to re-build a corner or a section of unsupported wood with just a small area for an anchor. If the new repair is not bordered on at least three sides, the cured putty could snap off if it is bumped hard. Secure the new fill by first setting a few headed nails or screws into the old wood. Leave the heads sticking out into the area to be filled, but below where the new surface will be. As you cast the filler around them, the nails anchor the new patch to the old wood.

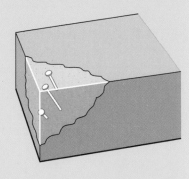

Repairing a Broken Corner
To add stability to a corner repair, hammer several nails into the wood to create an anchor that holds the filler in place.

Use two-part epoxy wood-filler if you plan to apply a clear finish. Use auto body filler, such as Bondo, if the repair will be hidden by paint.

Caulk

Caulk helps seal your home, keeping out mois-ture, hot and cold air, and bugs. Check old caulk-ing and remove any that is brittle or raised, then clean the surface with a wire brush or scrapers and recaulk it. Any time you put in new frames or trim, caulk around them as well. You should also caulk along seams, both inside and outside corners, and wherever the siding meets the foun-dation, doors, and window frames. Don't forget dryer vents, water faucets, and holes for electrical outlets and fixtures. In short, use caulking wher-ever the siding ends or is breached.

Types of caulk. Let's start with what not to use. Don't use caulk that is unpaintable, even if you are applying it after you've painted. You (or someone else) may want to paint it some day. That eliminates pure silicone caulk; save that for the bathroom. Also, pass on butyl caulk. It is the cheapest of the caulks and will most likely say "flammable" on the label. Butyl tends to dry too

quickly, skin over, and shrink too much, which can make the caulk fail prematurely. This leaves you with three good choices:

- Latex, acrylic, or siliconized acrylic is the cheapest of the three choices. It works best on clean wood surfaces and cleans up with soap and water.
- Tripolymer is an excellent all-around choice. It is in the medium price range, is very durable, bonds to most materials, and cleans up with lacquer thinner. You'll often see it sold as caulk/adhesive and sometimes as a clear ver-sion in a clear tube.
- Polyurethane is by far the most expensive and most durable of the three caulks and is capable

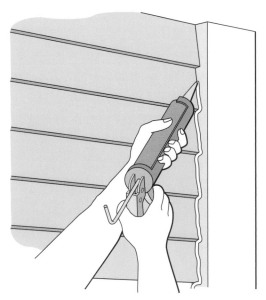

The Correct Way to Caulk
The natural tendency is to start at the top of the wall and pull downward. The proper way is to start at the bottom and push upward.

"Caulk helps seal your home, keeping out moisture, hot and cold air, and bugs."

TRADE SECRET

Some filler materials are thick enough to act like moldable putty and stay where you put them. Others tend to sag or flow. When you fill a missing upper edge on a piece of wood, you can rein in the putty with a dam made of masking tape. Use a long enough piece of tape so that you can stretch it across the void and anchor it on both sides. Let it sit higher than the area you are filling so you can overfill a bit. The weight of the putty deflects the dam so that it will be just proud of the final level.

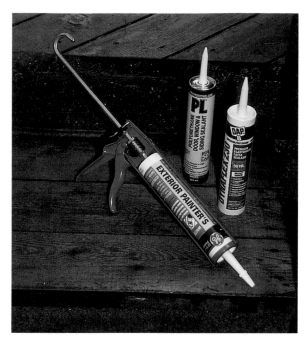

Use paintable acrylic, modified acrylic, tripolymer, or polyurethane caulk for exterior work.

inside the cartridge. Some caulk guns come with a folding metal rod to pierce the seal, or you can use a long nail or a straightened coat hanger. Once the seal is broken, the caulk should flow smoothly with each pull of the trigger.

When caulking, the natural tendency is to start at the top of the wall and pull downward. The proper way is to start at the bottom and push upward, a technique that fills the underside and seals the two surfaces to each other. If you don't have much experience with caulk, it's a good idea to practice first on scrap wood, even if you have to cobble up an angled practice board. If you push the gun forward while pulling the trigger, pushing the bead of caulk in front of the nozzle, you can make a very neat bead with just the gun. Fill any gaps or openings deeper than G in. with polyethylene backer rope or a piece of flexible foam and apply a bead of caulk over that.

of lasting up to 40 years. While it is also the most difficult to use (it's very sticky and harder to shape), it bonds to almost everything, including glass. It cleans up with acetone and adheres to itself, so you can recaulk over it.

How to caulk. Apply caulking to dry wood when the temperature is at least 50°F and the humidity is not too high. Use a good caulking gun (one that feels solid and not flimsy), load the caulk cartridge, and pull the trigger a few times until the plunger is against the caulk. Cut the end of the nozzle at an angle to create a hole. Start with a small hole first, as you can always make it larger (but not the reverse). I've found that a K-in. hole works best for most exterior caulking. Pierce the foil seal at the base of the nozzle

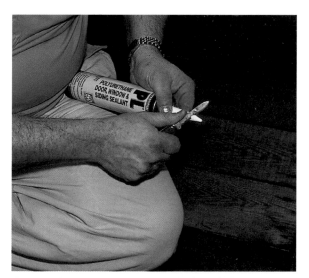

Cut the tip at an angle to create a hole. I find a ³/₈-in. hole works well for exterior caulking.

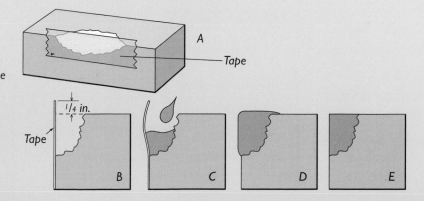

Repairing an Edge

A. Place masking tape along the edge of a gouge.
B. The tape should be about ¹/₄ in. higher than the top of the wood surface.
C. As filler enters the dam, the masking tape bulges.
D. Filler should be about ¹/₁₆ in. proud on both sides.
E. When dry, sand the filler level with the surface.

A — Tape

¹/₄ in.

Tape

B   C   D   E

WHAT CAN GO WRONG

Clear Finish Means Perpetual Care

Wooden entry doors and garage doors look wonderful in clear coatings, but beware of those that face strong, direct sunlight. One painter described clear coating a wooden door that received southern exposure as "taking up refinishing as a hobby." Even the best clear exterior finishes with UV absorbers can't stand the sun's onslaught for long and soon fade, peel, and turn cloudy. If you are not willing to recoat every year or two, pass on the clear finish and go with an opaque paint.

Garage and entry doors fade and peel in bright sun, so be prepared for more frequent recoating if you choose to apply a clear finish.

A sturdy caulking gun like this one won't flex or break and feeds caulk smoothly.

Selecting Stain and Clear Sealer

Wood highlights add a warm, natural look to a house. Staining or clear coating wooden garage doors and entryways adds a classy touch to an otherwise painted backdrop, and Tudor architecture could not exist without those distinctive wood beams angling across the façade. Clear coatings and semitransparent stains don't hold up as long as paint does, so if you decide this is the look you want, make sure you are willing to perform the regular maintenance they require.

Fade-resistant stains

Your choices for staining exterior wood are somewhat limited. Avoid interior wood stains, because they often contain dyes as well as colored pigments. Dyes fade in strong sunlight but pigments don't. Make sure you purchase all-pigment coatings, which are clearly labeled as exterior or interior/exterior stains. Fortunately, there are also a couple of other options.

Exterior semitransparent stains. Those same semitransparent stains that you buy for your deck or fence can also be used on doors and windows. However, they have severe limitations that could sour you on the idea. Deck stains usually contain paraffin wax. You can't coat over them with a clear protective finish because the wax prevents them from drying and sticking. Of course, you could use a deck stain and reapply it every year, but that means a lot of maintenance for a door or window that can survive on less.

Custom-mixed stains. Many stores offer pigmented exterior stains in custom-mixed colors. You choose a color chip, just as you do with paint, and they mix it on the spot. In most cases, these stains do not contain wax, so cover them with a clear protective coating. Make sure you check with the store clerk and let him or her know what you intend to do with the material. Another option is to buy custom-mixed latex or oil-based paint and thin it with solvent (water for latex, mineral spirits for oil) until it is the consistency of skim milk, then use it just as you would a stain. Once it dries, you can top coat it with a clear protective finish.

> *"Clear coatings and semitransparent stains don't hold up as long as paint does, so make sure you are willing to perform the regular maintenance they require."*

IN DETAIL

Finishing Off Caulk

Once you've applied a bead of caulk, finish it off by running down the seam with your finger, a tongue depressor, or a plastic spoon dipped in the appropriate caulk solvent. Use slightly soapy water for latex and acrylic caulks or mineral spirits for polyurethane and tripolymer caulks. In one swipe you can smooth the caulk, remove any excess, and ensure that it makes good contact with the other surfaces. This technique also leaves a slightly concave surface that looks neat and professional.

Some stores now mix custom exterior stains from a carousel of pigments.

Clear coatings

Whether you choose to stain wood or keep its natural color, you'll still want your front door to have a finish that brightens it up and keeps out dirt and water. In this case, you have three good choices: exterior alkyd varnish, exterior polyurethane, and spar varnish. They all hold up decently, but if the sunlight is harsh, expect to recoat every two to three years. Doors that are recessed or shaded from the sun by an overhang can go somewhat longer.

Polyurethane is the toughest exterior finish and resists scuffing and scratches best, but my favorite is spar varnish. The others may start to delaminate in strong sunlight, peeling where the wood meets the finish. If that occurs, you have no choice but to scrape or strip it off and refinish. Spar varnish tends to deteriorate from the

top down, becoming chalky but not delaminating, so you can usually sand the surface lightly and reapply another coat.

Selecting Paint

Take a good look at the front of your house. The primary wall color is only part of what gives the house its look and character. The windows, doors, shutters, and trim break up the lines and transform the exterior into a complex and interesting structure. To set them off even more, we generally paint trim elements a different color. Choosing the right colors can be at least as important as buying the right paint.

Clear finishes for doorways work best in protected areas where the finish doesn't bear the brunt of the weather.

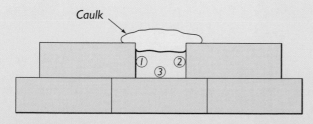

Caulk

Caulk Two Surfaces, not Three
Don't use caulk to fill a large void, and don't let it contact a third surface behind the other two.

WHAT CAN GO WRONG
Caulk Two Surfaces Only

Caulk works by forming a flexible bridge between two surfaces that move or present a gap. Don't use caulk to fill a large void or let it contact a third surface behind the other two, which can make caulk crack instead of stretch. Fill large voids with polyethylene backer rope and avoid filling smaller voids with large puddles of caulk.

IN DETAIL
Paint Duration

These days paints offer 10-year, 20-year, and even lifetime warranties—for a price. Of course, there is no real guarantee that any paint can last a lifetime, but the current paints certainly outperform their precursors. In my opinion, paint should last long enough so that we forget how much work painting was by the time we have to do it again. Unless you live in an extreme climate, a good paint job should last at least 10 years, provided you properly primed and prepared the wood and used good-quality paint.

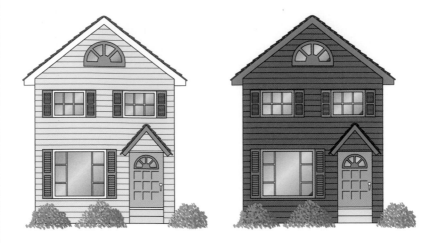

Light House, Dark House
Light colors make a house look larger and more open, while dark colors tend to make a house look smaller and more compact.

Color choices

You can give your home an entirely new look by borrowing a few good tricks from an artist's perspective. For instance, paint your house white or another very light color to make it appear larger. Darker colors tend to make a house appear smaller and more compact. A house that is painted a light yellowish or pinkish beige looks larger and draws more attention than one that is painted a dark greenish gray.

Once you've selected the basic color, it's time to think about coordinating trim colors. Take a close look at the overall design of your house with an eye to how you can bring out its strengths and hide its weaknesses.

For instance, artists look at colors in terms of warm tones, such as reds, yellows, and oranges, and cool tones, such as blues, greens, and grays. Warm tones tend to stand out and draw attention; cool tones tend to fade into the background. Emphasize the most special or appealing architectural elements, such as dormers and bay windows, with bold colors in warm tones. Apply cool tones to less interesting areas. Using two complementary trim colors often makes an ordinary house design look more complex and interesting to the eye.

There are some other tricks you can employ as well. Painting shutters a very dark color makes the windows look smaller, while white and light-colored shutters enlarge and draw attention to them. Painting a house and all its trim elements the same color makes it look flat and uninteresting because the architectural elements disappear into the monochromatic background.

Drive through some neighborhoods with a sketch pad and a box of crayons or colored pencils. When you spot a house that catches your eye

"You can give your home an entirely new look by borrowing a few good tricks from an artist's perspective."

IN DETAIL
Remove Doors and Shutters

When you are able to, remove doors to strip or re-coat them. It's a whole lot easier to coat them if they are in your workshop or on sawhorses in the garage. Pad the table or sawhorses with something soft, such as rolled-up old towels. Do the back of the door first if you are planning to coat both sides. Let it dry completely, then you flip it over and coat the front.

The effective use of contrasting trim and wall color emphasizes the best aspects of a house.

Be careful to select colors that blend with the unpainted parts of your house, such as the roof, brickwork, or stonework. A color wheel can help you determine how colors interact with one another. The colors opposite each other on the wheel go well together but make one another stand out more. For example, green trim accentuates red brick, making it more noticeable, while blue tones bring out the beauty of orange-hued brick or roof shingles.

The right paint

In the last chapter we talked about staining a house with a colored opaque stain rather than with paint. You have the same two options for applying color to trim and doors. From a distance, an opaque stain looks the same as a painted surface, but up close it shows more of the wood grain. Stained surfaces lack sheen and always have a matte or low-luster appearance. Trim treated with opaque stain, which is applied in a series of thinner coats, is not as durable as a primed, painted surface.

and looks appealing, make a quick sketch with color codes. Take your sketches to the store and match the colors to paint swatches. If you see a color that you really like but that is too intense or vibrant, the paint store can tone down the color. If you are not comfortable choosing colors that go well together, select a color you like for the siding and use a darker or lighter shade for the contrasting trim.

Opaque stains sold specifically for siding are usually waxless. That means you have the option of adding a coat of clear finish on top for more

Painting architectural elements the same color as walls minimizes their impact.

TRADE SECRET

Most people try to scrape off excess paint on the lip of the can. That actually has the effect of removing most of the paint you've just put on the brush. Instead, follow the pro's method. First, dip your brush about one-third of the brush length into the paint. Let the excess drip for a moment, then lightly tap the brush against the inside of the container. That leaves the brush fully loaded, but not dripping.

If you want to play it safe, choose a lighter and darker value of the same color for painting the walls and trim.

durability and greater sheen. The clear finishes described previously (see pp. 134–135) can be applied over water-based opaque stains.

For greater durability and sheen, you're better off with paint. Prime the trim with latex primer and add two coats of house and trim paint. Typically, this comes in satin, semigloss, and gloss finishes, not the flat-finish paint commonly used on walls. In part, this is a durability issue, since very low-luster paint doesn't have quite the same resistance to constant abrasion as the shinier ones do. Whether you go for satin or gloss is a matter of personal taste.

Most paint manufacturers offer several lines of paint at different prices. You'll notice that the best, most expensive, water-based trim paints are 100% acrylic. Acrylic resin offers excellent resistance to sun, abrasion, and weather, and is far less likely to support mildew growth than the oil-based coatings it replaces.

Applying the Finish

Whether you've decided on a clear finish, an opaque stain, or paint, the application method is still the same. Unlike large surfaces (such as walls), doors, windows, and trim present the challenge of smaller but more intricate elements.

From a distance this coating looks like paint, but up close opaque stain lets more wood grain show.

"In most cases, it is fairly easy to paint the trim without getting any on the wall, especially when the trim ends in an edge."

TRADE SECRET

Windows, doors, and trim need to be painted more often than walls do. They get more wear and abuse and, because they are portals to the house, often suffer more movement due to moisture. Instead of waiting for paint failures, which can mean a lot more work than simply repainting, look for the telltale early warning signs. Fine cracks and fissures in the paint surface, areas with wear on the edges and corners, and sections that repeatedly sport mildew stains are indicators that it is time to recoat the wood. Typically, you'll need to recoat trim areas about three times as often as you would the walls.

You'll need different brushes, some new techniques, and a strategy for masking.

Masking

More often than not, the trim on a house is a different color than the walls. There is no sense masking twice. Paint the walls and don't worry about getting wall paint on the trim. After the paint is dry you can mask if you need to. However, since you'll be using a relatively small brush for the trim, you can probably pass on masking. Trim colors usually highlight architectural features, which have sharp lines that delineate them from the rest of the wall. In most cases, it is fairly easy to paint the trim without getting any on the wall, especially when the trim ends in an edge. Don't be afraid to substitute a paint pad for a brush if the face of the trim is flat.

Painting around glass is another matter. On garage doors, entry doors, and windows, the wood goes right up to the glass. In most cases, there is a bead of caulking between the two. If you used paintable caulking, you can paint it when you do the muntins or moldings that hold the glass in place. You have three masking options. Which one you choose depends on your preference and skill with a brush.

- **Use a shield:** Holding a paint shield against the glass helps you paint a straight line. Just remember to wipe the shield after every brush stroke or you will smear wet paint onto the glass when you set it down again. For this reason, some folks find a shield more trouble than it's worth.

Color Wheel

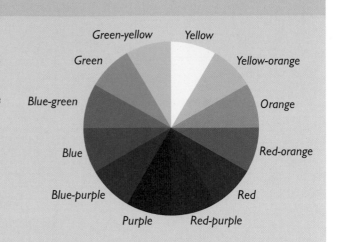

A color wheel is a very basic teaching tool for understanding how colors relate to one another. It can also help you understand how to choose paint and trim colors that go well together. Colors that are opposite one another (orange and blue, for instance) are complementary colors and look nice together. You can also choose three colors that are equidistant from one another (such as blue-green, yellow-orange, and red-purple) to create a triad scheme. My favorite grouping is the split-complementary scheme. Here's how it works. Choose a color, then find its complement—the color directly across from it on the color wheel. Select the two colors on each side of the complement. In other words, the combination of yellow (first color) with blue-purple and red-purple (the colors on each side of purple), is a split-complementary group.

- **Mask with tape:** Painter's masking tape gives you a clean line, but it takes some time to apply it, especially when there are several panes in each window. Use 1H-in.-wide tape to give you enough room for slipups; that way, you don't have to paper the center of the window. Remove the tape as soon as you finish the window and while the paint is still somewhat wet in order to get a clean line. If you wait until the paint is fully dry, you run the risk of lifting off the paint.

TOOLS AND MATERIALS
Wall Paint vs. Trim Paint

In the past, it was fairly common to find houses that had siding coated with latex paint and trim coated with more durable oil-based paint. After all, doors and windows get more abrasion and abuse than walls do. These days, you're more likely to see water-based paint used on both walls and trim. Some companies call their flat exterior paint *wall paint* and their satin, semigloss, and gloss versions of the same thing *wall and trim paint*. Other manufacturers don't differentiate. High-quality satin, semigloss, and gloss paints work well as trim paint for doors and windows, but leave the flat paint for the clapboards.

TOOLS AND MATERIALS

Trim Brushes and Paint Trays

A really good trim brush makes all the difference in the world when it comes to painting around glass or the raised panels in a door. Here's another case where quality and price go hand in hand. I find I can work wonders with a chisel-end 1-in. or 1½-in. angled sash brush coupled with a small, plastic paint tray. Soak the brush first in water (for latex) or mineral spirits (for oil-based paint), shake out the excess, then dip the first third of the bristles in the paint. Touch the tips gently to the side of the tray to prevent drips before you take the brush to the wood.

The combination of a good, angled sash brush and a portable plastic paint tray make detail work a breeze.

"The best way to approach a multi-paneled door is to paint it from the inside out."

Don't bother masking the trim if you are planning to paint it afterward.

It's usually pretty easy to paint a clean, freehand line on the trim, but you can mask if you need the extra protection.

When it comes to flat areas, a paint pad may be quicker and easier than a brush.

- **Clean up with a razor blade or by hand:** By far the quickest way is to forget masking altogether. Work with a good quality 1-in. or 1H-in. sash brush that is easy to control, carefully painting to a freehand line where the wood meets the glass. This sounds harder than it is. With a bit of concentration and a steady hand you can do a very clean job. By the second or third window you'll be an old hand at this and may wonder why you ever thought it was worth the time to mask. For spots where you do slip up, wait until the paint is fully dry, and then remove it from the glass with a single-edge razor blade.

TRADE SECRET

Here's a time-saving tip for when you need to caulk and paint glass at the same time. Use 1½-in. masking tape to lay out clean lines on the glass. Apply the caulk, smooth it, and remove the excess, leaving the tape on the glass. Make sure you smooth the caulk to the edge of the tape and not beyond it. Paint the wood. While it is still wet, pull off the tape to remove the excess paint and caulk at the same time. You'll get a clean caulk line that is painted right up to the edge. This works best when the caulking is the same color as the paint, such as white. If the paint is a radically different color, you may get a pinstripe line of caulk showing at the edge.

Painting paneled doors

The best way to approach a multi-paneled door (for an example, see the photo accompanying the sidebar Trim Brushes and Paint Trays, facing page) is to paint it from the inside out. With a 1-in. or 1H-in. angled sash brush, start by painting the bevels on the panels (see drawing, p. 142). Use the pointed tip of the brush to get into the tight inside corners. If you get too much paint in the corners, wipe the brush off across the edge of your paint tray and pick up the extra paint by going back over it with the unloaded brush. Now move on to paint the fields or panels. By painting each panel separately, you can take your time and get them perfect. You'll be able to paint

A paint shield is one way to mask without masking.

Two-Sided Masking Tape

This clever gun speeds up the masking process by laying down two strips of tape at once—one sticky side facing down and one sticky side facing up.

There are lots of interesting masking guns on the market. Some apply tape, some put up masking media, and some do both at once. One of the slickest is a tape gun from 3M that applies two strips of tape at once—a sticky side facing down and another one facing up. In this photo, the blue tape adheres to the wood and anchors the red tape with its sticky side facing out. Once the taping is done, you merely have to press the masking film onto the red tape. The blue tape gives you a clean line and easy removal, while the red tape gives you quick tack for masking film.

TOOLS AND MATERIALS

The Right Brush Makes a Difference

Picking the right brush is not as complicated as it may seem when looking at the store display. Reading the label often tells you the best uses for the brush you're holding in your hand. Generally speaking, natural bristle brushes are best for oil-based finishes and paints. Synthetic bristles are better for water-based finishes and paints. Obviously, the brush size should be appro-

priate for the coverage area. Small brushes are best for fine work and trim, while wide brushes make sense for clapboard. Don't always go for the most expensive brush. For doing quick touch ups or priming small areas, a cheaper brush may be fine and can be pitched instead of cleaned.

TRADE SECRET

Brush control is key to avoiding drips and minimizing brush marks. Always hold the brush near the base of the bristles rather than by the handle. This makes it easier to control your strokes, because the bristles become an extension of your fingers and nearly as easy to maneuver.

Take special care with your finishing stroke, too. After spreading the paint evenly over a small area, brush lightly in one direction, overlapping the section you just painted. Lighten up a little as you complete the stroke to avoid leaving a hard edge at the end.

Let any paint slipups dry, then remove them with a single-edge razor blade.

each one up to its seam line and get the whole frame done without generating the overlap marks that come from stopping in the middle. Once all the panels are done, paint the rails and internal stiles and, finally, the edge stiles. I use a sash brush for the bevels and a paint pad for the panels, rails, and stiles. It's easier to work to a sharp outside line with a small paint pad.

Painting double-hung windows

If your windows are old and the caulking is starting to go, follow the advice on pp. 132–133. Remove any old or loose caulking and recaulk with paintable caulk. The caulk is not there just to look good; it forms a seal between the wood and the glass that keeps out cold air and water.

If you have double-hung windows that come out easily, take them out. It's always easier to paint something as a separate unit on sawhorses than to have to work around an item suspended in a

frame. Otherwise, the key to painting double-hung windows is to find a way to cover all the parts, including those that are behind other segments, without painting the window closed.

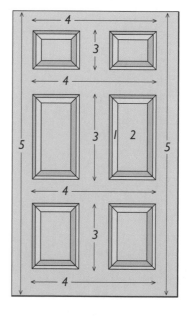

Door Painting Sequence
To paint a multi-paneled door, first paint the panels one at a time. Paint each bevel (1), then the panel (2). Next, paint the internal vertical stiles (3), the internal horizontal rails (4), and, finally, the external vertical stiles (5).

"The caulk is not there just to look good; it forms a seal between the wood and the glass that keeps out cold air and water."

IN DETAIL
Painting in Tight Spots

There's no bigger waste of time than cleaning hardware slopped with excess paint. If the hardware is easily removed, that's the cleanest solution. Detach the screws and fasteners and put the pieces in individual plastic bags separated by type of hardware. If you have a lot of hardware, label the bags by writing the location on a strip of masking tape and sticking it on the bag. In situations where hardware can't easily be removed, keep a stash of artist's brushes handy for painting around it. These small, fine tipped brushes allow you to do detailed painting quickly and neatly.

Here's one way to do it. Lower the upper sash about 4 in. from the top and raise the lower sash the same distance from the bottom (see left drawing, below). Paint all the exposed areas on the lower sash, then the entire upper sash. Do the muntins, then the outer sash. Paint the upper edge of the lower sash and the lower edge of the upper sash. Now reverse the sashes. Paint the unpainted half of the sash farthest from you, the top portion of the upper sash, and the bottom edge of the lower sash. Paint the frame and windowsill, then let the window dry completely. When it is dry, push both sashes all the way down and paint the upper half of the jambs. After the paint is dry, push the sashes all the way up and paint the lower half of the jambs. Avoid painting the metal channels and make sure the windows move easily after each painting session.

Painting Shutters

Remove shutters before you paint the house so that you can cover the areas behind them. Take the shutters into your shop or garage and drive a large nail partway into each of the corners. That way you can suspend the shutters by their nails on two sawhorses, paint one side, flip them over using the nails as handles, then immediately paint the other side. By painting the second side of the louver while it is still wet, you are less likely to get overlap marks. When the paint is dry, pull out the nails, putty the holes, and put a dab of paint on the putty spots before you rehang the shutters.

Use nails as handles to flip wet shutters.

Painting a Window Exterior

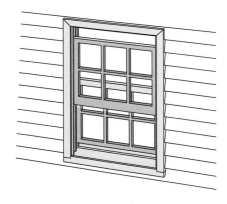

Open the window with the two sections overlapped. First paint the entire outer sash, and then paint the exposed areas of the inner sash.

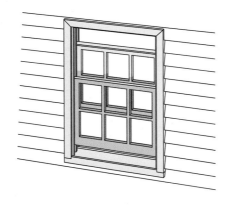

Reverse the position of the windows and paint the remainder of the inner sash.

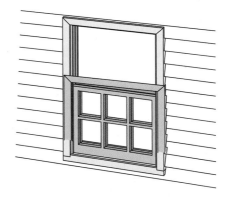

Push both sashes all the way to the bottom and paint the upper half of the jambs. Let it dry completely before you move the sashes up and paint the lower part of the jambs.

WHAT CAN GO WRONG

Drip Control

Drips are most common at the edges and outside corners. Always brush toward an edge. Brushing away from an edge causes the brush to drag over the sharp edge, depositing too much paint on the opposite side. When brushing a corner, make sure the strokes near the periphery don't run in and leave excess paint. While the paint is still wet, use a damp but unloaded brush to retrace where you've painted and mop up any excess.

IN DETAIL

Keep the Tracks Clear

Too much paint in window jambs makes it difficult to open and close the window. Over the years, it is easy to build up coats of paint. If that happens, strip or scrape the old paint off the jambs before you repaint, then prime and paint them with thin coats, applying just enough finish to achieve a uniform color. After the paint is dry, lubricate the metal tracks with silicone spray. (*Note:* The popular WD-40 is a great moisture chaser, but it is not the best choice for lubricating double-hung windows.)

Decks, Porches, and

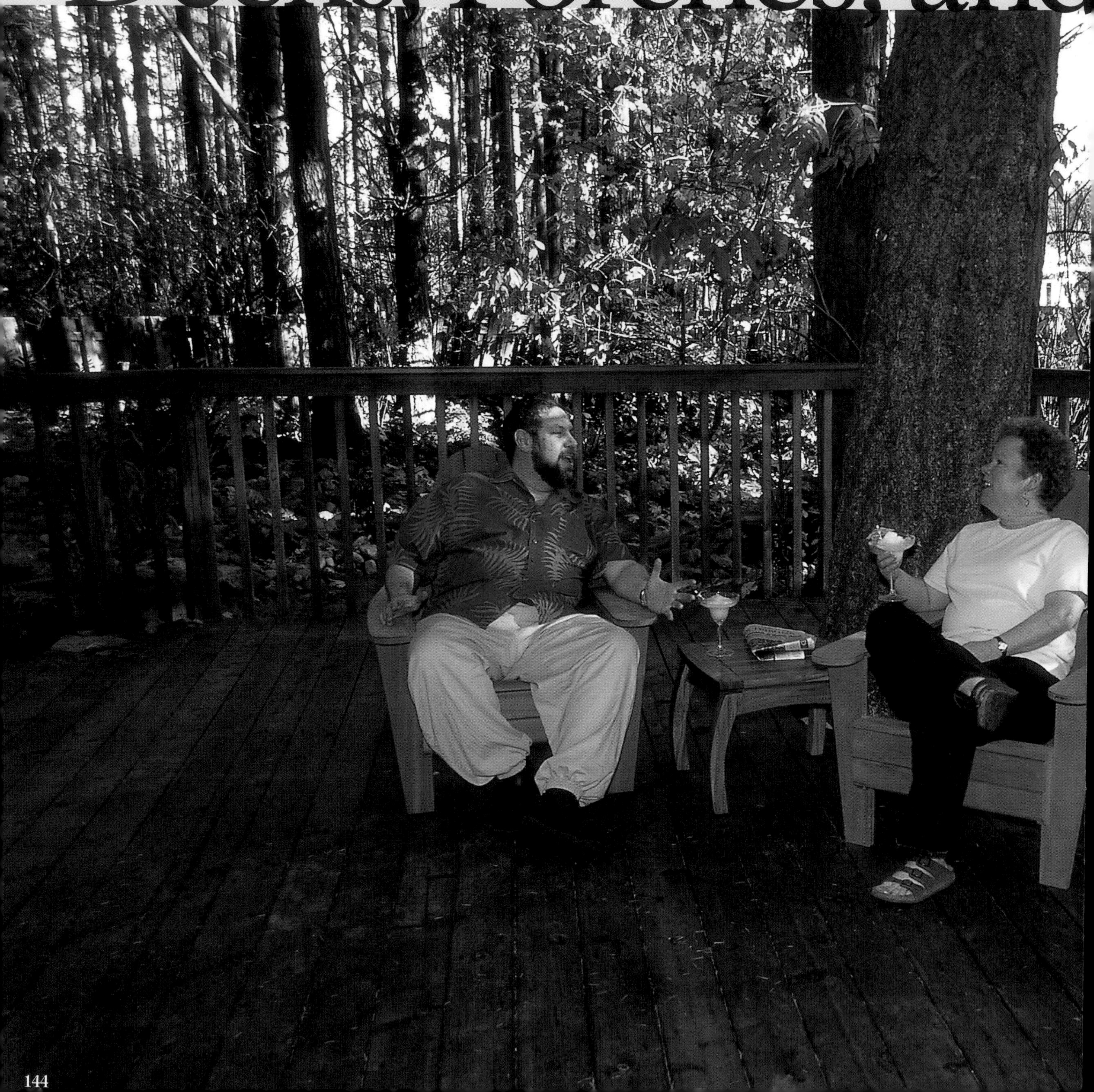

CHAPTER NINE

Fences

A well-designed deck or porch extends your living space, adding areas that have the comforts of home along with the beauty of the great outdoors. Like the exterior of the house, these add-ons are subject to the whims of weather, so it is tempting to simply use outdoor paint to coat them. Some folks do just that, and exterior paint works fine on fences and railings. Decking, though, faces another challenge: We walk on it. Surface paint is simply not up to that sort of wear. Decks built from attractive woods, such as cedar and redwood, look great naturally, but it takes some strategy and know-how to keep them looking as good as new. There are several ways to do that, but they all require more regular maintenance than the rest of the house.

TOOLS AND MATERIALS

What You'll Need: Deck Stripping Gear

- Old clothes
- Waterproof shoes
- Deck Finish Remover
- Dipping pan and applicator (roller, pad, mop)
- Long-handled, stiff nylon scrub brush
- Garden hose with small, high-power nozzle

WHAT CAN GO WRONG

The Right Stuff

Choose decking wisely and don't expect a finish to compensate for poor wood. If you build with wood prone to cracking and splintering, the finish won't change that. Finish can vastly improve how wood looks, but it has limited abilities when it comes to adding durability.

> *"By far the simplest, lowest maintenance choice is what I call the gray option."*

Deck Strategies

The real question for decks, porches, rails, and fences is not so much how to apply sealer but what to use. Store shelves abound with different products at different price points that make more or less the same claims. You have to wonder which features, if any, are really needed. A lot depends on the look you prefer and the amount of periodic maintenance you are willing to perform.

The gray option

By far the simplest, lowest maintenance choice is what I call the gray option. Cedar, redwood, mahogany, teak, and some pressure-treated woods can simply be left alone to weather naturally. Within a year they lose their original color and gain a patina of silvery gray. The wood may be a bit rougher than sealed wood, but for a surface that is going to be walked on anyway, that may not be a big deal. In fact, it may mean slightly better traction in wet weather. Of course, you need to decide if you like that style. To some people, weathered wood looks rustic. To others, it just looks unkempt.

Maintenance. The obvious beauty of the gray option is how easy it is to maintain. There is no initial work involved, no regular (or irregular) recoating, and no finishing costs whatsoever. In some areas, raw wood can develop some mildew, but it is often less than similar wood coated with oil-based sealers. If mildew does develop, you can remove it with a wash of one part laundry bleach to three parts water. This will not take away the

Letting the deck "go gray" is the easiest of the finishing options and quite appropriate for some woods.

gray color, only the blackened mildew. You also need to clean the surface once a year or so, just to remove collected dirt, but you'd have to do that anyway, whether it was coated or not.

Endurance. If you opt out of finishing are you sentencing your deck to premature deterioration? The jury is still out on that question, but it certainly seems that sealing does not significantly extend the life of woods with a natural resistance to bugs and weather. Decks made with less resistant species may not fare so well. Ipe, mahogany, teak, cedar, and redwood do well with the gray option, but pine, fir, and spruce do not. Weathered wood shows more of the subtle signs of aging, such as fine surface cracks and end checking, but there's no strong evidence that your deck will fail sooner if it is not sealed. It is a close enough call that I would not hesitate to let the wood go gray if that were the look I favored.

WHAT CAN GO WRONG

Different Shades of Gray

If you build a fence with cedar boards and pressure-treated posts, be aware that they will turn gray at different rates. The boards will turn quickly, within one year, but it may take several years for the pressure-treated wood to change color. Eventually it will catch up and be uniformly gray, but you'll have to be patient in the interim.

The untreated cedar boards on this fence turned gray more quickly than the pressure-treated posts, but eventually they will all look the same.

"Temporary" finishes

Even if you decide that you would rather go for the finished look, bear in mind that, by their very nature, all deck finishes are temporary. Any finish thick enough and tough enough to withstand the regular assault of shoes is not likely to tolerate the expansion and contraction of outdoor wood. Finishes that are flexible enough to deal with that much wood movement are not likely to put up with shoe wear for long. As a result, the best strategy for decking is a minimalist finish that is renewed each year. It's a perfect compromise. There is too little finish to peel, chip, or show worn areas that correspond to the traffic pattern, but there is also not enough finish to last more than a year before needing rejuvenation. If you work it right, you'll never have to strip off a deck finish. On the other hand, this option does require perpetual care.

Fences and railings are another matter altogether. They don't get walked on (except perhaps at our house, where our cat walks on our fences all the time). Since a fence or railing doesn't get the same abrasion wear as a deck under foot, you are free to treat them just like wood siding. You can leave them alone to gray, seal them with deck coating, apply a thicker clear finish, or coat them with opaque wall stain or paint. The gray option needs no care at all. If you choose a deck sealer, expect to renew it periodically. You probably won't need to do it every year, as you would with decking, but you should recoat every two to three years. If you favor solid or semisolid colors, your best bet is the new 100% acrylic stain/sealers

After 25 years, this fence is silver-gray but still solid.

Regional Considerations

As with house paint, you need to consider the climate you live in when choosing a deck treatment. You'll notice that some finishes contain UV blockers and absorbers to diminish the effect of intense sun. That's a good idea if you live in Florida or Arizona or if the deck is in direct sunlight for much of the year. Other finishes have mildewcide and fungicide added for very wet areas, such as the Pacific Northwest, and many deck coatings contain all of these additives. While the additives increase the per-gallon price, they really do work and are well worth the added expense.

Water and sun are a deck's enemies; good sealers contain mildewcides and UV blockers to deal with them.

TRADE SECRET

If the deck coating you want to use lacks the mildew and fungus protection your area demands, you can add them. You'll find mildewcide and fungicide in the paint department at your local home store. They are usually sold in packets or tubes that can be added to either one-gallon or five-gallon containers of oil- and water-based coatings. The packets are a bit expensive, currently about $3 per gallon of finish, but in the end they are roughly the same price as coatings with mildewcide and fungicide added during manufacture.

Mildewcide is sold in premeasured packets and bottles that can be added to a gallon of coating.

TAKE YOUR PICK

Oil- vs. Water-Based Finishes

Most deck treatments are oil-based, but some water-based ones have recently come on the market. They are designed to work the same way, but with some differences. Applicators used with water-based coatings can be cleaned with soap and water, while oil-based treatments require cleanup with mineral spirits. Water-based finishes dry faster and can be walked on sooner. They also smell less, though that is not usually a big issue outdoors. Even so, I prefer oils, since I feel that water-based resins do not soak into the wood as well. They tend to sit on the surface, making the finish easier to abrade with foot traffic.

The cleaning instructions on a label tip you off that it is a water-based material.

A 100% acrylic semiopaque stain/sealer, like this Wolman Extreme, is probably your best option for a long-lasting fence treatment.

on the market. They come in such colors as cedar, redwood, driftwood, and white. Two coats of acrylic sealer holds up as long as paint and requires no primer coat.

Yearly maintenance

Get used to the fact that no matter which coating you choose, you will still have to do some yearly maintenance. At the very least, you'll need to clean and possibly remove mildew from a deck each year, even if you choose the gray option. Thin or absorbed coatings should be reapplied each year, and even the most durable, semi-opaque, pigmented coatings rarely go more than two years before needing to be recoated. How much maintenance you need and how long the finish holds up depend on the climate you live in and the wear the deck receives. Our main deck, which is off the family room, gets lots of wear

and must be recoated every year, but the smaller, cantilevered deck that is off the second-story master bedroom gets almost no wear, and can go two years with a semiopaque stain/sealer before it needs attention.

I generally recoat the main deck railings and the wall around the hot tub every year when I do the decking, but I could probably do them every other year instead. However, the top railing on a deck or porch receives more wear and should be recoated every year, just like the decking. Fences can usually go up to three years with semitransparent stains and up to five years with acrylic stains or paint.

Choosing the Right Finish

If you prefer the finished look to the gray option, your next task is to untangle the confusing array of finish offerings. There are deck treatments in both tinted and clear versions, semiopaque and solid colors, and a wide range of prices. All of them make many of the same performance claims, but there are differences. It isn't easy to tell these finishes apart, so read the labels carefully.

Although they don't fall neatly into distinct categories, they can be divided into four general groups. The first three work by soaking into the wood and reinforcing it, so they leave the deck surface looking and feeling like natural, uncoated wood. The fourth acts like paint or varnish, protecting the wood by forming a film that sits on top of it. Each type has its strengths and weaknesses.

> "Get used to the fact that no matter which coating you choose, you will still have to do some yearly maintenance."

IN DETAIL

How Drying Oils Add Protection

Deck treatments based on drying oils look like they have done nothing except bring out the color of the wood. They absorb into the wood, leaving the surface looking and feeling like wet, natural wood. Yet they really do keep out dirt and water, prevent graying, and make the wood fibers near the surface a bit tougher. This is because they soak in, then cure to a solid after they have impregnated the wood. The one drawback is

Oil soaks into wood and impregnates it below the surface.

that mildew is fond of oil, so if you live in a wet area and choose an oil-based deck sealer, make sure it contains mildewcide.

Water repellents

Usually clear (as opposed to tinted) water repellents are the cheapest materials on the shelf. Not surprisingly, they offer the least protection, and typically must be reapplied in three to six months. They consist primarily of solvent (usually mineral spirits), a bit of oil, and paraffin. After the solvent evaporates the oil soaks into the wood and looks "wet," which brings out the wood's color and improves its appearance. The paraffin wax helps shed water by making it bead up rather than soak into the wood. This constitutes the sole protection of water repellents. It is cheap and short-lived but very easy to apply. It also provides the most natural look possible and never needs stripping. It is a good option if you are willing to recoat frequently.

Deck sealers

Take a water repellent, add more oil and resin (and perhaps a bit of pigment), and you have a more durable deck sealer. This type of treatment, available in both clear and tinted versions, costs about 50% more per gallon than basic water repellent, but it lasts a good deal longer. Claims on the label vary, but sealers typically last a year before they need recoating. Like water repellents, sealers usually contain paraffin to bead up water, but the extra oil or resin is what makes the difference. It soaks into the wood and cures, providing greater protection from graying. The oil also helps prevent dirt from being ground into the wood, making it somewhat easier to clean the surface.

Water beads up on the side of this board where it was treated with water repellent (right) but soaks into the untreated portion (left).

Sealers with additives

Although sealers with additives aren't called anything different, you'll recognize these enhanced deck treatments by the price—they generally cost twice as much as water repellents. Usually oil-based (and sometimes water-based), these buffered sealers contain mildewcide, fungicide, and UV absorbers and blockers. These additives make them more expensive, but they also result in longer resistance to graying from the sun and better resistance to moss and mildew growth. In parts of the country where sun or moisture is a problem, buffered sealers are practically a must. Like other sealers, these deck treatments soak into the wood and do not leave a surface film on top. Many claim to resist mildew and graying for two to three years, and they do. However, there is

WHAT CAN GO WRONG

Synthetics Only

Some deck strippers contain sodium hydroxide, better known as lye, which literally eats through natural bristles. When you buy a scrub brush and applicator for stripping old finish, make sure you purchase synthetic bristles and pads.

Deck stripper ate through this natural bristle broom. Use a stiff synthetic bristle brush instead.

TAKE YOUR PICK

Tinted vs. Clear Deck Sealers

Pigmented (colored) sealers offer more protection against fading and graying than clear versions do. A moderate amount of pigment can also improve the UV resistance of a finish. For example, some brands' top-of-the-line clear deck sealers claim two-year protection against graying, while semitransparent stains with the same materials claim three-year protection. Bear in mind that pigments only improve UV protection; they do not offer better resistance to wear or mildew. If you prefer a clear sealer, don't be afraid to use it since the protective difference tinted sealers offer is not that great.

Notice that this clear deck sealer boasts two-year protection, while the colored version of the same thing claims three-year protection.

"*Read the weather report carefully and try to choose a block of time with warm, dry weather for several days on end.*"

also traffic wear to consider, so I still advise recoating annually. In spite of the higher price, this is the product I use on my own deck.

Film-forming finishes

This last group contains very tough, film-forming sealers that act more like a paint than a deck treatment. Most often, they are water-based acrylic-resin coatings with enough pigment to place them somewhere between semitransparent and fully opaque. The acrylic resin is quite tough and highly resistant to mold and mildew. The high-pigment content gives these coatings good UV resistance as well.

The problem with these coatings is that they form a film on top of the wood, much like paint

Look for words like "resists mildew" and "UV protection" on the label to identify sealers with additives.

IN DETAIL

Picket Fences

What about fences? Paint and film-forming stains/sealers are perfectly acceptable for fences. If you want a wood tone, acrylic sealers look more woody than brown paint. For white pickets, both products are fine and last about the same amount of time. If you choose paint, you must wait until wet or pressure-treated wood dries out for a few months before you can coat

Tough, film-forming sealers are great for fences, but I would not use them for porches and decks that receive foot traffic.

and siding stain do. I wouldn't hesitate to use them for a fence or a railing, but I would think twice before putting them on a decking surface. The assault of shoe treads is likely to cause the finish to wear off in high-traffic areas, making the deck look uneven and spotty. It may take a while before that happens, but once it does, it will be difficult to get the deck looking really good again unless you strip off the old finish and start anew.

Applying Finishes

After you've selected the finish, applying it is rather easy. As with all finishing jobs, you must first prepare the surface, choose the application

it. Then it requires primer and at least one coat of paint (though two is better). Water-based 100% acrylic sealers need no primer and can go over wet cedar and pressure-treated wood. These sealers come in only white and woodtones but not in other bright colors, so if you want the fence to match your house, paint is the way to go.

method, and then have at it. Each step needs a good bit of drying time, so read the weather report carefully and try to choose a block of time with warm, dry weather for several days on end. Try to avoid working in direct sunlight, as it can blister the coating. If you can't avoid sunlight, at least apply the finish in the early morning or evening when the sun is low in the sky and not directly overhead. Coverage for deck coatings is about 400 sq. ft. per gallon for recoating but about half as much for new wood.

Surface preparation

The nice thing about finishing decks and fences is that new ones require no particular preparation except cleaning. There's no sanding, puttying, caulking, or random acts of tedium that other types of finishes require. Cleaning the surface with a jet nozzle on a water hose is usually enough. If that doesn't do it, make a solution of ½ cup of TSP in 1 gallon of warm water and scrub the wood with a stiff bristle brush to dislodge the dirt. Rinse it off with plenty of clean water and let it dry thoroughly. In my area, that means from three days to a week, but it may be as short as overnight in drier climates.

Wet wood. Brand new cedar decking and fence wood is often attached soaking wet. So wet, in fact, that water may squeeze out when you drive home the screws or nails. Some deck treatments, such as water-based coatings, can be applied over wet wood. Read the instructions on the label. If you are not sure, let the deck dry for a few weeks in good weather before you coat it.

Pressure-treated wood. The same story goes for pressure-treated wood, but the waiting time is usually longer. Some deck treatments go over fresh, pressure-treated wood and say so on the label. Others tell you to wait three to six months before coating. As usual, read the label.

Applicators

Deck coating has to be the most forgiving material in terms of application methods. You can put it on with almost anything—garden sprayer, roller, brush, mitt, or spaghetti mop—but my personal favorite is a floor or deck pad. It's essentially a long mop handle attached to an oversize 4-in. x 18-in. paint pad. The pad, which is replaceable, comes in natural lamb's wool and synthetic sponge-backed nylon nap. Lamb's wool works for oil-based coatings; synthetic materials work for both oil- and water-based finishes.

Pads are the bee's knees for flat decking, but you'll want something else for the railings, planters, benches, and trellises. A brush or roller works for walls and planters, but I like to use either a mitt or a cheap garden sprayer for slats and rails. A mitt is like a glove made out of lamb's wool, and using it is as easy as running your hand over a surface. It is particularly "handy" for awkward items. Just dip the mitt in sealer, wrap your hand around a post, and wipe it down. The mitt

Scrub the wood surface with TSP and a stiff bristle brush to clean it.

TRADE SECRET

If you're like me, you seal your deck once a year and do it all in one day. If you use an oil-based sealer, it isn't worth the money to clean a floor pad. You'd spend more in mineral spirits than the cost of a replacement pad. Let it dry, and then throw it away. Keep the applicator, though. You can buy a replacement pad for it next year.

Just One Coat

Here's some good news: Most deck finishes require just one coat. The idea is to let the coating soak into the wood and provide protection below the surface. Products that allow or suggest more than one coat often advise a wet-on-wet coat. In other words, you add another coat right away if too much is soaking in and the wood still looks dry. You may need two coats the first year; once the wood is somewhat sealed, you'll probably need one coat per year thereafter. The one exception to this rule is 100% acrylic pigmented fence and siding stain. It needs two coats the first year, but can go several years without recoating. While it is great for vertical surfaces, I don't advise using it on decks.

comes with a vinyl or latex glove; be sure to put that on first, because finish goes right through the cloth-based mitt.

Rails first, then deck

Start with railings, planters, benches, and privacy walls. That way you'll be able to walk on the deck in order to get to them. Besides, they are the most time-consuming pieces. The decking itself goes very fast once you pick up that big 18-in. pad. Apply the sealer evenly. If you create any drips or runs, wipe them up with the applicator as soon as you see them. Don't forget to coat the exposed edges of the deck. While you are at it, hit any inside corners where the railings or walls meet the deck. Apply finish a few inches in from the railings and walls so you can overlap those areas when you switch to the pad. The finish stays wet long enough so that the perimeter blends completely, assuming you do it immediately after you finish the rails. Applying sealer should take only a couple of hours, even for a fairly large deck.

When all the peripherals are done, fill up the pan and start with the big pad. Begin at one corner and cover the whole deck as you go, working away from the wet edge and standing on the dry part. And remember not to paint yourself into a corner. Plan your coating pattern so that you end up at a doorway or stairs.

One reason I like pads better than rollers and garden sprayers is that they put on less material. Applying too much is a bigger problem than applying too little, since it is easier to add more

Almost any applicator—a mop, mitt, brush, pad, roller, or sprayer—can be used to apply deck coating.

finish than to remove it. Deck coatings are relatively slow drying materials; if the surface is too wet or puddled, it will be tacky for days or even weeks. To make matters worse, a thick coating that sits on top of the wood, even after it dries, is much more likely to wear or peel off over time. Here's a case where less is more. If after about 30 minutes the coating still has not been absorbed in some areas, spread it around to thin it out or pick up the excess with a dry pad or roller.

Drying time

Be patient. Many deck coatings take days to dry completely, even in good weather. If the weather is cool or very humid, it could take longer. I once

> "Be patient. Many deck coatings take days to dry completely, even in good weather."

Buy Another Dip Pan

Floor and deck pads often come packaged with dip pans that fit the pad. Do yourself a favor and toss out that cheap, undersize pan and buy a larger, sturdier one. At my last job, the cheap pan tipped over immediately and cracked within 10 minutes. The replacement pan cost a couple of bucks, worked better, held more coating, and lasted throughout the entire job.

Toss out the small, cheap pan that comes free with the paint pad and invest a couple of bucks in a larger, more stable one.

Maintaining Finishes

Plan to maintain your deck by cleaning and recoating it every year. I know that some products point out that they resist graying and mildew for two or three years, but that only accounts for a portion of the wear that decks experience. Shoe abrasion, dirt, wind, and rain also take a toll. The bottom line is that if you keep after it, your deck will look great year after year with very little effort on your part. If you let it go for a few years, the amount of work and time to bring it back into shape will most likely convince you that regular maintenance is indeed the way to go.

Thankfully, fences and railings are less critical. Keep an eye on them and recoat them when they start to look a bit shabby. In most cases, you'll find that fences can go three to five years between treatments. That's partly because they are vertical surfaces and partly because they don't receive the same abuse. If your fence has a solid

A painter's mitt is ideal for coating awkward, four-sided shapes, but make sure you have a rubber glove on underneath.

applied a deck coating a bit on the thick side in the cool, wet, Pacific Northwest and found to my horror that it took three weeks to dry. As with all finishes, warm, dry weather speeds things up and thin coats dry much faster than thick ones.

Coat the perimeter of the deck a few inches in from the walls and railings before you switch to the large applicator, which won't get into tight corners.

Plan your coating pattern ahead of time so that you don't paint yourself into a corner. That's only entertaining in cartoons.

IN DETAIL
Degraying vs. Cleaning

Oxalic acid removes gray from bare wood. Cleanser removes dirt from both bare and coated woods. Some companies offer mixtures with both so you'll buy their one-application-treats-all product regardless of your needs. I'm a proponent of using a cleanser, such as TSP, for cleaning, and a degraying liquid, such as oxalic acid, only if you need it.

SAFETY FIRST

TSP (trisodium phosphate) is very effective for cutting grease and removing dirt, but it can be mildly irritating to your skin and can burn your eyes. Wear gloves and goggles when you handle it. If it comes in contact with your skin, wash it off thoroughly. If it splashes in your eyes, flush them with lots of water for 15 minutes and call your doctor immediately.

TRADE SECRET

If you prefer, you can make your own mildew remover by adding one part fresh laundry bleach (for example, Clorox) to three parts water. It works great, it's cheap, and it's usually available by simply raiding the laundry room. You can also mix up your own degraying solution. Buy some oxalic acid crystals at the hardware store or pharmacy and add one ounce per pint of warm water. No, you can't mix both solutions together and kill two birds with one stone. One is an acid and the other is a base, so they neutralize each other.

To make a mildew-cleaning solution for wood, mix one part laundry bleach with three parts water.

flat-top rail, check it carefully. You may need to recoat it more often. Standing water on slightly cupped top rails and frequent bird and tree droppings can prematurely wear the finish.

Yearly schedule

Set up a yearly schedule to take care of your deck and stick to it. Plan to wash the deck, remove mildew and graying (if necessary), and recoat it each year. While the job may stretch out over several days due to drying time, the actual procedure requires only a couple of hours each day. You'll need to time it right and plan ahead, because you can't finish the same day you wash or strip, and you need good drying weather for the entire process. By the third year, the wood will be so well sealed that it will never need more than one thin coat to rejuvenate it. Eventually, the deck will be sealed well enough so that even if you skip a year, you'll be able to get away with it.

Dirt removal. Dirt, evergreen needles, tree sap, bird droppings, pollen, and spilled food all manage to leave their marks on our deck each year, and yours probably suffers a similar fate. Clean it thoroughly before you recoat it or you'll simply seal in the dirt. If you have a pressure washer, use it on its lowest setting. Otherwise, a garden hose with a high-pressure nozzle is more than adequate. If the dirt does not wash off easily, go after it with a long-handled scrub brush and ½ cup of TSP in 1 gallon of warm water. Rinse it well and let the deck dry for several days before you recoat.

This well-used, well-maintained deck is six years old and still looks like new.

Mildew removal. While mildew often looks like black dirt, it doesn't come off easily the way surface dirt does. Mildew is a parasitic plant that grows in moist areas and is particularly fond of oils. There are several commercial mildew removers that kill mildew along with other molds and moss, removing the black color all at once. In most cases, you won't need to scrub, so you can sponge or spray on the material. Rinse the area well with water as soon as the mildew is gone.

When good wood goes gray. Deck brightener is a liquid wash that brings grayed wood back to its true color. As with mildew remover, it doesn't require any scrubbing. If you do this step last, you can wash the deck, remove the mildew, and kill the gray—in that order—all in one day. Sponge, mop, roll, or spray on the

"Set up a yearly schedule to take care of your deck and stick to it."

Full-strength bleach works faster but can also damage the finish.

WHAT CAN GO WRONG

Saponification by Excessive Bleaching

When you see how well bleach removes mildew, you may be tempted to use it at full strength instead of watering it down. If you do, it will work faster and better, wiping out the mildew as fast as you apply the bleach. Resist that temptation. Full-strength bleach can saponify some deck finishes, causing them to turn white. There is no easy way to bring them back and, unless you fancy the white pattern of randomly splashed bleach, you will have to strip the finish off completely. Stick to the proper ratio. It does the job, albeit more slowly, and leaves the finish intact.

deck brightener and let it dry overnight. Wash off any white residue with a hose the next day.

Strippers

Perhaps you went too long without maintaining your deck and some areas are bare or peeling while others still sport finish. Maybe too much finish has built up or you've decided to refinish a painted deck or fence. If the only thing that will save it is to take it back to the bare wood beneath, it's time to strip the wood. Before you start, wet down nearby plants with water and cover them with a tarp or plastic sheeting.

Let me warn you that stripping a deck is a very tedious job that requires time, patience, elbow grease, and lots of water. You'll need to buy some deck finish remover or stripper (which, by the way, is not the same thing as deck bright-

A garden hose with a high-pressure, tapered brass nozzle usually creates enough pressure to rinse off a deck.

ener). It takes about 1 gallon to strip 150 sq. ft. While we are on the subject of warnings, be aware that once the stripper starts to work on the old deck finish, it gets *very* slippery. Wear shoes with excellent traction, and work a small enough area so that you can always keep at least one foot in a section without stripper. If you have an old 24-grit cloth-backed sanding belt or disk, duct tape it to your shoes to make gripper soles.

Work a small area at a time, soaking it and keeping it wet with stripper, even if you have to keep reapplying it. Let the stripper do the work. Don't mess with it until the finish softens, then scrub the gunk loose with a stiff bristle brush. When all the finish has been loosened, wash it off with a garden hose with a high-power nozzle or a pressure washer on the lowest setting. Once it is clean, let the deck dry for a week before you recoat it.

Mildew killer works immediately, removing the dark stains as you wipe.

IN DETAIL

Stripping a Deck

- Follow the instructions on the label!
- Concentrate on a small area that is no larger than 10 ft. × 10 ft.
- Be sure to keep the entire area wet with stripper for the recommended amount of time (I use a simple kitchen timer to keep track).
- Don't strip in direct sunlight—it dries way too fast.
- Wet down nearby bushes, shrubs, flowers, and other vegetation before you begin, then cover them with plastic.
- When the finish starts to lift or dissolve, scrub it with a stiff brush.
- Combine scrubbing with hosing off—it's faster and more efficient.

CHAPTER TEN

Ornaments

1 Clear Finishes
page 158

2 Solid Colors
page 160

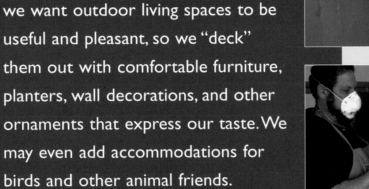

3 Painted Gems and
Ornaments
page 162

I n warm weather, a deck, patio, or porch is the most delightful room of the house. As with other rooms, we want outdoor living spaces to be useful and pleasant, so we "deck" them out with comfortable furniture, planters, wall decorations, and other ornaments that express our taste. We may even add accommodations for birds and other animal friends.

Items that live outdoors deserve the elegant look of finished wood, but they present some challenges their indoor cousins don't share. Exterior finishes must endure harsh sunlight and extremes in temperature. Wide humidity swings, rain, and snow mean that wood expands and contracts substantially as its moisture content varies, and the finish has to move with it. In short, the finishes we use must be flexible, waterproof, and resilient.

TOOLS AND MATERIALS

What You'll Need: Finishing Outdoor Furniture

- Wiping rags
- Nylon abrasive pads
- Brushes
- Latex or acrylic paint or stain
- Spar varnish or exterior polyurethane
- Drop cloths or tarps
- Furniture glides
- Epoxy

Professional estimate
Adirondack chair, 6 hours

IN DETAIL

Linseed Oil and Tung Oil

Drying oils, such as boiled linseed oil and tung oil, are another option for exterior coatings. Two or three coats help seal the wood, shed water, and prevent graying. The problem is that mildew loves these oils. Fortunately, you can buy mildewcide in packets that can be added to finishes. If you choose a drying oil for your exterior finish, add mildewcide before applying it or you will be forever fighting mildew.

> *"Cedar, redwood, teak, and mahogany do quite well with no finish at all."*

Clear Finishes

As luck would have it, most of the woods that tolerate outdoor conditions well are also quite attractive. Cedar, redwood, teak, and mahogany can tolerate humidity changes and are able to fend off invading insects. Since they look so good just as they are, we're inclined to coat them with clear finishes that take advantage of their natural colors and patterns. Unfortunately, clear coatings don't withstand the degenerative powers of the sun as well as paint does, and that translates into occasional maintenance. Considering how nice some of our outdoor furniture is, that may not be such a high price to pay.

Left untreated, cedar adopts a rustic, silver-gray appearance.

IN DETAIL

Fading Exotics

Most woods change color over time when exposed to strong sunlight. This can be especially troublesome with highly colored exotic woods, such as purpleheart, padauk, and bubinga. Often chosen for their vivid purple, red, and orange hues, these woods soon lose their bright colors when they are placed outdoors. You can't prevent that entirely, but you can slow it down by using clear coatings that contain UV blockers and ab-

sorbers. These invisible additives bar the sun's UV rays in much the same way suntan lotion does. Many of the exterior varnishes sold at paint stores and marine supply stores contain these additives and say so on the label. They are your best bet to keep things from fading. However, don't expect miracles—they merely prolong the inevitable (see photo, facing page).

The gray option

Cedar, redwood, teak, and mahogany do quite well with no finish at all. They form a silver-gray patina and can go year after year looking more or less the same. If you like the look and the woody, rustic feel of uncoated wood, this is by far the easiest "finishing" method. Sand the wood to 180 or 220 grit, then simply let nature take its course. Once a year, wash the furniture thoroughly to remove accumulated dirt, then treat it with a bleach solution or mildew wash (see formula, p. 154) if mildew has developed.

Clear sealers and semitransparent stains

In a sense, clear sealer is one step above the uncoated gray option. It leaves the surface feeling woody and natural—as opposed to slick and glossy—but brings out the depth and color the way film finishes do. For decorative planters, hangings, and furniture, use any penetrating deck sealer, such as Penofin or Flood CWF, in clear or tinted colors. Brush on a liberal, even coat and let it dry. This method helps the piece shed water and keep its true color, but you'll need to rejuvenate it every year or so with another coat. One good strategy is to recoat sealed furniture each time you reseal your deck.

Exterior polyurethane

Exterior polyurethane, a perennial favorite, provides a more finished look. Make sure you select polyurethane designed for exterior use, as interior

This outdoor bench is washed and recoated with deck sealer each time I refinish the deck.

polyurethane is not the same thing. A polyurethane finish lasts for several years (more or less), depending on the amount of sunlight and wear it receives. Exterior polyurethane is waterproof and tolerates the wide humidity and temperature swings experienced by outdoor items. Like interior polyurethane, it provides a good deal of abrasion resistance and has a long life. Polyurethane's one weakness is the sun. As polyurethane ages, it may start to separate from the wood and eventually peel. When this starts to happen, there is no good solution other than to remove the old finish and recoat.

Exterior polyurethane comes in both oil- and water-based versions, so you can choose which one you prefer. Both have an equal ability to stand up to the rigors of the great outdoors. Oil-based polyurethane tends to darken a bit more over time than water-based polyurethane does. No matter what you choose, sand the raw wood smooth to 180 grit. If you use water-based

Over time, strong sunlight and creeping moisture can make polyurethane delaminate and peel away from the wood.

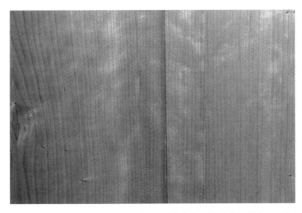

The left half of this board was finished with oil-based polyurethane, the right half with water-based.

The left side of this purpleheart board was masked, but the untreated right side shows the change in color after only a week of exposure to strong sunlight.

TOOLS AND MATERIALS
Spar Urethane

Combine the wear characteristics of polyurethane with the flexibility and UV-stability of spar varnish and you have spar urethane. This is a good option for projects that require just a bit more abrasion resistance than plain spar varnish can provide.

Spar urethane combines the characteristics of spar varnish with polyurethane.

polyurethane, sand the wood lightly after the first coat dries to remove the raised grain. Otherwise, sand between coats only if you wait more than a week between applications. Simply brush or spray on two or three coats, one coat per day, and let the finish dry at least a week before you press the items into service. No special sealer is needed.

Spar varnish

Wooden benches built into the sides of boat decks are undoubtedly coated with spar varnish,

The first coat of spar varnish brings out the beauty of this mahogany Adirondack chair.

and you can do the same for furniture at home. Although spar varnish is too soft and slippery for flooring on a deck or porch, it is just right for tables, chairs, number plaques, and fancy birdhouses. Clear and flexible with natural UV stability, spar varnish is just the thing for year-round outdoor protection. In fact, it has one characteristic that gives it an edge over polyurethane—it does not delaminate with sun exposure. Instead, it wears from the top down, turning cloudy or chalky in a couple of years. When that happens, simply sand the top surface lightly with 220-grit paper and add another coat of spar varnish.

Apply spar varnish as you would any clear finish. Sand the wood up to 180 grit and brush on two or three coats, one coat per day. Wash the items every year and recoat them as needed. If mildew develops, scrub it with a bleach solution (see Trade Secret, p. 154) and add mildewcide to the spar varnish the next time you recoat (see Trade Secret, p. 147).

Solid Colors

Not all wood is pretty enough to show off. Solid colors hide a multitude of sins, coordinate furniture and accessories with your home's exterior color scheme, and add a bit of pizzazz to your deck. An added bonus is that opaque and semiopaque colors resist the deteriorating effects of UV rays much more effectively than clear finishes do. Assuming you don't wear through the finish, solid colors can last twice as long as clear coatings.

> **"Wooden benches built into the sides of boat decks are undoubtedly coated with spar varnish, and you can do the same for furniture at home."**

TOOLS AND MATERIALS
Latex Wall Stain

If you use wall stain, make sure you read the label carefully and buy products that are 100% acrylic. Cheaper latex wall stain is fine for walls and even some trim but is not durable and smooth enough for tables and chairs. A picnic table sealed with 100% acrylic stain is more wear resistant and easier to clean. Wall stains discolor and start chalking with the same sort of wear and tear.

After three coats of semitransparent stain, the pressure-treated post (center) on this fence is identical in color to the cedar boards on each side of it.

Acrylic siding and fence stain

Strong, fast-drying, and highly resistant to mildew, 100% acrylic siding and fence stain is a fine choice for picnic tables, chairs, and wooden wind chimes. Unlike paint, it can go over even wet wood and requires no primer coat. Due to the durability of acrylic resin, it easily outlasts oil-based stains designed for decks and siding. You'll find that it has better wear resistance and far better mildew resistance, so you won't need to recoat as often. It is available in both semitransparent and fully opaque versions. A semitransparent stain lets some of the wood's character show, but after three coats it looks more like paint than stain.

Acrylic stains dry fast because they are water-based, but the first coat raises the grain of the wood. That doesn't matter on fences and siding, but it does make a difference on benches and tables. Start by brushing or spraying a liberal coat onto the raw wood. After the first coat has dried, sand the surface lightly with 220- or 320-grit sandpaper to smooth the roughness. Follow up with a second coat. If you are working with a semitransparent color, leave it at that. For opaque colors, feel free to add a third coat. Don't be surprised to find that this rather durable "stain" lasts three or four years before it needs any attention. When it does need a facelift, sand the surface lightly to promote adhesion, then add another coat.

Exterior paint

House and trim paint, which is tougher and glossier than wall paint, also works for outdoor items. If you don't mind the shine, lean toward semigloss and gloss finishes, as they hold up a bit better than matte finishes. Treat the wood just as if you were coating trim. Start with latex primer to seal the raw wood, then follow up with two coats of paint. If you are working on wood that bleeds into water-based coatings (cedar, for instance), choose a specialty sealer, such as Kilz or 1-2-3. The color may bleed into the primer, but it will not continue into the top coat. Once you

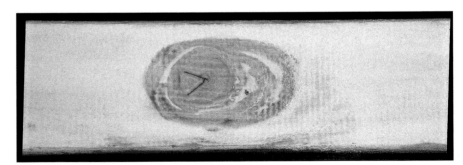

The knots and sap of some woods bleed through paint unless you prime them first with special sealer.

Don't Caulk All Four Sides
Caulk along the top and sides on the back of a wall plaque to let water drain off. Leave the bottom edge open so water doesn't become trapped between the plaque and the wall.

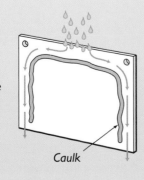

Caulk

TRADE SECRET

Do you have a welcome sign or numbered plaque attached to the side of your house? If so, it is best to use nonrusting, stainless steel or brass screws and a special caulking method for extra protection. Put a bead of silicone or siliconized latex caulk along the top and sides on the back of the plaque where it contacts the wall. Leave the bottom edge uncaulked. The caulking on the top and sides keeps water out, but if some water does happen to get in, it can drain out the uncaulked bottom edge.

TRADE SECRET

Caulk is for more than just seams. Seal screw holes with silicone caulk when you hang security lights, house numbers, hanging planters, hooks for holiday lights, and anything else that requires putting a screw into an exterior surface. The easiest way to do this is to dip the screw, point first, into the end of the caulking tube. That will get enough caulk onto the screw to seat it and seal the hole. Silicone caulk glues the screw into place and, more important, prevents water from seeping in through the screw threads.

Water won't seep through screw holes if you first dip the screws in silicone caulk.

go through the bother of priming, paint is quite durable and outlasts even the best of the stains and clear finishes. Other than washing it now and again, it needs almost no attention. Treat it as you would the house, repainting as needed if it starts to show common signs of paint deterioration or wears through at the corners and edges.

Painted Gems and Ornaments

Perhaps you go for whirligigs, highly decorated birdhouses, or fanciful mounted plaques to let your friends know which house is yours. Or maybe you are inclined to add decorative artwork or stenciling to outdoor projects to set them apart from the mundane. Here's where you can let your sense of color run wild, but you also want to do what you can to make sure that those colors last as long as possible.

Decorative paints for outdoors

It should be obvious that you can use any outdoor house paint for ornamental work. Just remember to follow all the rules of painting: Start with a clean, smooth surface and seal it with a coat of primer first. In this case, you could use either oil- or water-based primer, but I have to admit a fondness for water-based materials. The primer is not absolutely necessary, but it is likely to extend the life of your artwork by providing better adhesion to the wood beneath it. If you plan to decorate a large painted surface, do the background color with custom-mixed house

My son made this birdhouse as a replica of our house, and he even painted it with the same coatings.

paint. It makes a fine base for decoration and is much less expensive than coating the whole thing in artist's paints.

With the surface properly prepped and primed, you can now decorate it with any exterior acrylic art paint. There is an endless variety of colors in the craft section of stores (or in craft and hobby stores), or you can mix your own colors using

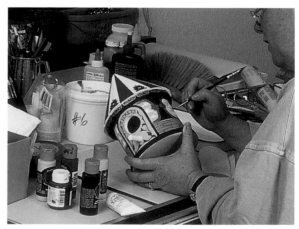

Craft stores sell an endless array of artist's acrylic colors for decorating birdhouses, hangings, and wall plaques.

"Once all the painting is done, protect your work with a couple of coats of clear finish."

TRADE SECRET

Furniture glides (like the kind probably gracing the feet of your kitchen chairs and table) work great on outdoor furniture. I put them on the feet of my deck furniture to keep them dry. This preserves the ends by preventing water from seeping up and destroying the finish. Another advantage is that glides make heavy Adirondack chairs and picnic tables easier to slide from here to there. Use the largest dome-shaped glides that will fit. Small "pork-pie" glides can catch in the spaces between the decking.

Two coats of exterior water-based polyurethane add protection to this painted birdhouse.

keep an eye on it. If it turns dull, appears hazy, or starts to erode, recoat it. Clean it with soap and water, rinse well, and go over it lightly with a fine nylon abrasive pad (Scotchbrite, for example) to roughen the surface. You can use sandpaper too, but it is likely to sand right through some of your painting, and you certainly don't want that. Add another coat of clear polyurethane and let it cure for a week (bring it indoors to avoid a rainstorm). With proper care, your painted gems will last longer and reward you with years of satisfaction.

artist's acrylic colors or universal tinting colors. To add variety to your work, use stencils, hand-painted designs, or antiquing and texturing tools from the paint department of your favorite store.

Clear-coat your masterpiece

Once all the painting is done, protect your work with a couple of coats of clear finish. Once again, either oil- or water-based coatings work, but oil-based materials add an amber cast to the paint beneath it. White becomes off-white, blue becomes greenish blue, and pink turns down-right orange. You'll get the same protection without altering the colors by using water-based exterior polyurethane. Make sure the paint or decoration is fully dry, then apply two thin coats, one per day. Use either satin or gloss poly-urethane, depending on the amount of sheen that you prefer.

The combination of acrylic paints and clear polyurethane should last a good long time, but

Pot the Feet

The feet of wooden patio and garden furniture, picnic tables, and Adirondack chairs get the worst of the weather. They sit, end grain exposed, directly on wet ground. Water wicks up through the end grain, de-laminates the finish at the feet, and starts to rot the wood. You can prevent all that at the finishing bench by potting the feet with epoxy. While you can use

Pot furniture feet with epoxy to prevent water from wicking up through the end grain. Remove the masking tape while the epoxy is still tacky.

any two-part epoxy, the thin, easy-penetrating versions made for rotted wood repair work best. Turn the piece bottom-side up and soak the end grain with epoxy until it absorbs no more. Let it cure, then apply the finish. The epoxy seals the wood and prevents water from entering through the feet.

WHAT CAN GO WRONG
The Limits of Finishes

When you build outdoor items, such as storage sheds, patio furniture, and birdhouses, use exterior wood products. There is no finish that makes interior plywood suddenly become suitable for exterior use. The adhesives used in interior ply-wood delaminate in the presence of water and

high humidity, and no finish can prevent that. The same is true for things you build with solid wood. If you want them to hold up, use waterproof glue and choose woods that have a natural resistance to insect attack and rot. Finishes help protect woods but do not change their nature.

Index

LEARNING RESOURCE CENTER
ALAMANCE COMMUNITY COLLEGE
P.O. BOX 8000
GRAHAM, NC 27253-8000

19.95

Taunton's

BUILD LIKE A PRO™
Expert Advice from Start to Finish

PAINTING *and* FINISHING

DISCARD

DISCARD